Gymnastics Psychology

WHAT Coaches, Gymnasts, Parents, and Gymnastics Enthusiasts just like YOU are SAYING…

The sport of Gymnastics has always been about having a strong mind to support a strong body. In my career as a coach, whether I am working with a Level 4 or an Elite National Team Member, I find myself frequently returning to Doc's papers, lectures, and articles. He manages to take complex topics and write in a way that is easily understood by the reader. His passion for gymnastics comes alive in his writing which really holds something for everyone-Coach, Gymnast, or Parent.

Tony Retrosi

2010 USA Gymnastics' Educator of the Year

Owner and Coach-Atlantic Gymnastics

www.GymMomentum.com

Understanding where and how to focus your time, energy and effort, are tools that will serve you in sport, business and life. Learning to focus on performance (things you have control over) instead of outcome (results over which you have no control) is a skill that I have seen make champion gymnasts and drive success both personally and professionally. 'Gymnastics Psychology: The Ultimate Guide for Coaches, Gymnasts, and Parents' immediately makes the "must read" list for parents and coaches of all sports.

Bob Colarossi

Federation Internationale de Gymnastique (FIG)

Past President, USA Gymnastics (USAG)

I highly recommend 'Gymnastics Psychology: The Ultimate Guide for Coaches, Gymnasts, and Parents' to every coach whether you're just starting out or have been around for a while. I believe the knowledge I have gained from understanding the psychological aspects of the sport have helped further my career and the accomplishments of my gymnasts. I would suggest that every coach takes the time to read the book in its entirety and then go back and pick out parts to begin incorporating into their own training programs.

Patrick Palmer

Head Coach & General Manager

Massachusetts Gymnastics Center

I have been grateful for the knowledge and insights into sports psychology that Dr. Sue Massimo has provided for my gymnasts and me in her workshops during gymnastics camps and clinics. I continue to use many of her techniques in mastering fear with my gymnasts today.

Cheryl Spillman
Coach and Former Gym Owner

Dear Doc…We are so fortunate to have you in our region. You're always there to help us and I truly appreciate all that you do for us. Kathy O, for all of Region 6.

Kathy Ostberg
USA Gymnastics, National / Region 6
Administrative Committee Chairman

My role model…I have learned so much from 'Doc.' I have learned how to stay calm and collected in high-pressure situations. I can stay focused during a competition even when it is not going my way… 'Doc' is a great role model and I am so glad he is my mentor.

H.G.
International Elite Gymnast

Dear Doc…You have been an unbelievable influence in the life of our daughter; Mary…She is a strong, positive, and independent person. She learned how to set realistic goals for herself, and follow through on them. Somehow, saying a simple thank you does not seem to let you know what grateful hearts we have for you.

Bill, Diane and "Bear"
Gymnastics Family

Dear Doc…Thank you for your guidance, whether it was giving me advice about how to be a better gymnastics teacher or helping me figure out what I wanted to do with my life.

Heather
Gymnastics Instructor

How fortunate I am to have a mentor, a coach, and a constant listening ear that has been there during my formative years and my adulthood, as both a gymnast and more importantly, as a person.

Growing up in the gym and hearing amazing stories of gymnastics breakthroughs and groundbreaking psychology research as well as anecdotes from personal experiences was a regular occurrence. And out of these stories came priceless messages. Messages that helped shape mine and my teammates perspectives, work ethic, and overall outlook. We referred to these messages as 'Doc-isms.'

These messages became engrained in me so much that as a beginning coach, I heard that message verbalized to my athletes…from my own mouth… and immediately knew where it came from…my favorite Doc-ism: 'I care more about you as people than I do as gymnasts.' What a fantastic message from coach to athlete.

Doc, thank you for consistently continuing to impact every person who is lucky enough to cross your path. The world is fortunate to have this book, "Gymnastics Psychology" as a resource to apply Doc-isms into their lives.

Nicole Langevin
Owner & Director
Precision Choreography, Precision Los Angeles
www.precisionlosangeles.com

Dear Doc…In our 'fast paced' society, it is easy to forget to thank those who have influenced our lives in some way. In my pursuit of a doctoral degree, I needed a statement explaining my interest in sport psychology. Thank you for exposing me to the cognitive and affective techniques for improving athletic performance.

Beth Lancelotti
Sport Psychology Doctoral Candidate

Although he lived six hours away…'Doc' has had a significant impact on my life. He has helped coach me in gymnastics as well as teach me lifelong lessons. He was there as I grew from a shy recreational gymnast into a confident young adult. I learned how to apply the strategies he taught me in gymnastics to several other aspects of my life.

Annelise H.
Gymnast

Dear Dr. Massimo…We wanted to let you know how much we enjoyed your lectures…We are implementing many of these ideas into our program.

Elaine, Paul, Kathy and Brian
Coaches

For my Competitive Team Parents, I recommend they read the articles in 'Gymnastics Psychology: The Ultimate Guide for Coaches, Gymnasts, and Parents'. Parents are more knowledgeable today about their children's sports and are becoming more involved every year. However, there are also boundaries which need to be established and understood by the parents. The sections for parents in this book will help educate them as well as help me to be able to communicate with them better on certain issues.

Patrick Palmer
Head Coach & General Manager
Massachusetts Gymnastics Center
www.massgymnastics.com

"Thank You" Letter and a Reply

This is a bit of a departure from a normal "testimonial," but we were so moved by this "thank you" letter sent to the editor of *International Gymnast Magazine*. It was written by a prominent gym owner and coach, Mr. David Holcomb and we have reprinted it in its entirety along with our reply to Mr. Holcomb.

"Thank you for reprinting the 20 Commandments of Coaching ('Chalk Talk,' Nov. 2007). You note that the commandments are an adaptation of a 1987 article written by Dr. Joe Massimo, but I think Joe's Coaching Commandments go back even further than that.

I know that I all but memorized his sage advice on coaching many years earlier, when I was just starting my coaching career back in the mid-1970s. When I started Buckeye Gymnastics in 1982, I used these same commandments as the foundation of our teaching and coaching philosophy.

As we celebrate 25 years of landing on our feet at Buckeye Gymnastics, Joe's advice to coaches can still be found in our staff handbook. We still train our teachers and coaches using the 20 principles as our guiding light.

Tens of thousands of children in Central Ohio (and who knows how many around the country and the world) have benefitted from the coaches and teachers who carry forward Joe's principles in the gym every day.

I think it's possible that the repeated publication of these 20 Coaching Commandments has had a greater positive impact on gymnasts in this country than anything you have ever published.

Thank you for sharing them with us one more time and thank you to Dr. Joe Massimo for helping generations of young gymnasts train under the direction of teachers and coaches who are safe, effective, positive and gentle, because you touched their hearts."

David Holcomb, Westerville, Ohio
Reprinted from:
International Gymnast Magazine, Letters to the Editor.

Dear Mr. Holcomb,

Thank you for your letter to the editor in International Gymnast (IG) Magazine. We were very moved by your comments. It is so satisfying to know that sometimes just one thing we do as coaches, teachers, and mentors can have a significant impact on the lives of the young athletes in our charge.

In fact, you were correct in your letter that you had first learned of the commandments when you were starting your coaching career because the originals were part of a two part series published in 1975. The original list was just referred to as "Massimo's Big Twenty." In 1987, the two articles were rewritten and the coaching philosophy and guidelines were presented in more detail. Several versions of the guidelines were reprinted over the years and soon were referred to as the 'Coaching Commandments' by you and other coaches, as well as Dan Millman, and IG magazine.

We also want to thank you for your work in training hundreds of teachers and coaches using positive principles and sound philosophy. As a way of doing this, we are going to republish these principles and guidelines in our new book entitled, 'Gymnastics Psychology: The Ultimate Guide for Coaches, Gymnasts, and Parents.'

We truly appreciate the fact that you are committed to helping generations of young gymnasts through ensuring that your teachers and coaches adopt these twenty principles as their guiding light. We also thank you for sharing your story with us and bringing this to our attention, so that the new generations of coaches to come, in our country and around the world, can also gain some insight from the commandments as they develop their own coaching philosophies to positively influence a new generation of gymnasts.

Best regards,
Joe and Sue Massimo

Gymnastics Psychology

THE ULTIMATE GUIDE
for Coaches, Gymnasts, *and* Parents

DR. JOE MASSIMO
DR. SUE MASSIMO

New York

Gymnastics Psychology
THE ULTIMATE GUIDE
for Coaches, Gymnasts, *and* Parents

ISBN 978-1-60037-948-2 paperback
ISBN 978-1-60037-949-9 eBook
Library of Congress Control Number:

Morgan James Publishing
The Entrepreneurial Publisher
5 Penn Plaza, 23rd Floor,
New York City, New York 10001
(212) 655-5470 office • (516) 908-4496 fax
www.MorganJamesPublishing.com

Cover Design by:
Rachel Lopez
www.r2cdesign.com

Interior Design by:
Bonnie Bushman
bonnie@caboodlegraphics.com

In an effort to support local communities, raise awareness and funds, Morgan James Publishing donates a percentage of all book sales for the life of each book to Habitat for Humanity Peninsula and Greater Williamsburg.

Get involved today, visit
www.MorganJamesBuilds.com.

Books & More

Dr. Joe Massimo & Dr. Sue Massimo

⁓

COLLECTED PAPERS
Psychology and Gymnastics: Vol. I
Psychology and Gymnastics: Vol. II

⁓

COMMANDMENTS
Coaching Commandments
Parenting Commandments
Gymnast's Commandments

⁓

BOOK SERIES
Gymnastics Guidebooks & eBooks

⁓

Gymnastics History & Research
Coaching Psychology
Coach/Gymnast Relationships
Motivation
Fear
Health & Well-Being
Stress & Anxiety
Mental Gymnastics
Goal Setting
Psycho/Physical Training
Performance Psychology
Meet Preparation and Competition
Psychological Preparation Program
Gymnastics Parents

DEDICATION

"The compilation of material offered in 'Gymnastics Psychology: The Ultimate Guide for Coaches, Gymnasts, and Parents' are dedicated to the thousands of young gymnasts along with the guidance and support of their coaches and parents, who strive to express their creative energy through this art; many with small success, some with considerable, and a very few with much, but all with inspiring dreams and abiding love."

Doc & Dr. Sue

TABLE OF CONTENTS

A Thought While Watching Warm-Ups

(1979 WORLD CHAMPIONSHIPS)

What is it that brings them all together once again; these creative, hearty young people showing their athletic prowess sharpened to a fine art through hours of difficult practice? Who, but for some special calling, would endure the waiting, suffer the unpredictable fortune that rests on one slight error with no reprieve, tolerate the salty taste of tears and silently bear the pain within? Could it be for the love of victory, as simple as that, for the thrill of the hunt, for the exciting feeling of movement, for the pleasurable side of tension which we curse, yet pursue? Or is it something far more basic, something inherited from the past that is part of us now, a drive within the human spirit that still demands personal expression; not as part of a tribe, but singularly, as it was millenniums ago when our ancient ancestors struggled one by one to establish their own individual identities in an indifferent and hostile world?

An Observation While Watching Finals

(2011 WORLD CHAMPIONSHIPS)

The thoughts used to describe our athletic youth while watching warm-ups at the World Championships in 1979 are just as relevant today. Now, some 30 years later, observations show us that some endeavors never change when it comes to expressing oneself through the art of gymnastics. It may be that, despite changes in society, science, and technology the elements of athletic prowess today are much the same as they were at the first Olympiad.

PREFACE

Gymnastics Psychology: The Ultimate Guide for Coaches, Gymnasts, and Parents is the culmination of our passion with gymnastics and the people involved in it. Our combined experiences as gymnasts, judges, coaches, educators, and sport psychologists have been vast and varied and have encompassed over 100 years in the sport.

In the process of paying our dues, we recognized from our interactions with those marching to achieve physical competence that the mind/ body connection was of prime importance. We are very gratified to be able to pass on our acquired knowledge and experiences surrounding the undeniable importance of the mental aspects of the sport of gymnastics.

Doc & Dr. Sue

ACKNOWLEDGEMENTS

There are many people who contribute in unique ways to any careers which span the decades. The names of those we have learned from are so numerous as to require a separate volume. Therefore, wherever you are in the world, we thank you for giving of yourselves.

However, we need to mention a few without which this volume of papers would not have come together. We'd like to thank the late Mr. Glenn Sundby, the original publisher of "Modern Gymnast Magazine," "Mademoiselle Gymnast," and "International Gymnast Magazine," who strongly believed in the mind-body connection in gymnastics. He published the first article on this concept in 1969 entitled "Psychology and the Gymnast" which we have included in this collection. Mr. Sundby subsequently and faithfully ran a column with the same name for the next 25+ years publishing nearly 60 articles which provided much of the material for *Gymnastics Psychology*.

We also wish to thank USA Gymnastics, the United States Association of Independent Gymnastics Clubs, and the National Open Gymnastics Program who always fostered our research and supported our efforts here and abroad to educate and train coaches and gymnasts as well as their parents on the importance of the mind-body connection in gymnastics.

Doc & Dr. Sue

Foreword

Dr. Len Zaichkowsky

I am pleased and honored to have this opportunity to write the foreword for the book "Gymnastics Psychology: The Ultimate Guide for Coaches, Gymnasts, and Parents" authored by Drs. Joe "Doc" Massimo and Sue Massimo. My association with "Doc" and "Dr. Sue" goes back quite a long time.

While at Boston University in the early 1970's I discovered to my chagrin that I was not the only one doing sport psychology in the Boston area. There was this Harvard educated clinical/school psychologist who, in addition to working with school children in Newton, Ma., also worked with world-class gymnasts. At that time the field of sport psychology was beginning to emerge and few faculty members and graduate students had heard of Dr. Joe Massimo-except of course those in the gymnastics community. But the gymnastics community was blessed because they had in their camp the very best sport psychologist in North America, bar none. In my opinion "Doc" was right there with the very best early pioneers in sport psychology such as Bruce Ogilvie, Bob Nideffer, Bob Singer, and my mentor Murray Smith at the University of Alberta.

Joe's teaching, and writing about psychological concepts in gymnastics were brilliant, taking complex psychological concepts and simplifying them so coaches, athletes, and parents could understand them. Although Joe's work often flew below the radar, primarily because he was not in the world of higher education, it did not escape me. He was most gracious in sharing his ideas and writings with me and of course I generously shared them with my students at Boston University as well as with coaches and athletes I worked with world-wide. So it was no surprise to me when Joe was elected to the Gymnastics Hall of Fame, for he was already in my "hall of fame." When Joe retired as a school psychologist I hired him to work with me at Boston University as an adjunct professor so that he could share his wealth of knowledge with the next generation of sport psychologists.

Dr. Sue came to me as an enthusiastic graduate student in the early 1980's, after studying with one of those early pioneers in the field of sport psychology, Dr. Bob Singer, and completed her doctorate in 1986. Her dissertation research was titled, "Identifying specific cognitive and affective attributes of female junior elite gymnasts." Some of her research findings are presented in this manuscript. To this day, I tell those in the field, that based on Sue's research elite gymnasts have extraordinary short term visual memory skills and extremely high internal locus of control.

Although I have read earlier versions of the extraordinary chapters in this book, most of you have not had this privilege. Those of you that are coaches (experienced or novice), gymnasts, and parents of gymnasts will derive extreme benefit from reading this very thorough handbook. In fact, the topics covered in the twelve chapters deal with the essentials of performance psychology and as such are pertinent to coaches, athletes, and parents that have interest in high performance outside the sport of gymnastics. As well, students interested in learning about true "applied" sport psychology will also derive great benefit from reading this book.

Nowhere will you learn more practical information about such concepts as the psychology of fear, anger, motivation, stress, mental preparation, ethics of coaching, coaching commandments, eating disorders, recovery from injury, transition to elite sport, or the unique aspect of leaving home to train, than in this book. With each topic, Joe and Sue were careful to provide a brief theoretical overview of the concept, but quickly deal with case examples, practical suggestions or "tips" written in point form, and a concluding summary in an easy to read format. Although references are provided at the end of the book, the chapters are not cluttered with citations.

One of my research interests is to better understand how individuals become "experts" or "extraordinary" in their field. The Drs. Massimo are truly experts in the psychology of performance, particularly in gymnastics. Dr. Joe has more than six decades in the field, and Sue is approaching four decades. This incredible time frame of experience as performers, educators, researchers, coaches, judges, and sport psychologists, far exceeds Anders Ericsson's "10 year/10,000 hours of deliberate practice" rule for becoming an expert. In reading about the psychology of gymnastics, rest assured that you are learning from two of the very best in the world of gymnastics psychology.

Leonard Zaichkowsky, Ph.D.
Boston University
Professor of Education and Graduate Medical Sciences
Director of Sport Science, Vancouver Canucks (NHL)
Past President-Association for Applied Sport Psychology

Dr. Len Zaichkowsky is a licensed psychologist who specializes in sport, exercise, and performance psychology. He has made more than 300 professional presentations worldwide and makes frequent expert commentary on television, radio and the print media such as the New York Times, Boston Globe, Chicago Tribune, LA Times, Washington Post, Wall Street Journal, and Edmonton Journal. Dr. Zaichkowsky has also consulted with the U. S., Canadian, and Australian Olympic Organizations, the NBA (Boston Celtics), Major League Baseball Players Association, NFL, NHL Players Association, New England Patriots, Calgary Flames, Sydney (Australia) Swans, and most recently with the Spanish World Cup Soccer Team, and Real Madrid soccer club.

INTRODUCTION

The following papers on gymnastics psychology represent a compilation of material written and published between 1969 and the present. Several of the articles began in the field of Men's Gymnastics and many were focused on Women's Gymnastics, but for most, the information is relevant to coaches, gym owners, judges, athletes and their parents regardless of the genders or the discipline of gymnastics. In addition, although their focus is primarily gymnastics, the basic content can be applied to any competitive sport.

Much of the collection is based on original articles which appeared in *Modern Gymnast*, *Mademoiselle Gymnast*, *International Gymnast*, and *Technique* magazines. Some of the articles are based on material prepared for or presented at regional, national, and international training clinics as well as research conducted at various United States Association of Independent Gymnastics Clubs, National Open Gymnastics Program's camps, and international competitions. Since their initial publication, many reprints have appeared in other journals and in several books on sport psychology, however, the information is as relevant today as it was in years past and some even more so in the 21st century. From letters we have received over the years, some of the papers have also provided the impetus for numerous doctoral dissertations.

Our primary objective in the writing has been to reach the largest audience possible with concrete ideas which would have immediate and practical value. The collection of the papers begins with the history of psychology in the sport of gymnastics including the first article ever written in this area entitled "Psychology and the Gymnast." Some of the papers are more specifically directed towards parents such as "My Daughter, the Competitive Gymnast," others towards coaches in general such as "Coaching the Team" and "The Art of Feedback: A Model for Coach-Gymnast Communication," and still others for the athlete such as "Goal Setting Guidelines" and "On the Beam: A Gymnast's Guide for Staying There." In addition, several of these articles, such as "Coaching Commandments" and "Parenting Commandments" are used in training manuals for coaches and as required reading for athletes and parents in gyms across the country.

We trust you will enjoy reading the papers as much as we enjoyed writing them and that everyone will find something of interest. Ultimately, perhaps they will serve to assist future generations of coaches, gym owners, officials, gymnasts and their parents as they strive for mastery in gymnastics as well as in life.

Doc & Dr. Sue

Chapter One

———— ɰ ————

BRIDGING HISTORY
AND RESEARCH

In 1969, the first of 60+ articles written over the decades by your authors concerning the psychological aspects of gymnastics was published in *Modern Gymnast Magazine*, known now as *International Gymnast Magazine*. From that point on and for the next 30 years, an international column with the same name as the article was devoted to this field. That article, entitled "Psychology and the Gymnast," provided insights into the beginnings of the notion of the mind/body connection in our sport.

We begin this chapter with a copy of that historic article. We have also presented a few articles of a historic nature which supported and aided the growth of gymnastics in the U.S. and helped our competitive presence abroad. Lastly, important surveys and research-oriented articles concerning a variety of psychological and personality issues are discussed which set the stage for the advancement of conducting additional research, suggesting promising directions for the sport, and providing guidelines for coaches and athletes of the future.

- Psychology and the Gymnast
- The Role of a Psychologist in a National Training Program
- An Open Letter to Dan Millman: Personality and the Gymnast
- The Gymnast's Perception of the Coach: Competence and Coaching Style
- Psychological Characteristics of Jr. Elite Gymnasts

1

PSYCHOLOGY AND THE GYMNAST

The significance of clinical and applied psychology in all sports is relatively obvious. The mystique which surrounds certain well-known coaches is usually attributable to their extraordinary capacity in their overall approach to interpersonal relationships as they pertain to the individuals on the team.

The gymnast, for all practical purposes, is on his or her own—a loner. Although he may be a team member, once he leaves the bench and approaches the apparatus he becomes a single entity "competing," in a sense, with himself against an inanimate object. The objective: to execute a polished work of art which meets technical as well as aesthetic demands and which is to be evaluated by a panel of experts. Each gymnast, referring here to both men and women, has a particular style or approach. Some are aggressive and attack the apparatus as if to throttle it into submission. Others approach the challenge more delicately, with a kind of finesse reminiscent of a person pacifying an unpredictable animal. Both methods can meet with success, each, and many other such styles, reflect the gymnast's personality. The wise coach will build on such differences to emphasize the uniqueness of delivery and personal expression so important in gymnastics.

Due to the individual nature of this sport and the performance demands made upon the gymnast, there are few other activities where the coach-athlete relationship is more crucial. It is given that a good coach evaluates the athlete's physical readiness. In addition, however, the successful coach should carefully study the individual gymnast's behaviors in an effort to determine some psychologically significant facts which will help define the nature of their relationship and even appropriate coaching techniques.

Identifying Individual Behaviors
The coach should consider, for example:

1. **What is the gymnast's preference in regards to communication?** Some gymnasts require long explanations of a given stunt before attempting it— they want to know everything about mechanics and ask for relevant details of Newton's Laws of Motion to be spelled out at length! Others want a minimum of verbiage and prefer to feel out the trick relying primarily on courage in the initial attempt. A happy medium, of course, is probably best. Some other gymnasts must simply see the trick with little verbal dialogue needed. This is the "show me" school. The coach strives to discover the mode appropriate for each individual. (In some cases pure operant conditioning is all that is needed!)

2. **What is the gymnast's tolerance for ambiguity?** Probably in no other sport are things less definitive. The rule and regulations are quite clear, but the learning of movements and their expression proceeds at a "play it by ear" rate. The individual variables in terms of mastering an exercise are inexhaustible.

3. **How does the gymnast deal with fear versus anxiety?** These are distinctly different concepts. Fear is specific and object directed. Gymnasts can state specifically what they are afraid of and be helped over this block. Some, however, have a diffuse, general anxiety which predominated and which implies a state of tension which is irrational and cannot be related to a specific situation. ("I'm afraid of hitting my head on the bar" vs. "I'm psyched out.") The anxious gymnast can be very productive with the coaches' help, but an over-determined amount of anxiety can cripple any effectiveness. The art of spotting is pivotal in this area. It is through this support that the gymnast gradually gains confidence in his coach. Again, each athlete is different in terms of the amount of spotting he desires or needs.

4. **When does the gymnast work best—structure, schedule, conditions, etc?** Some gymnasts can practice their art under any and all circumstances. There are others who become immobilized if it is too cold, too hot or any one of dozens of other such excuses. Many gymnasts thrive on a rigid schedule which is predictable; others demand a greater sense of autonomy. It is important that the coach consider the individual patterns preferred by the majority of his athletes and plan his program accordingly. The over-understanding coach, however, will be devastated by strong-willed gymnasts. A middle-of-the-road position, again, is usually most desirable. It should be remembered in passing that some gymnasts prefer a real boss and to work under a "dictatorship" where little decision-making on their part is necessary.

5. **Is the gymnast compulsive?** Observing gymnasts working out can be very amusing. Many develop idiosyncratic rituals which suggest their mental sets. Some such concerns—e.g. the gymnasts who always must approach the apparatus from the same direction, etc.—if carried to extremes can lead to real problems. Repeated mannerisms, such as blowing on the closed fists after chalking up, touching the apparatus in a special way, etc. although not necessary important in and of themselves, represent means of dealing with stress and can help the sensitive coach better understand his gymnast. The coaches' observation and quiet acceptance of these things can tighten a good relationship just as does the controlled use of humor. Too many such habits on the part of the gymnast may suggest inflexibility and a difficult coaching problem indeed.

6. **How does the gymnast respond to frustration, constructive criticism, and failure?** Some gymnasts become so angry at defeat in any form that they throw the equivalent of a temper tantrum. Others sulk and become depressed, even unable to continue a workout. There are a few, if any sports, which can equal the frustration experienced in gymnastics. The gymnast's response in these situations is a sample of how he copes with life in a general way. Often the coach may have to spend many hours listening to his gymnast's concerns and problems, supporting him and helping him negotiate difficult periods. A critique of the athlete's exercise is part of the coaches' responsibility. Some gymnasts like the "hard line" and have a psychological need to be severely "scolded" at times. The resulting anger is displaced and channeled into the next effort, often leading to progress. Some gymnasts, on the other hand, are psychologically fragile and only become discouraged when treated roughly, requiring a "softer" approach. The coach must remain flexible in his methodology and cognizant of the specific needs. Observing a gymnast's response to success is also revealing. Overreaction is often an ominous sign.

7. **How does the gymnast handle pain?** This is a fruitful area for observation. Some gymnasts seem oblivious to discomfort and work on under situations which would long ago have stopped the weaker. Others go into a near state of shock over a minor injury, suggesting an immaturity and egocentricity which is somewhat atypical. Again, such knowledge about the individual gymnast's response pattern can help guide the nature of the coaching interaction.

8. **How does the gymnast relate to other members of the squad?** This is really self-explanatory. It is through this dimension that the greatest useable information can be gained about the individual athlete.

9. **Many, many others** too numerous to articulate in this paper.

In most cases gym teams are relatively small, enabling the conscientious coach to pay attention to such considerations and apply growing psychological insights about individuals to his coaching technique with them. It is well worth the effort. It is important to remember that the coach-gymnast interaction is a relationship, but that the coach is not a relative! Although he will become involved with the gymnast, he cannot allow himself to over-identify with the competitor. That is, the coaches' personal success or failure is not contingent on the success or failure of his gymnast. It is interesting to note here that the mature male coach working with the female gymnast can often produce wonders; it would be naïve not to recognize that such a relationship partially re-creates the father-daughter and/or classic male-female constellation. The astute coach can utilize this involvement in a positive fashion. Needless to say it can also be disastrous if poorly handled or if the emotional transference is highly neurotic in character! Refer to the article "Male Coach–Female Gymnast" for further insight.

Summary

Many good coaches working today already practice, almost on an intuitive level, principles of psychology as suggested herein. The point is simply: the more knowledge the coach can gain in this area and the more aware he can become of just what he is doing and why, the better he will be able to function and assist his gymnasts. This does not suggest that gymnastic coaches become clinical psychologists or psychotherapists, but that they give more conscious thought and study to this aspect of their behavior as it applies to their everyday coaching.

It may well be that when the young gymnasts of today protest that there is a "lack of good coaches," they may not be referring so much to technically incompetent instruction as they are the absence of men and women who are able to communicate what they know and demonstrate a personalized understanding which is a deeper and possibly more important component of coaching. The article entitled "The Gymnast's Perception of the Coach: Competence and Coaching Style" provides much more detail on this subject.

In summation, it is clear that psychology plays a major role in all sports. For the gymnast and coach it can be sensitively applied in a meaningful way which facilitates the enjoyment of the multiple benefits of gymnastics and even, perhaps, in the eventual achievement of real excellence.

THE ROLE OF A PSYCHOLOGIST IN A NATIONAL TRAINING PROGRAM

Author's Notes: In the late 60's and early 70's, Dr. Joe Massimo received several inquiries concerning the use of a clinical psychologist in the training of gymnasts. In 1970, he developed a paper which was used to describe this kind of work preliminary to his own efforts of being named as a consultant to the Men's U. S. National Coaching Staff. The following material is partially taken from that document and from others which discussed the existing use of applying psychological dynamics in the training arena being used by other nations competing on the international scene.

In both the United States and Europe, early studies in motor learning and capacities have contributed in indirect ways to the general understanding of the international level athlete. In the United States, relatively few pieces of research, and even fewer scholars, have turned their attention to superior athletes in a direct way. More concentrated focus has occurred in Europe during this same period of time in an effort to understand the psychological nature and problems of athletes engaging in international competitive tournaments.

The increasing interest in the psychological aspects of the athletic performance probably reflects several things:

- The search by coaches and athletes themselves to identify the elusive nonphysical determinants of success,
- The discovery by clinical psychologists that the athletic experience is a fruitful laboratory for behavioral research
- A growing attention to such concepts as self-actualization and positive psychiatry rather than a continuing preoccupation with pathology and remediation.

It would be a mistake, however, to assume that psychological insights into the personality structures, motivational patterns and general performance of athletes have had to wait for the modern methods of evaluation and research.

The mystique surrounding many outstanding coaches can be attributed to their innate ability to use sound psychological principles in an intuitive manner with their teams. As a matter of fact, the Olympic archives contain detailed records of their observations. Much has had to wait, however, for the establishment of the International Society for Sports Psychology in 1965, which provided for the organized exchange of opinion, research and information between serious researchers in sports psychology from many parts of the world. It legitimized the work of these men and women and provided a vehicle for the dissemination of relative data. There appears to be growing evidence that their common interest in this field has brought together psychologists from many countries and different psychological orientations, and that this collaboration has been extremely beneficial.

Despite this increasing exchange of ideas, a careful review of the literature reveals that little is really known concerning the psychosocial aspects of high level sports training and competition. A vast majority of past efforts in sports psychology have focused primarily on the experimental aspects of this discipline, such as studies of bio-physiologically and psychologically determined behavior under various conditions of training stress and performance. In recent years, emphasis has shifted to a more clinically-oriented stance where team psychologists are concerning themselves with individual motivation, intra-team communication, psychological aspects of the sport unit, and general mental and emotional preparation for the competitive experience through use of various forms of psychological intervention. In some cases, the techniques utilized are even similar to those employed for purposes of therapy. Professor Ferruccio Antonelli, president of the International Society of Sports Psychology, puts it strongly when he states in Vanek and Cratty's, "Psychology and the Superior Athlete:"

> *The sport psychologist must assume important and difficult tasks: he must establish an empathetic relationship with each athlete and get in touch with the conscious and unconscious concerns of each; he must establish a real psychotherapeutic relationship with each member of the team as he attempts to understand the different personalities of the* athletes. In any case, his behavior cannot follow common and habitual rules.

In addition, it seems apparent that the sports psychologist must recognize the interpersonal relationships and interactions between the athletes and the coaches in his efforts to help establish a more cohesive sport unit.

There appears to be substantial evidence that such procedures, carried on by highly trained professionals, can make a genuine contribution to the overall performance of specific athletes and maximize the consolidated effort of a competitive team. It is clear that any work in this area must:

> *"… Have a scientific basis constituted by serious professional training in psychology, based upon the results of specific experimental research including a comprehensive testing program, and upon deep knowledge of the motivations*

which induce individuals to practice sports, to seek to win, and to exceed the limits of their own human nature."

At the 1968 Olympics in Mexico City and the games in Munich in 1972, a number of eastern European national teams utilized psychologists in preparation for and during the competition. Even with the increasing involvement of such professionals (some of whom have more than a passing acquaintance with the particular sport), the concept is still very much in infancy and much is yet to be learned about procedures, methodology and evaluation. Many English speaking coaches may be skeptical about attempts to scientifically apply principles of psychology with their athletes. As Vanek and Cratty pointed out in their book, "Psychology and the Superior Athlete", "They (coaches) may claim that winning depends upon hard training methods and the availability of superior facilities rather than upon close attention to the emotional climate of the training camp or to the personality characteristics of their athletes."

The number of medals won by American athletes, particularly in Olympic competitions, would seem to add weight to their words. However, it may be true, as Vanek and Cratty suggested that Americans win in international events, in spite of insensitive coaches, because of the large number of participants, the superior training facilities, as well as the diet to which they are exposed since childhood. These writers are of the belief that even more superlative performances could be evidenced if coaches, given the other assets mentioned above, would become more cognizant of the techniques involved in the psychological training of individual athletes and become more sensitive to their role in the psychosocial dynamics of a team's interaction.

It's possible at this point to enumerate some areas that would be fruitful to explore. These might include such things as:

1. Utilization of psychological assessment techniques with groups and individuals to clarify relevant personal and team dynamics and to identify personality trait patterns of this particular group of elite athletes.
2. The gathering of other basic information concerning attitudes, motivation, intelligence, motor learning, etc.
3. The improvement of individual communication and overall personal relationships between gymnasts and their coaches and within each respective group using special observations and collected data referred to in numbers one and two (the establishment of a climate of trust and mutual respect).
4. The carrying out of relaxation-activation training designed to produce significant changes in complex psychological and physiological indices (peaking for competition, psychotonic training).

5. The development of performance prediction studies involving pre-competition and competition psychological stress training ("model training," anxiety, projection, etc.)

6. Intellectual training (participating when appropriate) – ample evidence indicates that intellectual pursuits related to the specific activity (gymnastics) which are accomplished during preparation may take the form of discussions, lectures and readings about the physiological, psychological and biochemical demands of the sport.

7. The keeping of records and statistics on elite gymnasts involving notation of response to practice, differentiated coaching approach, speed of recovery, etc.

8. The development of a system of information feedback for both coaches and gymnasts (group process).

9. The provision of specific educational and career consultation for the athletes.

10. Participate in the formulation of an appropriate research design to evaluate this aspect (psychology) of the national program.

11. Work with other disciplines interested in maximizing performance (sports medicine, hypnosis influence, etc.).

12. Provide a series of ongoing papers describing the work for dissemination in the sport community.

It is apparent that the task outlined here is of considerable magnitude and would require an extensive period of time. The objectives are presented in this paper only to illustrate the potential such an assignment might hold. There is a great deal that would need to be demonstrated before an investment of time and energy becomes feasible. Progress will only be made if an atmosphere of cooperation among the staff and athletes can be achieved along with a readiness to venture into the uncertain. This preparation in itself would be a separate challenge. The dialogue which would most likely ensue from such an endeavor would perhaps provide us with valuable information as to direction in the future.

In any event, it seems appropriate to begin to explore how athletes might heighten their level of achievement through the development of a productive psyche in relation to the use of personal talents and capacities in this type of demanding athletic and artistic expression.

AN OPEN LETTER TO DAN MILLMAN "PERSONALITY AND THE GYMNAST"

Author's Notes: The following is a letter written by Dr. Joe Massimo to Mr. Dan Millman, who at the time was the director of gymnastics at Stanford University. As both coaches and authors, the two were very interested in the mind-body relationship in the sport of gymnastics and providing the U.S. gymnasts with the best possible training. Mr. Millman is currently well-known for his seminars, books, and movie.

Dear Dan,

I enjoyed reading your article on the philosophical and psychological aspects of gymnastics. Thank you for your reference to my work, as I need the support of gymnasts and coaches such as yourself in order to continue my own efforts.

You make some interesting statements in your article. The questions concerning the longitudinal studies of the gymnast (academic career, lifestyle, etc.) are intriguing and my current work would facilitate this kind of follow-up in coming years.

Your article reminded me that we are collecting a tremendous amount of data which sheds light upon, and eventually may answer, some of the questions you raise regarding fear, motivation, aggression, general attitude and other issues related to personality and the gymnast. Perhaps now is a good time to begin to share some of this material.

Early in 1968, I applied for membership in the International Society of Sports Psychology. The objective of this organization is to coordinate and share a growing body of research into the area of psychology in sports. Essentially, there are three factors which account for the expanding interest in this area: 1) the discovery by clinical psychologists that the athletic experience is a fruitful laboratory for behavioral research, 2) the search by coaches and athletes themselves to identify the elusive, non-physical determinants of success, and 3) the growing attention to such concepts as self-actualization and positive mental health rather than a continuing preoccupation with pathology and remediation.

As you know, I joined our national staff in gymnastics two years ago as a special assistant, specifically, as a clinical psychologist with the men's program. I have not only been concerned with applying clinical skills in work with our national staff and gymnasts, but have also focused on a national/ international testing program, as well as other data gathering procedures.

Since joining the staff, I have collected a considerable amount of data, not only on U.S. gymnasts, but also on some top foreign competitors in this sport. It has been possible to solicit such material through the cooperation of personal and professional colleagues in different parts of the world. This is a lengthy process, because of the language difficulty and *the necessity of formulating clinical objectives and methodology. Despite these limitations, we are beginning to make real progress.*

Incidentally, you should read the report of the eight-year work of Ogilvie and Tutko in the October 1971 issue of "Psychology Today"—"If You Want to Build Character, Try Something Else." They have worked, as you know, with 15,000 professional and amateur athletes and their observations on this large "N" are quite revealing indeed. It would also appear that they have used a similar device for evaluation, besides interviewing, as myself which makes our work quite related at an important level. Also, they have provided some broad-based data which will be extremely helpful while I am zeroing-in on one specific sport. The issue they raise about winning vs. "joyous pursuit of aesthetic experience" is open to considerable debate! That is, are they mutually exclusive, etc.? Surely our competition in Eastern Europe has a different focus.

My basic operational premise is very close to your point concerning the harmony of mind and body. The more knowledgeable and understanding the gymnast is of his own psychology, the more efficient and successful will be his performance. I also happen to believe that the most successful coaches are those who can best communicate with their individual gymnasts, because of sensitivity about the athlete's specific personality. (Research has already shown that coaches who are most skilled at articulating the personal "sociology" of their teams have the most successful records.) Such skill (many coaches don't have it) cannot be a substitute for technical knowledge, but it can help maximize the entire relationship and its outcome. The discipline of psychology can help in the development of this ability.

As of this date, I have collected autobiographical material, including many questions dealing with the nature of the individual's conscious motivations and other aspects of his participation in gymnastics, and personality test data on practically every superior U.S. gymnast. For my purpose, I mean those men who, for the past two years, have made our training camps and/or international teams. In addition, I have accumulated data on less successful gymnasts currently competing. I am also, and this is most important, in the process of attempting to gather the same material (questionnaire and testing) on top gymnasts from other parts of the world. (Hopefully a substantial number as time allows.) Although only a small number is involved at this time, it is a beginning and the prognosis is good.

Individually, this material is, and will remain, confidential. However, it is possible to speak of trends and perhaps now is an appropriate moment to state some preliminary observations. Much analysis and further collection and refinement is necessary, but certain aspects seem to have some validity at this time.

More research (basic and applied) should point out future directions for investigation in this area. Personally, I am more interested in applying clinical knowledge and technology to the actual gymnastic experience and to the interpersonal coach-gymnast interaction (this is surely needed on our national scene). This does not, of course, diminish my desire to remain as scientifically oriented as possible in so far as evaluation and research are concerned.

First of all, it should be stated that all past literature strongly suggest that it is extremely difficult to select out from a general population, in terms of psychological variables, athletes from non-athletes. It is also quite difficult to determine from a general psychological profile the different sports a group of athletes may participate in (e.g. weightlifter from basketball player), leaving out physical dimensions of course! I am beginning to feel, however, as I collect data on top athletes other than gymnasts, that this specific group may, in fact, be differentiated. I will need time and clearer evidence, but there are indications that this is quite feasible.

Ogilvie and Tutko feel that they have collected enough data now to state that it is possible to distinguish between participants in team and individual sports (based on personality configurations) and even to distinguish between athletes participating in different sports. I have not studied all their material, but I respect their conclusions. This is, of course, exciting news. It is interesting to note that among woman, Ogilvie and Tutko found less trait variation from sport to sport than men with the exception being in fencing, gymnastics and parachuting.

One thing I am prepared to state with growing confidence is that we can distinguish the top, world-class gymnast, via personality variables and overall profile, from the simply "good" performer. (These criteria include scores and national/international performance records.) There is some evidence that this may even be true not only within our own country, but cross-culturally as well! Obviously, instrumentation is of prime importance and presents the biggest problem (translation, etc.) when working with athletes in other cultures. Some progress is definitely being made in this area.

Should such a differentiation prove valid in coming months (i.e. 1972 Olympics) it may represent a significant contribution to our understanding of the gymnastic effort and to sports psychology, generally. This is an aspect of research the Russians are particularly interested in: distinguishing, from a psychological point of view, the top competitors from those just below them. Included in their work are interesting performance prediction studies.

In time, we should be better able to answer the question as to whether or not these personality factors and attitudes are the result of becoming a superior (top) athlete or are casual factors in achieving such excellence (chicken or egg inquiry). Current evidence suggests that they are characterological in nature and contributing variables in the individual personality, rather than purely acquired traits gained through training and competition. In other words, you have it to begin with and in most cases, those athletes who have the highest achievement and persist the longest have stronger personalities (by the way, "stronger" may not necessarily mean "healthier!"). As Ogilvie points out, competition does not appear to build character. More research is needed to clarify this comment.

Let me whet your appetite at this time with a few specific observations from my own work. It is clear from my research to date that certain personality variables are found among virtually every superior gymnast. These variables, although found in other athletes in varying degrees as well, have a very strong presence in the personality profiles of top gymnasts (I would need access to Ogilvie and Tutko's work in order to make definite quantitative comparisons). What is most striking is the fact that our top elite performers in the U.S. appear to be closer in their "psychological appearance" (tests and questionnaire) to their foreign counterparts than they are to their less successful American peer gymnasts. This supports the notion that these traits tend to be an aspect of the athlete's intrinsic, personal fiber. Perhaps of even greater interest is a preliminary observation that the higher a gymnast ranks as a competitor (those closest to the top) the more predictable is the personality profile along certain dimensions. Clarification of this finding must wait upon a more careful data analysis, but it is an intriguing trend.

In general, the protocols of gymnasts vary from man to man as one would expect in any group of human beings. In the top men, however, the variables alluded to above appear in a striking progression in terms of intensity, spread and interrelationship.

Top gymnasts appear to have a relatively high need to achieve. Although this need is present in the profiles of gymnasts in varying degrees, it is more prevalent than in any general population sample and may be higher than another group of athletes. However, it is not a predominant need. Gymnasts, however, do continually strive to accomplish tasks requiring great skill and sustained effort and to be successful in these attempts. Their reasons for doing this vary from individual to individual, but their need to do so is constant.

Along these same lines, and much more dominant, top gymnasts exhibit an extremely high manifest need (in comparison to even less adequate gymnasts) for psychological and physical endurance. That is, a powerful drive to finish a job which is undertaken at almost any cost.

A similarly strong and somewhat surprising characteristic of top gymnasts is a strong tendency to follow directions closely and do what is expected then to experience acute guilt when something goes wrong. In this situation, they seem to be willing to accept the blame for miscalculations themselves, rather than project responsibility upon someone else (coach, judge, etc.). An interesting point to observe here is that in the material of those successful gymnasts where this deference-abasement needs were not prevalent, there is a proportionately higher degree of need-aggression expressed, which may suggest the existence of some specific type of compensatory relationship may be operating.

An additional high-valence variable found in the protocols of most top gymnasts is one pertaining to a need to have external and internal order in their lives. In this case, what is sought is a sense of predictability, not rigidity, as it pertains to the concept of order.

The questionnaire data from top gymnasts is very stimulating. Besides descriptive material concerning personal motivations, styles, idiosyncratic manifestations, peaking, anxiety control, etc., the gymnasts provided their operational definition of the characteristics of an outstanding coach. Again, in all of this material, top gymnasts (given latitude for normal variance) "look" alike. What is impressive here is the phenomenal similarity given in the "coach's profile" by the best gymnasts. It may surprise some of our coaches to know that, although technical know-how is imperative, there are other factors which the top athletes are enlightening. For example, the top men evaluated (U.S. and non-U.S. to date) all mention, as a positive coaching personality variable, the control of one's verbal output; in other words, the ability of the coach to keep quiet unless he has something of real value to say. As I have indicated in an article in "Mademoiselle Gymnast," our predisposition to chatter may be culturally determined. In any event, the best gymnasts see this as a highly negative factor in coaching.

There are other equally challenging aspects to the questionnaire data collected so far, but I wish to reserve comment until further work is completed. An additional inquiry on the questionnaire concerned how the gymnasts felt a psychologist might be utilized on a national staff. Needless to say, this was personally highly informative and revealing.

There is much more to say, but time limits me at this point. I hope you are as "stirred with curiosity" as I am.

In the future, a complete report of this work will be prepared. Perhaps I will have continued opportunity to apply some of the things that are now coming into focus in my work with our national staff. Much will depend on our leadership's vision and willingness to explore new areas as they relate to gymnastics.

Sincerely,

Dr. Joseph L. Massimo, Special Asst., Men's U.S. National Coaching Staff

C.c. Mr. Frank Bare, President, U.S. Gymnastics Federation

THE GYMNAST'S PERCEPTION OF THE COACH

COMPETENCE AND COACHING STYLE

Many of the articles on gymnastics psychology that we have written have been more practical than research oriented in nature. In terms of research development, applied psychology seems to be where continued action is needed. Applying psychological principles to our training and coaching efforts remains important, but in order to continue to improve, we also need to persist in the area of basic research.

This article is designed to share with the gymnastic community some of the results of these efforts in research. Material will always be presented in a general way and individual gymnasts will not be identified. In all our work to date, the promise was made to participating athletes that their individual responses, test results, etc. would be held confidential, and that commitment will be honored. We will try to avoid jargon and statistical detail that will narrow the interest value of the article. One thing is certain: the endeavors of the past have opened the door for many doctorate studies.

Data collection on hundreds of world-class male and female gymnasts as well as information gathered on competitors at the intermediate and advanced levels were conducted personally by your authors and/or by foreign colleagues working in the competitive arena. The main focus was to look at the personalities of gymnasts from a variety of perspectives in an attempt to:

- Identify a psychological profile for these athletes distinct from other competitors
- Understand the psychological issues gymnasts face such as fear, motivation and attitude
- Develop more sensitive training approaches based on comprehensive individual assessments, in order to maximize performance by addressing the non-physical (mental) variables associated with excellence

In the process, and through the collaborative efforts of other disciplines such as medicine, physical science, sociology and others, a considerable body of information has gradually emerged. Additional research and findings on young developmental gymnasts can be found in the article "Psychological Characteristics of Jr. Elite Gymnasts.:

One of the various techniques utilized in the data collection phase was that of an "Elite Gymnast Questionnaire" specifically developed for elite male and female competitive gymnasts. This five +page instrument, designed by Dr. J. Massimo, is quite detailed and covers a wide range of information about the individual and his or her gymnastics. The questionnaire has been slightly modified to accommodate for the particular experience of Western and Eastern European gymnasts and to facilitate translation in the future. Basically, however, the questionnaire seeks the same material wherever it would be administered. Participation in filling it out, as with all aspects of the work, was voluntary, and the gymnast was told in either a cover letter or in person that they could ignore items they did not wish to answer. As one can imagine, there is an enormous wealth of material that has resulted from this one approach, but in this article we will deal with one particular question and an analysis of the answers received.

Part of the questionnaire included inquiries concerning the qualities you feel (look for) are important in a coach (trainer) including style of teaching (training, coaching), personal characteristics, etc. The coaching characteristics given reflected a deeply felt need in the gymnast and indicated his/her feelings about the importance of certain attributes in the coach. A careful analysis of the responses to this item revealed some remarkable findings, which even the statistician found striking.

Coaching Characteristics

The overall pattern that emerged in response to this question clearly showed a trend suggesting that the gymnast's view of what was important in a coach bore a close relationship to his or her own level of performance competence. It was evident that the more competent gymnasts were naming (seeking) a somewhat different set of qualities in their trainer than were their less successful colleagues (competence in this report was determined by regional, national, and/or international performance records).

Variation was present in the lists compiled for both highly successful, as well as less successful gymnasts. However, the degree of variation was considerably higher in the athletes whose actual performance record was not indicative of current competence. Further data analysis revealed the fact that for the most part, the better athletes always listed the same specific qualities among the top characteristics named. Although they varied in placement, they were always present near the head of the lists.

For the top performers, the major characteristics listed were in the general area of psychological motivation and support. The higher skilled the individual gymnast, the more important were these kinds of elusive characteristics in the coach. The more skilled and successful gymnasts appear to psychologically need and seek greater personal interactive closeness and motivational incentive based on an emotionally supportive relationship. Although the less competent gymnast also needs "motivation," it was not specified in incorporated terms, but in very task-oriented, concrete language such as, "a coach who wants me to do well," "who wants to win," etc., versus "a coach who will help me realize my potential."

The further down the success ladder, the more scattered the expressed attributes became, except that in the less proficient athlete, technical knowledge was almost always identified as very critical. Technical knowledge was also given a relatively high priority by top performers, not for its own sake, but always in terms of an ability to communicate to the gymnast information of a technical nature. It was rarely the most important characteristic identified in contrast to the less competent performer, where it was a key ingredient sought. There appeared to be an inverse relationship in this regard, that is, the less successful the performer, the higher significance the coach's pure technical ability and the more successful the competitor, the less crucial that quality was based on its placement and description in the list of trainer characteristics.

As previously indicated, in the vast majority of cases the number one characteristic sought by top performers was the coach's willingness and desire to get to know the gymnasts as an individual, and in a way that suggested care and emotional support. The verbal expression of this quality varied in construction, for example, "a coach interested in me as a person," "a trainer who would respect and know me as an individual," "a person I could trust and who cared about me," but the characteristics all suggested the same general theme. This kind of coach-quality was rarely indicated, as of highest significance in the lists of less successful gymnasts. For that group, as discussed earlier, the major quality sought and identified was technical knowledge. This was indicated in such phrases as, "a coach who knows how to teach difficult and skills," "a person with knowledge of the mechanics of tricks," "an individual who is able to show me how to do various moves," etc.

Other high-regarded characteristics named by the more competent gymnasts were the ability to motivate and maintain motivation, the ability to manage the sociology of a team, and the ability to develop meaningful interpersonal relationships on a one, to one as well as group basis. In the less successful gymnasts, more concrete attributes such as physical strength, skilled spotting and the provision of discipline were seen as more critical and most often mentioned. It is interesting to note that two characteristics having high valence for all gymnasts were the ability to organize training efforts (time management) and a clearly shown love for the sport.

Behavioral Qualities

It may be of interest to our readers to know what some of the other observations that were identified by gymnasts. Although some of these qualities might appear as behavior objectives many thoughtful coaches strive to develop, it is encouraging to have them confirmed by the athletes themselves. These are given with no attention to order of importance in so far as they appeared on the gymnast's lists, but they do represent the most frequently mentioned attributes identified by the most successful youngsters. In addition to the emotional and social factors, the capacity to communicate technical knowledge on an individual basis, a genuine dedication to gymnastics and organizational ability, the primary qualities discussed were: the ability to get a concept across with an appreciation for the individual gymnast's learning style, a minimum of excess verbiage (talking), consistent limit setting and the firm establishment of authority, an applied sense of humor while still taking gymnastics seriously, the absence of sarcasm and negativism as a general mode of response, hard work and enthusiasm on the part of the trainer, personal predictability, fairness in dealings with gymnasts, mature way of relating (not as a peer), good control of individuals and team at competitions, the ability to translate theory into action, honest critique of work being done and not being afraid to say the truth about one's performance, the ability to make a firm decision without dwelling on it, exemplary behavior (practice what you preach), ability to stay calm under stress, capacity to allow others to take responsibility, a person who will direct the spirit, not break it, an individual who is open to suggestions and willing to admit error, one who provides the opportunity for gymnasts to socialize with one another and who listens to the gymnast's concerns and problems, reliable attention to safety factors, and an overall positive attitude about training and competition. The above listing is not exhaustive and there were others, including some totally unpredictable, and even bizarre, notions, but the characteristics given represent a reasonable summation of the majority of responses.

There are several rather interesting issues raised by the material reported herein. It would be most enlightening to see if the task-oriented characteristics identified by less successful gymnasts at a given point in their careers shift to more emotional-caring ones as their own level of ability improves. Another related and intriguing inquiry would be to see if those less successful gymnasts at the time the questionnaire was completed, who did not fit the pattern associated with their level, but in fact named characteristics more in harmony with those expressed by better gymnasts, became more successful themselves over time. In essence, which comes first, the chicken or the egg: the success or the particular coaching approach associated with it? What is really going on here? Is there some specific psychological cluster reflected in a deeply held conviction and statement concerning the nature of the teaching-learning relationship which is predetermined in the personalities of successful athletes? If this is so, and it isn't present in a particular gymnast, can it be acquired or developed? This is not just a matter of intellectual curiosity for it has implications concerning the training of all gymnasts.

Coaching Styles and Skill Level

The material reported in this article strongly suggests that homogeneous ability grouping of gymnasts is a wise way to construct programs. Although it is true that some positive benefits from the performance of more skilled gymnasts might "rub off" on less competent members of a group, our results suggest that the more highly functioning youngsters need a different type of coaching style and approach which warrants segregation. Unless the coach is a Renaissance man or woman who can easily shift technique moment to moment depending on who he or she is working with, it is far more efficient to form groups whose members are very close to one another in ability. This may appear like an obvious fact which anyone could figure out without much fanfare. Experience suggests, however, that when such a grouping does occur, it is haphazard or done for overtly valid, but not thoroughly understood, reasons, such as that they are easier to work with, require less spotting and the like. The essential question is, "Why is this the case and what does it say about the kind of training interaction needed?" Our gymnastic history is replete with examples of how we do the correct thing, but for a less-than-informed reason. It may seem to some that it is a subtle difference indeed between a coaching approach to a group or individual that says, "Alright, I want you to do 20 compulsories each and watch execution on the back walkover," and the coach who says, "Let's see where we need to look in this exercise for perfection, what would you say we have to focus on at this point?" but, as a matter of fact, these represent a difference in both mentality and approach.

It is important to note that many of the better performers come from well-established programs where several coaches and combination of coaches are employees. Very often the coaching responsibilities are divided along performance level lines, one coach responsible for beginners, another for intermediates, etc. Obviously, from material reported here and elsewhere, such training organization makes sense. Coach selection, however, should not be random or simply based on seniority, but should be made on the basis of who can provide the kind and quality of input and leadership needed at a specific point in the gymnast's development. In most cases, the more experienced coach ends up working with the top youngsters. As has been pointed out, it is not only experience that is important, although it often accompanies the ability to motivate, but what is needed is a special personality and instruction style as well.

The relationship sought by top performers is sometimes already present, particularly if the coach and athlete have been together a number of developmental years, during which time this interaction has emerged quite naturally. Many top youngsters were reporting on the kind of coaching they were receiving already, but this was not the case in all situations, and from comments made on questionnaires it was apparent that sometimes the characteristics mentioned were those desired, but not necessarily present in their current training experience. It is at these junctions that progress may come to a standstill. This is the time when "driving" is still needed, but to a substantially lesser degree than an empathetic, personalized system of motivation and communication. Some coaches simply don't have the skill. They continue to rely on the old, faithful, standby techniques that worked at a prior time, failing to recognize that their gymnasts have grown and that the older methodology is no longer appropriate or effective. At that level of competence, much support is gained from comparable peers and the depth of talent and self-determination is such that it wins out over a less-than-ideal coaching situation. Loyal gymnasts "hang in," but their gymnastics becomes a maintenance operation at best, rather than a creative, forward surge at a time which often coincides with the peak learning and performance years. How much better the athlete could do, should the coaching conditions be more favorable to the development of excellence, remains unknown. Perhaps this is one reason we see a considerable amount of team changing at the higher levels in this country.

Some additional comments are appropriate at this time. The gymnasts responding to the questionnaire were all twelve years of age or older. You will note that there has been no differentiation in this article along sex lines. The explanation is simple and somewhat surprising, considering that the personality configurations of male and female gymnasts are different. However, there appeared to be little difference between the identified characteristics sought in a trainer by female or male gymnasts. Small variances can have large implications, but our first inspection suggests that what differences did exist were primarily a matter of emphasis rather than content. The articles "Coaching the Team–Part I & II" provides more information and coaching recommendations on this topic.

Implications for the Future

If we accept the hypothesis that the more skilled gymnasts need a different applied coaching style, one which is more highly personalized and motivational in nature, as suggested by this paper, it follows that we need to pay careful attention to the background, level and kind of expertise brought to our training camps at the national level. Coaching staffs that work at this level should be well balanced. Not only is it important to have our most technically competent coaches present, but equally, if not more critical, those coaches with a demonstrated capacity to relate to and motivate gymnasts in an emotionally supportive and psychologically caring manner. The coaches must be able to do this with gymnasts other than their own.

It would seem appropriate to consider the development of a master blueprint for the training and evaluation of coaches on a national level along the lines suggested by our observations. Currently, time in the sport is often a major criterion for selecting training camp personnel. Although this factor may be correlated with coaching ability, longevity does not necessarily ensure the presence of the specific characteristics named in this research. Another common, and perhaps more reliable criteria, is to nominate the coaching staff from among those coaches who have the top gymnasts (the assumption being that if they have the best youngsters, they must be the best coaches). Again, this may be a very erroneous assumption. There may well be some coaches working in our program today who may not have a top competitor in the current gymnastic ranks, but who, nevertheless, are superb trainers with excellent style-shifting and relationship building ability. Conversely, it is quite possible that some coaches with current top gymnasts may not be as sensitive and appropriate at a more finely tuned level as it may appear on the surface.

Giftedness along the dimensions suggested in this report is not as mysterious as it may seem; the desired characteristics can be identified and should be prerequisites for selections. Some individuals will resist this notion perhaps for selfish reasons, but somewhere along the line, priority will soon have to be given to the overall welfare of the gymnasts above any other factors and/or adult motivations.

In this same regard, it is interesting to contemplate what would happen if we asked our top performers, all of who know most of the coaches working on the national scene, who they would like to see at the training camp. If this were done anonymously, there is considerable evidence that some gymnasts would not endorse their own current coach. Without recourse to a secret ballot, this could be accomplished by asking each gymnast to nominate two coaches, one from their own gym and one from another. Although this might result in some painful ego blows, it would assist in the process of weaning from the single coach model and would help our top athletes to get the type of assistance they felt was important from whom they felt could deliver it at a crucial time.

In Conclusion

The body of research which we have amassed over the years is quite extensive. For this article, we offered information concerning the qualities a top level gymnast looks for in a coach. You may also be interested in a few related articles entitled "The Psychologists' View of Coaching: Part I & II," and the "Coaching Commandments."

PSYCHOLOGICAL CHARACTERISTICS OF JR. ELITE GYMNASTS

Authors' Notes: The psychological characteristics of Jr. Elite gymnasts was based on the findings from data collected and evaluations conducted at various training camps of the United States Association of Independent Gymnastic Clubs. Over 500 gymnasts have participated in our data collecting procedures over the years at these training camps. The following represents a typical descriptive report given to club owners and coaches to help them understand the personality of their gymnasts along with some recommendations for facilitating training in the future.

Report from the Sports Medicine Advisory Board–Psychology

TO: United States Association of Independent Gymnastic Clubs
ATTN: Coaches-USAIGC Jr. Elite Development Program
FROM: Dr. Joe Massimo, USAIGC Sports Medicine Advisory Board–Psychology, assisted by Dr. Sue Massimo
RE: Summary of Data Collection & Evaluation

General Description of Group

Sixty-five gymnasts participated in our training and data collecting procedures during the week at the training camp. All of the gymnasts appeared in excellent health and mainly ranged in age from 6-13. Here is a report of one of the camps which typifies the data gathered and the results found. An additional observation of a general nature seems in order. Although it was a factor not directly measured by any paper and pencil test, it is clear that these youngsters are fiercely competitive. This is not an unusual characteristic in such a group of young elite gymnasts, but it is important to keep in mind when dealing with them individually or in a group situation.

Specific Profiles

In response to a training questionnaire, the following results were obtained:

- Average age of female participant at camp ....10.7 years
- Average age for beginning gymnastics.....................................6.5 years
- Average number of workouts per week .... 5.0/wk.
- Average number of hours per workout.................................5.5 hours
- Weight training..................................(87% affirmative) 1+ hours/wk.
- Dancing.. (97% affirmative) 2.5 hr. /wk.

- Running...(48% affirmative) 1-5 miles/week
- Swimming.. (6% affirmative) No Time
- Biking.. (8% affirmative) No Time
- Average caloric intake reported... 1,750 cal.
- Taking of vitamin or diet supplement........................50% affirmative

Data Collection and Results

We personally administered a number of formal psychological instruments designed to measure visual-motor-perceptual coordination and functioning. We also gave the gymnasts a simple, but well researched devise used to determine their locus of control. This is a psychological construct indicating whether the athlete looks outside or inside of herself for critical motivation.

In all areas of visual-motor-perceptual functioning, this population scored in the above average to very superior range with the vast majority falling in the superior range of performance when compared to youngsters of the same age. In addition to the standardized normative data, we have collected hundreds of similar protocols from other athletes of the same age in other sports.

The data collected revealed that this extraordinary group of young people shows superiority in the following areas:

- Auditory sequential memory
- Short-term visual memory
- Freedom in receptivity, unhampered attention and contact with outside reality
- Planning, organization, and the capacity for sustained concentration
- Visual perception and spatial relations
- Capacity to synthesize concrete parts into a meaningful whole
- Internal motivators

One might suggest that the above characteristics would be predictably found in successful athletes in a sport such as gymnastics. Although such an observation would be reasonable, the marked degree of excellence found in this specific group is striking.

One of these areas is in the evaluation of short-term visual memory, that is, visual motor dexterity and speed under stress and the ability to learn new visual material quickly. In this measure, the gymnasts, in keeping with past results, are phenomenal and completely off the normative scale. It is now possible to begin to develop an entirely separate set of normative charts to be used with gymnasts alone. It is important to note that age does not appear to be a factor in this variable; that is, all the youngsters, regardless of their age, were outstanding in this area.

Another area, the locus of control measure of motivation yielded interesting results as well. The overwhelming majority of gymnasts evaluated were internal in locus of control. This finding suggests that, unlike visual memory, the degree of internal locus of control is dependent on age in gymnasts and becomes solidified at a later time. The fact that visual memory is a neurological function and locus of control is a personality characteristic supports this conclusion. This result tells us that actual behavior is the determining factor in terms of reward systems that motivate these gymnasts. In other words, what in their opinion they do well has a built in payoff or reinforcement. They do not look for motivational strokes from the coach, nor do they believe it comes from fate, chance, or any powerful others, but rather from themselves. They pride themselves on being independent and will avoid situations of dependency in their own manner. [For an in-depth look at this issue refer to "Locus of Control and Coach Effectiveness]."

Implications of Results and Recommendations

1. It appears advisable that we continue to gather information of a clinical nature on young gymnasts in order to better understand the nature of their unique psychological profiles and assist in maximizing their potential.

2. Our own personal relationships with your gymnasts appear to be quite good at this stage. In addition, it would be appropriate at this time to do more applied work with the gymnasts in the area of increasing attention, managing stress, and controlling levels of individual arousal, important parts of what we have referred to as the "performance connection." [You can get a greater understanding of this topic in the articles "The Performance Connection: Part I & II]."

3. Although this group is superior in many areas including the capacity to process auditory information, we have clearly seen that their strong suit is in the visual area. We believe that coaches are underutilizing this strength. We recommend that whenever possible coaches emphasize a visual presentation to go along with any verbal process for these youngsters. A most worthwhile (investment) project for a parents support organization would be to raise funds to purchase an excellent video-recording and playback system if one is not already in the gym. Beaming basic instruction and feedback to both visual and auditory modalities takes time, but it will be well worth it in terms of progress of these gifted athletes. American coaches have not been known for lack of verbiage, sometimes to a fault. It is important to remember that "show & tell" is a basic educational experience, but "show" comes first or should occur simultaneously with "tell." A further suggestion for use of video once it is available is to move the equipment to the actual site of the

apparatus when using it (beside the beam, next to bars, etc.). Using this system in close physical proximity to the event being considered can facilitate learning, as can the use of other gymnasts for demonstration purposes. [A look at the article "Right-Brained Gymnasts in Left-Brained Gyms" presents more insight into this area].

4. The fact that the majority of our youngsters are internal locus of control individuals suggests the following:

    a. These children will not respond well to overt, verbal coercion or conditioning. What they feel they do well is the determining motivation factor, not outside influence.

    b. These gymnasts will more likely respond to successful skill execution via personal self-competition (physical testing, skill level, etc.).

    c. Motivation schemes with these children should involve task-oriented, skill mastery feedback, rather than "cheerleading," or a "drill sergeant" approach. Encouragement in the form of positive reinforcement should be given of course, but be focused primarily on results with effort being somewhat taken for granted.

    d. An individualized skill-acquisition record book, or Personal Goals Notebook, with specific timelines and an overall blueprint for mastery should be part of each gymnast's personal belongings. [See "My Goal is to… A Gymnast's Plan" for more information on setting this up].

5. As pointed out earlier in this report, these athletes are extremely competitive. It is recommended that coaches and parents avoid making comparisons between gymnasts in the group as well as setting up any internal contests (which may become conflicts) with one gymnast against another. Skill and physical testing competitions as well as regular meet experience will provide all the formal competitive situations that are needed. A competitive attitude is important, but it would be wise to avoid over-fueling an already blazing fire!

6. It is important that parents be informed and involved in plans that are developed for their children. We do not imply by this that they should control the coaching of the gymnast nor dictate the overall effort. Most of the parents we have spoken to are not interested in this kind of participation. On the other hand, they are naturally involved and should feel a sense of respect from the people in whom they have placed their trust. We strongly recommend that coaches keep the lines of communication with parents open. A helpful and committed parent can be a real asset to a dedicated coach.

Chapter Two

— ΨＪ —

COACHING PSYCHOLOGY

Through our nearly combined 100 years in the sport as competitors, judges, coaches, and sport psychologists, we have amassed a considerable amount of experience on the nature of the coach-athlete relationship. In fact, much of the information presented in this effort is based on interviews and research conducted with hundreds of age-group, national, and international level gymnasts.

The chapter begins with an overview of the philosophy and principles surrounding psychology in coaching gymnastics. Some of the original guidelines for coaches set forth and revised through the years, were again recently published to much acclaim. In fact, the "Coaching Commandments" can be found in gymnastic clubs' handbooks across the country. Next we cover understanding leadership styles and communication skills as it relates to both the individual as well as the team. Lastly, other topics related to coaching psychology such as coach readiness and safety issues are discussed as well as ethical behavior and establishing a personal code of conduct, which are paramount to being a productive and effective coach.

- The Psychologists' View of Coaching: Part I: Philosophy
- The Psychologists' View of Coaching: Part II: Principles
- Coaching Commandments
- Coaching the Team: Part I: The Role of Adult Authority
- Coaching the Team: Part II: Democratic Leadership
- Safety Psychology in the Gym
- Ethics: A Personal Code of Conduct

THE PSYCHOLOGISTS' VIEW OF COACHING PART I: PHILOSOPHY

The job of coaching gymnastics has many aspects, but surely one of the most important and difficult, from the sports psychologists' point of view, concerns the psychological management of individuals and the overall shaping of the team as a composite of these same individuals. It would not be possible in one article to do justice to the complexities that a sensitive and committed coach faces on a daily basis. However, we will touch on the major qualities which form each coach's individual philosophy of coaching.

Coaching Philosophy

Communication

If one looks at the great coaches in any sport, it can be seen that their special mystique is not based exclusively on their technical knowledge of the sport alone. A great deal appears to rest on an ability to handle the interpersonal relationships and motivational issues involved within the team and between the coach and athlete. Our own research in past years examined the characteristics that world class gymnasts valued and looked for in a high quality coach. The results of these inquiries clearly demonstrated that one of the most important abilities, even above technical expertise, was skill in handling the personal interactions between coach and individual gymnast. See the article "The Gymnast's Perception of the Coach: Competence and Coaching Style" for a full report on these qualities.

It is clear that the more adequately the coach can communicate with the gymnasts, based on specific knowledge of their personality, the more productive will be the effort to increase high level performance on a consistent basis. For many this ability is a gift, for others a matter of trial and error, for some a result of special training and study as well as long experience, and for others a combination of all of these factors. Whatever the origin of such insightful, psychologically sound behavior, it is crucial in assembling the pieces of an individual and team effort into a finished product. The article "Coaching the Team" provides more information on this area.

Individual Philosophy

The coach's individual philosophy will, of course, have a critical impact on determining the character of the club. Many successful coaches premise their work on getting to understand each athlete on a personal level: what motivates each, what are the areas of special strength or weakness, how do they approach the sport, etc.? The objective is to promote the development of a sense of mutual goals, respect, support, and caring which will result in a disciplined individual and unit performance. Within small clubs or teams internal competitions quite naturally arise and it is important and useful to control these in a constructive way while at the same time monitoring them so they do not get out of hand and demoralize the group effort.

Discipline

In essence, the major challenge of the coach is to direct the spirit, not break it. Discipline is an important concept in this regard. Discipline is defined in most standard dictionaries as a special form of "learning." There are coaches whose discipline is irrational, harsh, over-determined and destructive. If a demand or decision is made in this context, which is unfair in terms of the individual or team, it will surely erode productivity in an insidious manner. There is nothing wrong with a coach changing his/her mind if it is in the format of rational behavior and not the result of weakness or manipulation. This kind of flexibility will be admired by the gymnasts rather than an authoritarian rigidity which is impenetrable regardless of the particular circumstances involved. On the other hand, fair demands and expectations must not be subjected to the whims of the athlete, but must be strictly enforced as part of a "disciplined learning." Most athletes will dutifully, albeit sometimes reluctantly, follow through on such demands since they respect and accept a coach who has demonstrated reasonableness and earned authority.

Work Ethic

In gymnastics, hard work is a universal guiding principal and successful gymnasts thrive on it. The psychological climate for this labor of love is most important. Extremes in this psychological atmosphere seem doomed to failure in the long run. The establishment of a positive environment is a subtle and on-going challenge. From the sports psychologists' point of view, what appears ideal is a purposeful setting where concentration and self-discipline is stressed. Coach control is gradually reduced as the acceptance and the recognition of a common purpose becomes clearer with each passing day. The group, and each individual within it, understands that the demand is for 100+ percent effort. This is the expected and explicit norm, the basis of all motivation. With time, the need to emphasize such a work expectation should be greatly reduced. Work volume and element count should be at a peak. If this is not the case in a higher level competitive program, something is wrong and the time has come to analyze objectives and what is happening with the overall training effort in the gym.

Coaching Dynamics

All coaches are called upon to make spontaneous decisions. It is quite often a matter of coming up with quick and instinctually calculated responses: when to pat on the back and when to prod forcefully, when to be gentle and when to be extraordinarily demanding, when to say "STOP" and when to say "I think you're ready to do this on your own." In addition, coaches must learn how to handle emotional meltdowns, frustrations, anger, fear, injuries, over-extension in training and underproduction in competition, and many others all under the watchful eyes of bright and sensitive young people! This is the true nature and excitement of the profession of coaching.

In some matters, consistency for all is important, for example the level of training demands, while in other cases it will depend on the specific circumstances and the individual involved, for example, an angry response from a certain gymnast. It is a never ending task requiring a considerable disbursement of emotional energy. Obviously, the more a coach knows about the individual dynamics of the youngsters under their charge, the easier the job will become and the less chance of premature coach burn-out taking place. You may refer to the article "Abuses of Anger in the Gym" for help in this matter.

Encouraging Individuality

Another imperative in coaching from the sports psychologists' view is the encouragement of individuality. Along with this is the awareness and appreciation of each gymnast's learning style. The task is to help a gymnast develop their own style, much like an artist tries to project a specific identity. This is much easier said than done. There is no way that the coach can totally keep him or herself out of the picture being painted and presented. We all have expressive preferences. Often we will hear a comment suggesting that all the routines look alike, or reflect a certain known coaching style. That is fine, up to a point, as part of the process. However, if "sameness" is over-present, then perhaps it suggests a situation where innovation is discouraged by an overly dominant coach who stifles the creative process and is threatened by originality. It is a psychological factor which needs to be looked at from time to time by the committed coach. Control of the training and creative control are different issues.

Technical Knowledge

In addition to these direct psychological kinds of coaching content, is the very essential requirement of knowing your business. The teaching and learning of gymnastic skills requires a coaches input in terms of technique, mechanics, execution, spotting and safety issues. Since our knowledge and the requirements in these areas grow each year, a coach must also keep abreast of the latest thinking in the sport as well. There is nothing worse than coaches who pretend that they know what they are talking about when the bottom line is clearly one of ego not mastered knowledge. This is the quickest way to bring a group down, not to mention the risk present in today's malpractice suit mentality which might result from such erroneous behavior. Some teams function amazingly well with a coach who may be technically less knowledgeable than another, providing that person is willing to recognize shortcomings and gradually take steps to learn what is needed. Gymnasts can accept this if they see an effort being made to learn from others, including the gymnasts themselves. Perhaps the coach's strongest current asset is his or her ability to motivate, and that is very valuable indeed. It is often difficult to hold respect under lopsided conditions, but it is far better than creating a transparent illusion of technical competence where everyone can be subject to emotional and perhaps even physical injury.

Developing a working comprehension of the technical and safety requirements of the sport are areas that require continual input and study by the coach. In addition to all these things that need to be monitored, there is the endless homework, planning routines, training schedules, competition calendar, traveling, funding, and dozens of other equally necessary tasks which are all part of the coaches overall responsibility. If you combine all of the above, along with the physical task of spotting, one can understand why many coaches are as exhausted as the gymnasts at the end of a workout.

Role Model

Finally, from the psychological point of view, the coach's most awesome challenge is to provide an acceptable and admirable model for impressionable young people who spend more time with them than any other significant adult in their lives. Coaches can and do exert a very powerful influence in the lives of their latency and adolescent age gymnasts. This responsibility must not be taken lightly. Gyms cannot be guidance or mental health clinics; that is not their mission or goal. They also should not be places where children experience negative feedback, blows to their emerging self-esteem, or emotional pain as the result of an insensitive, single-minded adult who may purport to "love gymnastics," but fails to carry the essence of this kind of feeling over to the youngsters who make it all happen. From our biased point of view, this is the most important non-physical aspect of all coaching. Refer to the article "The Issue of Ethics" for more insight on this very important subject.

Summary

Every individual who works with children in any capacity over time develops certain personal guidelines that result from their experiences. The introductory content of this article has been to briefly represent the views of sports psychologists concerning the profession of gymnastic coaching. We would all agree that it is a very difficult but rewarding job, involving both some heartache and much joy. If this were not the case, it is unlikely that there would be many coaches still around. In the last analysis, whatever is taken in must flow through the personal value system of the individual coach. Ultimately, what emerges in the way of philosophy, motivation, behavior and dedication to the young people in their charge will be more a result of the complex conditionings that go into the human experience than of anything read, seen or heard.

With that in mind, we have compiled a master list of general observations about the psychology of the coach-gymnast interplay which may assist the coach in developing a personal coaching philosophy of which they would be proud. In Part II of "The Psychologists' View of Coaching" we present these guidelines, not as "dos and don'ts," but as a reflection of a philosophy that governs an individual's work with their young gymnasts.

THE PSYCHOLOGISTS' VIEW OF COACHING PART II: PRINCIPLES

Part I of "The Psychologists' View of Coaching" presented an introductory statement about the nature of coaching from the viewpoint of sports psychologists working and coaching in the field of gymnastics. Several major themes were developed including the basic idea that coaching is an extremely complex activity involving technical knowledge, individual and team management, communication and relationship building skills, decision making, adult modeling, and others. Coaching was seen as a highly professional and sensitive task that was most successful when it involved positive approaches to the teaching-learning situation. It was further suggested that the more sophisticated the coach was in terms of a psychological awareness of the individuality of each athlete, the more successful and rewarding the outcome of mutual hard work in any sports endeavor.

Anyone who works with young people in any capacity over a long period of time eventually develops a set of principles or guidelines based on everyday experience, which they feel are most important in fostering a good working relationship designed to bring about maximum results. Part II of this series presents such a "list" from the perspective of sports psychologists who have been involved in gymnastics in various capacities as gymnasts, judges, coaches, and researchers for five decades. It is interesting to note that all of these strategies can be linked together and are not given in any order or priority. They can all be applied to any teaching-learning model whether it is parent-child, student-teacher, coach-gymnast or any other give and take interaction whose objective is to have an individual young person grow in knowledge, competence, and self-esteem.

Over the years, the following principles became referred to as the "coaching commandments" by many outstanding coaches and gym owners. In fact, many programs include these in their team handbooks for all their coaches to use as a guiding force as they develop their own coaching philosophy. In any event, it is hoped that coaches will find food for thought in relation to their own efforts in coaching young athletes.

Principles and Commandments in Coaching

1. **Establish your philosophy and authority early.** It is very important that from the beginning, and throughout the athlete's experience in your program, the lines of authority be made absolutely clear to gymnasts, assistant coaches, and parents. The coach needs to be firm and definite about these matters with limits and controls understood by all. This also

establishes a philosophical statement about the role of authority. This does not mean that a dictatorship needs to be in place, but evident structure does. Refer to the article "Coaching the Team: Part I" for more insight on the role of authority.

2. **Relate to your gymnasts in a warm, natural way, but not as a peer.** Although many coaches keep their distance, this should not mean indifference or obvious coldness. In fact, that is really counter-indicated in a sport like gymnastics. Show care and emotional support and interact with a mutual goal that should involve work and fun, but not the "coach" as a "big buddy."

3. **Minimize verbiage.** In some of our past research, comparing other nation's coaching style to that of the U.S., it has been evident that we have a cultural predisposition to chatter and talk in the gym. That is not to say that our competition doesn't speak to one another, but a verbal exchange count clearly suggests that we do much more. Our gyms can really become very noisy places. Don't add to this with endless feedback to the athlete. Observe the gymnasts carefully and comment on their effort only when you really have something of value to communicate. Make sure, for example, that an error you see is not just a single miscalculation, but is a chronic mistake. This requires time and silence. Don't comment each time your gymnast moves; look for a pattern to maximize learning. Use non-verbal tactics as much as possible like we point out in the article, "A Coaches Guide to Non-Verbal Communication." If you ask questions or make comments, do so one at a time. Don't force the gymnast to choose which one to respond to. Avoid small talk and, as the coach, remain focused and concentrated on the task at hand.

4. **Have a sense of humor,** but don't make a joke out of gymnastics. Nothing will de-contaminate a tense and potentially destructive situation quicker than a good sense of humor. You will help your kids keep themselves and their work in perspective. On the other hand, it is important that workouts are not a "laughing matter."

5. **Never utilize sarcasm and negativity in coaching.** This is an easy trap to fall into, for this style comes very readily to many coaches. Few latency and adolescent age youngsters have emotionally mature egos, which can manage and cope with anything that comes their way. We have known many coaches who feel that they can berate a gymnast with a continual bombardment of negative feedback and who feel this represents real "learning" and is good motivation. We suggest that they are 100% wrong and, although a negative comment from time to time is justified, the measured and unquestionably preferred approach from all points of view

is to be continually POSITIVE. Although some feel it is funny, it usually isn't to youngsters unless it is rarely used, and only then with clear humor. Basically, it isn't funny and should be consciously avoided, like a plague. Sarcastic comments represent the ultimate in disrespect for the other person no matter what your position.

6. **Be enthusiastic in your work and encourage the same thing among gymnasts.** A high spirit and energy level is difficult to maintain, but every effort should be made to do so. It creates a contagious atmosphere in the gym. Many coaches have kids applaud or ring a bell when a teammate accomplishes something very positive. This is a wonderful idea.

7. **Be fair in your treatment of each gymnast.** This applies in particular to the training situation where the number of turns on an apparatus, rotation time to events, etc. is concerned. Most coaches do in fact have favorites in the gym, although some will deny this natural tendency. Sometimes it is based on talent, sometimes on other not so easily recognizable factors. It is very important to guard against this circumstance interfering with the overall emotional climate in the gym. There are times when one athlete will receive special attention, perhaps because of a most demanding skill, etc. That is perfectly fine, as long as teammates know that in their time the same attention will be given to them. That is fairness at an important psychological level.

8. **Give each gymnast your complete attention** when you are working with them. Often we will be speaking with a youngster and, out of the corner of our eye, spot something someone else is doing that we wish to comment on. This is a natural distraction in a busy gym. Don't, however, allow that to interfere with the communication under focus unless of course, it's a matter of safety. So, at that moment the only person, as far as you are concerned, should be the gymnast you're speaking with. Make sure you are really listening and communicating with your athlete.

9. **Don't tell a gymnast that their work is "good" when it isn't.** Most gymnasts know when they have done a good job. They will not trust your critique if you praise them when they know in their hearts that the performance was inadequate. It is not necessary to say anything negative, but surely false praise is not warranted. However, you can continually stroke worthwhile effort. That kind of encouragement is always important and valid even if the gymnast has clearly failed but at least tried. Say such things as, "Better," "It's coming along," and "Next time, you need to…" to provide the corrective measure for the task.

For example, if a gymnast is running slowly on the vault, don't say, "If you ran any slower, you'd be going backward." That is a useless comment and hurtful. It would be better to say, "OK, good effort. This time explode at the start and keep the momentum going." This is a motivating statement. You must show your gymnast respect if you hope to get the top effort from them and expect the same degree of respect in return.

10. **Say "NO" without feeling guilty and "YES" without resentment.** These are very subtle but important matters. Very often a youngster will ask something such as, "Can I do another?" and the coach will answer out of affection, cohesion, etc. "Yes," only to hear a voice inside saying, " I really didn't want to say that."

Be careful of this issue, for if you are not, your true feelings will come out later, usually in a negative way. Think about the gymnast's request carefully when it is of the "can I?" type. Avoid a display of uncertainty or inconsistency about the issue. Make up your mind, and then be secure about your decision.

11. **Be a consistent spotter and pay attention to all safety issues.** Keep up on the latest equipment and safety guidelines. If you use a lot of physical assistance in your gym, then be consistent with its application. This builds confidence in your gymnasts. When you say you are going to be there, or you've got them, be there and get them. This may appear to be solely a physical recommendation, but has real psychological implications as well.

12. **Don't be afraid to say "I'm sorry" and "I don't know."** From time to time, coaches make blunders. Nothing will cement your relationship quicker with your athletes than your recognition and willingness to apologize for poor behavior on your part. The value is written on the faces of the gymnasts when you do so. You surely are not above making an error either. The coach whose attitude suggests that he or she knows it all is at risk. You will gain respect from your gymnasts if you are willing to admit there may be a limit to your technical knowledge at some level. They will not put you down especially if you are, in fact, competent and if you indicate your intention to find out and even search for the answer with your gymnasts. If you fake it for ego reasons, not only do you risk injury to the youngster, but in the long run you will diminish your basic image.

13. **Allot time for the gymnasts to socialize.** This should not take place during the workout except in a minimum way. Each day, however, the youngsters should know that this is possible within a particular situation (prior to warm-up, mid-workout break, after conditioning, etc.) Let them know you realize

this is important in a restricting sport like gymnastics and that it has a time and place in the overall training plan.

14. **Provide a forum for listening to your gymnasts.** We feel this is a most important variable. At least once a month the coach(s) should sit down with the kids to discuss any issues relevant to the smooth running of the training effort. Think of it as a "state of our team" dialogue. The rules for this meeting should be: LISTENING/LEVELING.
    - One person speaks at a time.
    - No one has to speak.
    - Anything can be brought up.
    - When one person is speaking the others will maintain eye contact with him or her.
    - No put downs allowed.
    - Questions are only used to clarify a point of view, not to criticize it.

This process takes time and patience to develop as basic trust is involved. It is well worth the effort in promoting a positive climate in the gym and avoiding a build-up of any difficulty. See the article "The Coach-Gymnast Conference: Listening and Leveling" for more information on running these meetings.

15. **Continually educate yourself.** Work extremely hard yourself in and out of the gym on educating yourself on the technical demands of the sport, safety and spotting issues, as well as child development and the physiological and psychological aspects of your sport.

16. **Delegate some responsibility to your athletes.** It helps the emotional climate in the gym when the gymnasts feel some sense of ownership in certain decisions, and that they complete assignments along with routines. Don't overdo this to the point of losing basic control. Gymnasts working with other gymnasts are a good way to spread motivational strokes beyond the coach and promote a sense of pride and responsibility.

17. **Be personally and emotionally predictable.** Coaches, as athletes, can be moody and gymnasts can accept this, but for best results a certain consistency in response is imperative. This is essential so the gymnasts can feel that external matters which affect their internal attitudes and consequently their output are being monitored in a stable fashion. This responsiveness provides an important sense of security for them. All youngsters, even highly discipline gymnasts, will test the limits from time to time. For example, they may slack off somewhat on their work, but they know just about how

long it will take before the roof falls in. What matters is they know and expect the boom will be lowered and that in fact this eventually happens in a predictable way.

18. **Be a role model at all times,** especially during competitions when the pressure is at the highest. Remember to practice what you preach! It is easy to overstate the coaching relationship, but it is equally easy to underestimate your influence on the lives of the youngsters in your charge. There is such a psychological construct as "identity formation," and coaches can play a key role in its development, particularly during the adolescent years. It is easy to tell your athletes that you want to see "style" at a competition marked by controlled behavior. It is another matter for the coach to stay calm during the heat of battle! Try to avoid setting a poor example.

19. **In the case of male coaches working with female gymnasts, be very careful not to sexualize your interaction** with your gymnasts. This should need no further elaboration. The article "Male Coach-Female Gymnast" provides more information on this issue.

20. **Have the ability to motivate and manage the team.** Top gymnasts look to their coaches for help in promoting and maintaining motivation among individuals as well as the team. They also rely on the coach to manage the overall sociology of the team.

21. **Be the type of coach who will direct the young gymnasts' spirits, but not break them!** Don't play with your athletes' lives and emotions. They may be "tough" youngsters in many regards, but they are not adults, and their external physical strength, resilience, and psychological endurance might lead you to forget that they are basically children. Encouragement, support, and praise will go a long way in directing your gymnast's spirits resulting in a happy, confident, and productive young person.

22. **Have a positive attitude towards training, competition, and life in general.** Here is what one famous American Olympian wrote in her "Elite Gymnast Questionnaire" describing three of the main qualities she looks for in a coach. She stated that the "things I look for in a coach" are a "desire that equals mine" and "one who really loves the sport." It can't be said better than that.

Summary

Overall, the coach's task is to "work with" the youngsters "not against" them, both in terms of physical learning as well as emotional well-being and development. To accomplish this you need to be a genuine person to your athletes, one who is capable of laughing, crying, sharing, committing, and above all, caring at a number of levels. You can be very interested in them as people, not just motor-wonders without being overly involved in their lives. It takes practice and patience as well as mature judgment.

Finally, it may help to remember that when the history of sport is written, it is unlikely that your coaching activities will be recorded. Keep things in perspective and enjoying the mutually satisfying rewards of a working relationship with these young artists and your sense of participation in the creative process. That alone should be your overriding objective, and with it will come unexpected benefits and satisfaction in the short-and long-term, for you and your gymnasts.

COACHING COMMANDMENTS

Anyone who coaches young athletes over a long period of time eventually develops a set of principles or guidelines based on everyday experience, which they feel are most important in fostering a good working relationship designed to bring about maximum results. Coaching is a highly professional and sensitive task that is most successful and rewarding when it involves positive approaches to the teaching-learning situation coupled with a psychological awareness of the individuality of each athlete. The full descriptions of the following commandments can be found in "The Psychologists' View of Coaching: Part I & II."

Coaching Commandments
- Firmly establish your authority.
- Maturely relate to your gymnasts, but not as a peer.
- Minimize verbiage.
- Have a sense of humor.
- Never utilize sarcasm or negativity.
- Be enthusiastic and encourage the same in the gym.
- Be fair in your treatment of each gymnast.
- Pay complete attention when working one-on-one.
- Don't tell a gymnast that their work is "good" when it isn't.
- Say "NO" without feeling guilty and "YES" without resentment.
- Pay attention to safety factors and be a consistent spotter.
- Don't be afraid to say "I'm sorry" and "I don't know."
- Allot time for the gymnasts to socialize.
- Provide a forum for listening to your gymnasts.
- Continually educate yourself.
- Delegate responsibility to your gymnasts.
- Be personally and emotionally predictable.
- Be a positive role model at all times.
- Be careful not to sexualize the interaction with your gymnasts.
- Motivate and manage team cohesiveness.
- Direct your young gymnasts' spirits; do not break them!
- Have an overall positive attitude towards gymnastics and life.

COACHING THE TEAM
PART I: THE ROLE OF ADULT AUTHORITY

Gymnastic coaches often struggle with the question of how strict or lenient to be in the management of the athletes they are training. The decision made in this area often affects the entire program and the quality of the relationships within it.

This series of two articles examines the important issue of the use of adult authority in the coaching of a gymnastics team. "Coaching the Team: Part I" considers some theoretical and practical implications that accompany the unique challenge of working with a group of young athletes versus focusing on a single individual. Research findings, which investigate different styles of leadership and authority in non-gymnastic situations, are discussed. These same findings are applied to gymnastic coaching, with a specific leadership style being identified, as being more favorable than others. In "Coaching the Team: Part II" of this series, this leadership model is elaborated in greater detail with suggestions offered for maximizing the effective use of authority within this preferred approach to coaching.

Individual vs. Team

Since individual gymnastic "stars" often steal the headlines and attention, it is easy to forget that most often coaches deal with a group of children on a team as well as with individuals within that group. This challenge, by its very nature, raises the question of just how much authority a coach should exercise at any given time. In discussing this question, two important points need to be made: (1) gymnasts in groups, in fact, children in general do not always behave the same as they do individually, and (2) as a result of this basic fact, it is one of the coaches' responsibilities to exercise guidance, leadership and specific authority in order that both the individual and group develop toward mastery, and that the "good of the team" not be sacrificed.

Coaches are usually aware that they cannot neglect the whole for any single part, unless the specifics of a high level competition dictate that this must be done in order to realize success. Intuitively, good coaches have long understood, at some level, that there is more complexity in leading a group than usually meets the eye. A group is not a constant organism and a team shifts in mood, competitiveness, cooperativeness, zeal, etc. from day to day, and often even from moment to moment. There are a number of reasons for such shifts.

Individual personalities both influence the behavior of groups and are altered by membership in a group or on a team. Most adults have had the experience as adolescents, for example, of seeing a change in their "best friend's" behavior when a third person joined what had previously been a twosome. Within a larger "team" situation, such changes also occur and can have quite dramatic effects on the group.

Being in a team situation can affect the individual gymnast's behavior in unpredictable ways. Since team life has particular intricacies, a coach needs to attempt to understand not only the forces within the group that may be activators for acceptable or unacceptable discipline, but also the psychological influences upon these forces.

Adult Leadership

Many forces act upon and influence the nature of the team group. Some of these are more or less self-evident. Surely, the quality and nature of the official adult figure (coach) is one of the most important influences. The nature of the unofficial leadership, the gymnast or gymnasts whom the group looks up to, is also a critical variable. In addition, the physical environment, whether it is limiting or spacious, underequipped or over equipped, and the nature of the tasks to be performed within it, can influence the team functioning. A team is also affected by personality problems of the individual gymnasts, by its size which is often dependent on goals, by the "spirit" of the team which can be influenced by such diverse factors as the weather, holidays, school pressures, etc., and finally by the kinds of control and authority that the individual gymnasts have been subjected to previously, such as a very stern teacher in school, or a permissive father or other parent figure outside of the gym.

As indicated earlier, the adult leadership of the coach is usually the most crucial of all these factors, because the effective coach is in a position to bring and weld together diversity, reduce the anxiety which often accompanies specific gymnastic challenges, stimulate and motivate for the task to be done, and smoothly control the reins which may have been held too loosely or tightly in the past. For example, an effective coach may act with greater assertiveness than ordinarily if he/she recognizes that the day before a holiday may mean the "team" will be somewhat high strung.

He may intervene more forcibly if a strong-willed athlete is acting up. He may vary the training regime if the work has been particularly demanding and difficult. These are crucial and often subtle decisions that the coach makes for the good of the group interaction. They come out of wisdom, experience, and an awareness of the psychology of group dynamics. Of course, what works well for one coach will not for another, for they too are individuals with personality organizations that affect their sensitivity and flexibility, as well as their level of need for dominance or control.

Recognizing the individuality of coaches and training circumstances, is there any more objective data that might assist in determining the nature and extent of adult authority that is appropriate in coaching a team and the individuals within it?

Classic Research

Although there have been a variety of studies in recent years considering the coach and coaching style as an important variable in team management, a research effort conducted by Lippitt and White with non-gymnastic populations, remains a classic work with considerable implications for the development of a workable coaching model. The study investigated the effects of different kinds of leadership on what was called the "social climate" within groups.

These researchers sponsored the organization of four different clubs of ten year old boys with the major purpose of the clubs being the pursuit of various crafts activities. Membership in each club was controlled by using different sociometric devices for obtaining a balance of similar personality characteristics, social relationships, health, socioeconomic background, and intelligence.

Each of the groups was led by one of three different kinds of leaders for a period of six weeks. At the end of this time the type of leadership style was changed, although the physical setting for each group remained the same. Carefully trained observers using one way mirrors noted, in exhaustive detail, the behavior of the group and its members. Research conclusions were formulated from these observations.

Leadership Styles

The three kinds of leadership which the youngsters experienced were labeled by Lippitt and White as, authoritarian/autocratic, laissez-faire/detached, and democratic.

1. Characteristically, the **autocratic leader** structured the situation, dictating what the activities were to be and assigning specific tasks to individual members. This approach, involved rule by an iron hand, and it tended to be personal with praise given to those individuals in favor and criticism to those who appeared to be disliked by the leader. Negative reinforcement was dominant.

2. The **laissez-faire leaders** tended to let the group, more or less, structure their own activities. Input and guidance was held to a minimum, and intervention only came when an activity was seen as potentially dangerous. In most cases, leadership was withdrawn and little encouragement or discouragement was given to group members to establish any kind of leadership on their own.

3. The **democratic leader** was much more involved as a leader-participant member of the working group. The leader provided a plan, but considered input from the members as appropriate. Goal setting was mutually accomplished with input from the leader, designed to achieve the stated

objectives. Although this leader was not impersonal, no favoritism was evidenced. Constructive criticism was given to all participants as warranted and positive reinforcement was continually utilized.

Coaching Implications

The results of this study have significant implications for leaders of other groups, specifically coaches with gymnastic teams. The major conclusion of the effort was that more of what Lippitt and White referred to as spontaneous cohesion, a kind of easy unity took place in groups led by the democratic approach than in the other groups. There was more mutual helping evidenced in setting overall goals and moving toward them, and generally more positive behavior. In addition, far less discontentment was seen in these groups.

Obviously, developing a competitive edge and running a high powered gymnastic training program requires forceful and structured leadership, but this should not be thought of as synonymous with a dictatorship which is often the case. A common fallacy of coaches, who wish to be more "democratic" in their coaching, is that they mistake the form for the content. A formal democracy is not always a democracy. A training program in gymnastics can be organized democratically, as the term is used in this article, without the gymnasts running the show or having a vote! Democratic control is as much a psychological and mental health concept as it is a social contract. Its core is in the feelings that exist between the leader and the group and within the group itself. If this kind of democratic control could be summarized in few words, they would most likely be feelings of mutual respect. This is an essential concept that needs to be elaborated.

The findings of this same study on the relationship between autocratic and laissez-faire leadership were quite provocative. The data strongly suggested that the young people in the groups preferred the autocratic model over the laissez-faire, somewhat indifferent leadership. Discourse and disruption was evident under the laissez-faire leadership, but groups under the autocratic leadership seemed to respond in two different ways. In one group, under autocratic leadership, there was considerable rebellion even when the leaders were present. In another group, however, when the leader was present, there was considerable submissiveness shown, but whenever the leader was not visible chaos often occurred. These observations may not be surprising to certain coaches. It is well known that a weak coach is often disliked by athletes to a point of contempt, and that such an individual in a high risk activity, such as gymnastics, can cause a good deal of anxiety in the gymnasts. A coach who exerts strong control and gives direction, even though it may come entirely from him or her is generally more acceptable. The coach who combines both coach-direction and athlete involvement is preferred. We also know that an authoritarian coach may be very successful in dominating a team as long as he or she is present, but that the team may "go to pieces" if discipline is relaxed or the coach is absent.

Leadership that constantly restricts psychological growth at any age is ultimately met by either retaliation or resignation on the part of group members; neither of these conditions will maximize the learning process. Psychological restriction can occur, not only where there is too much leader dominance and too little personal initiative, but also when youngsters are left more or less on their own and unguided.

Goal setting is an established psychological tool in the mental preparation for competition. In democratic groups, as was previously indicated, the goals were not unstructured as they were in the laissez-faire or superimposed, as they were in the autocratic groups, but were set by the total group with active assistance from the leader. In addition, because of a democratic leader's sensitivity, goals were constantly kept in view and youngsters were able to gain an ongoing perspective on their progress. They could clearly see that they were making measurable steps toward their objectives. This is how formal goal-setting in gymnastics needs to be organized and conducted. You can find helpful step-by-step guidelines in "Using Goal Setting as a Coaching Tool."

Summary

In this article several observations have been presented that have implications for the role of adult authority in coaching a gymnastics team:

- In a democratic model of coaching a team, responsibility for leadership rests with the coach. This is a notion often misunderstood.
- In this model the responsibility carries with it the obligation to sense when to be a very strong leader and when to step into the background to a calculated degree.
- Democratic coach leadership has as its objective, the teaching of group control and self-discipline which will increase with age and experience of the gymnasts while, at the same time, teaching skills needed to realize their maximum physical potential and support important emotional growth.

This last point is not easily achieved, and in "Coaching the Team: Part II" of this discussion, we will examine, in greater detail, some suggestions as to how a coach can adopt a democratic leadership style, while still getting the job done in this demanding sport.

COACHING THE TEAM
PART II: DEMOCRATIC LEADERSHIP

In "Coaching the Team: Part I–The Role of Adult Authority," we discussed arriving at some position about how strict or lenient to be in the management of gymnastic training. Some theoretical and practical implications that go along with the special challenge of working with young athletes in a group, as opposed to one individual at a time, were also examined. Research findings that investigated different leadership and authority models in non-gymnastic group situations were discussed and related to potential coaching styles. It was stated that any leadership model that constantly restricts psychological growth at any age, is eventually met by either rebellion or a kind of resignation and "giving up"; neither response being conditions that contribute to the learning process. It was stated that psychological restriction can occur not only where there is too much leader dominance and too little personal initiative, but also when youngsters are left too much on their own.

Of the various models presented in Part I, one was identified as being more favorable than others. This style was called "democratic" in nature and the myths surrounding this concept as a non-productive "coaching" approach, for high powered gymnastic programs, were examined. The most common fallacy addressed was that of coaches who wish to be more democratic in their efforts, but who are reluctant to do so because they have mistaken form for content and that a democratic approach meant a loss of control. It was pointed out that a basic democracy is not always totally democratic; nor need it be to be successful. Democratic control was shown to be as much of a psychological and mental health concept as it is a social construct. Most importantly, it was observed that at the heart of this democratic model is a core of feelings that exist between the leader and the group and within the group.

In Part II of this series, the democratic leadership model will be described in more detail with some suggestions offered for getting the most effective use out of authority, within this generally preferred method of coaching, while still maintaining the priority of high level gymnastic training.

Mutual Respect

If the type of democratic control being referred to in this discussion could be summarized in a few words, they would most likely be feelings of mutual respect. In a democratic gymnastic training setting the gymnasts "feel" and "sense," at a very fundamental level, that the coach respects them as individuals, team members, and most basically, as human beings, because he or she in fact really does.

This may appear, at first glance, to be a very simplified statement, but it says a great deal. In essence, if the coach does not have genuine respect for the athlete, the democratic approach will not work and both gymnasts and coach will have a very difficult time. This attitude cannot be faked with young people and it is quite hard to acquire, but not impossible, given time, commitment, and patience. In the true democratic gym, being proposed in this article, the athletes "know" that the coach feels this way, because they are sometimes directly involved in planning and decision making, and the evaluations of both discipline and direction, whenever it is reasonable to do so. This does not mean the gymnasts are in charge in any way, or that they get their way at all, but it does mean they are heard when appropriate and that their opinions are respected, although not automatically accepted. Knowing you have been truly listened to can go a long way in terms of positive motivation. Discussion soliciting the gymnasts opinions, take place when the decisions being considered are within their scope. Selection of the team leotard or uniform, fund raising, social events, and even some aspects of the actual training schedule, are examples of this kind of participation. Some coaches go too far the other way in these areas, and decide that democratic discussion must be formal. Parliamentary procedure, although of value in adult groups, usually stands in the way of the free interchange of ideas among young people.

Feelings of mutual respect, which characterize the democratic gymnastic setting, include, of course, not only respect of the coach for the athletes, but also of the gymnasts for the coach. However, this respect is based on coaching ability and maturity, not on the basis of being "the coach" alone. What is being said, in effect, is that the kind of respect we are referring to does not come from sergeant's stripes or a policeman's badge.

More precisely, respect in the democratic model comes as the gymnasts become aware of the coaches capacity to identify snarls, bugs, and issues relative to the training activity. He or she can also organize, in order that things may run more smoothly and effectively, while at the same time, remaining flexible enough to respond to the unexpected. He or she is adept at bringing out ideas from the gymnasts, yet strong enough to keep command and never allow things to get out of control. This last point is very interesting from a psychological standpoint. Youngsters, like many adults, sometimes act hostilely and in a manner in which they do not want to act because their own feelings get out of hand.

It is clear that in these cases, it is a great relief to have a leader-coach who can help them regain personal control, by using his or her own strength. There are often times when gymnasts are anxious and uneasy, during difficult skill acquisition and prior to a major competition being just two examples. At these times gymnasts need and want a strong coach who can effectively deal with such issues. The coach, who is democratic, is cognizant of when such times occur, and acts affirmatively. However, this same coach continues to look for the opportunity, even in these more difficult times, to return to the gymnasts as much decision making participation as is feasible, thereby confirming their individual value.

Finally, the coach is respected because he knows his stuff from a technical, biomechanical point of view. He comprehends his subject matter or most of it. A gymnast, who is motivated to learn, appreciates a coach who has command of the material he is attempting to teach.

Coach's Limitations

It is important to add that new coaches should not have any illusion that, in order to be respected by gymnasts, they have to know everything and know it perfectly. This expectation, suggests the idea of super-coach, as described in "I Have a Problem with My Coach," and it is not humanly possible (or desirable) to obtain this status. (It is indeed unfortunate that some coaches think they have achieved this level!) For a coach to pretend to be such a complete and total master of the art not only places such a burden upon that individual that the educative purpose is defeated, but also such a stance can result in serious injury to the gymnasts.

As a matter of fact, although gymnasts want and respect a coach who is very competent, they can also gain something from learning that a coach has some fallibility and some limitations and seeing how the coach manages these issues. These observations represent a mental-hygiene point of view which has implications for democratic control.

It is your authors' contention that sometimes a coach who can readily acknowledge his or her own imperfections, gains in respect and hence in discipline in the long run. A by-product, from the mental health vantage point, may be the learning-lesson gymnasts derive from working with a respected, but admittedly fallible human being. It is indisputable that for this to happen the coach must be more competent than incompetent. The point is that a coach's limitations can be turned to an educative advantage to some degree. A coach, who can admit that perhaps he or she has not yet achieved perfection in every aspect involved in teaching a skill or series of skills, can gain respect from the gymnasts because he is strong and confident enough to say there is something he still has to learn just as the gymnasts do.

In our opinion, democratic control is closely related to overall mental health. It contributes to the development, not only of controls from within, but also it increases self-esteem on the part of gymnasts as discussed in the article "Promoting Self-Esteem." A portion of this self-esteem may grow from seeing a respected coach who is imperfect, thereby creating in the athletes, awareness that they can be good without always having to be the best, although the ultimate goal may be to achieve mastery. In competitive gymnastics, psychological difficulty is often caused by a compelling need to be perfect and a feeling of misery and inadequacy that emerges if one is not.

The critical message of the last several paragraphs has been that a democratic coach has confidence in their ability and exercises it the majority of time, but need not be flawless, and moreover, may contribute to the emotional well-being of youngsters by being this kind of individual.

The democratic coach, therefore, is one who:

1. Appreciates the need that gymnasts have for adult leadership.
2. Understands, to the greatest degree possible, individual psychology in the various developmental states which influence the kind and degree of leadership that must be taken.
3. Recognizes that a group can be a powerful factor either positively or negatively in the training effort.

In regard to these points, a democratic lead team has the feeling of working together, pride in its accomplishments and a sense of real unity. It contributes to its own control and gradually reduces the need for authoritarianism.

Understanding Child Development

One final statement about a quite different characteristic of a democratic leadership style coach is warranted. Such a coach will be most effective in putting the principles discussed in this article into practice if he or she has an assimilated understanding of child development. This will enable the coach to know what can ordinarily be expected from six year olds or adolescents or whatever age group is being coached. The coach will not, for example, look for too much cohesion from five year olds who are not as socially developed as nine and ten year olds. The coach will be aware of some of the inner turmoil of high school students which make some of them capricious. Knowing what children are like at different stages of development, the coach will not be naive or over demanding in level of expectation or approach, which could prove self-defeating. If the coach combines this with knowledge of what makes for group morale and motivation and other elements that are characteristic of groups, a large step will have been taken in adopting a democratic leadership style.

Summary

In summary, a democratic style of coaching leadership with a gymnastics team is characterized by:

- Feelings of respect from the coach, for the coach, for the group itself and its individual members.

- The understanding of the coach of complexities of leadership and group interaction in relationship to the use of authority.
- The provision of a training environment conducive to an on-going interest in learning.

Not all coaches will be able to function in a model as described in these articles. However, whatever principles from the democratic leadership style that can be comfortably adopted by a coach, will most likely be of positive benefit to both that individual and the gymnasts being trained.

SAFETY PSYCHOLOGY
IN THE GYM

Many beginning coaches and instructors study long, hard hours to master the technical complexities of gymnastics coaching. Terminology, spotting techniques, basic safety "thinking," and organization (i.e. physical layout, mat use, and other aids) are critical components in the preparation of professional coaches. In fact, all registered coaches must pass the USA Gymnastics Safety Certification course as part of their membership.

An important area that often does not always receive the attention it deserves in coach readiness has to do with the relationship between principles of psychology and safety education. This brief article is designed to introduce a higher level of psychological and safety awareness which not only promotes a happier gymnastics environment but also one that is safer for young athletes on several levels.

Coaches and instructors eventually develop an individual philosophy about their interaction with youngsters as well as a personal style for approaching the task of coaching. Hopefully this methodology contains a high degree of understanding about child growth and development both physically, and of equal significance if not more so, the stages of emotional and psychological growth associated with different chronological ages. This type of knowledge is indispensable in establishing and maintaining an overall productive and healthy learning environment for gymnasts. Professional coaches should be concerned with the whole child not only with their physical progress. This attitude has a direct relationship to the psychological factors associated with safety in the sport.

Motivation and Safety

First and foremost is the development of both physical and mental performance feedback (information about what needs to be done in order to accomplish the skill) and continuous positive reinforcement (+CR) which is rewarding the individual for the display of the desired behavior. This combination of communications in a mutually respectful climate motivates the gymnast to continue to strive for mastery. This coaching approach not only provides rewards for efforts on an on-going basis, but at the same time enhances positive self-esteem. What is the connection between this psychological model and safety? Children who feel good about themselves are usually focused when training and more apt to feel personally "safe" in such a setting. This feeling of well-being in a gymnast can contribute to physical safety. Such athletes are attentive, more open to corrections, and generally more in tune with what is going on around them. Gymnasts who train in a negative training atmosphere and who are constantly subjected to put-downs, ridicule, sarcasm, and demeaning interactions are more distracted and potentially in emotional stress. These youngsters are accidents waiting to happen because they are focused on the emotional messages they are receiving rather than on the physical instruction. Athletes who don't feel good about themselves may be prone to punish themselves on a pre-conscious level. What better way than sustaining a physical injury? See the article "Behavior Change: Part I" for more information on this topic.

Communication and Safety

Another important area which is psychological in nature but has a direct connection to physical safety involves the openness of communication between the coach and student. Gymnasts who are inhibited in their ability to tell the coach what they are feeling need to be encouraged to do so. A dictatorial approach on the coach's part may close the avenue of needed communication where the gymnast feels he or she cannot approach the teacher. Many times a gymnast may not feel ready to perform a particular skill or is aware of that physically uncomfortable feeling called "fear." Some are afraid to tell their coach that they are experiencing that emotionally loaded response. Often the non-verbal signs will be evident, but the coach must be open to seeing these indicators in addition to being willing to hear this kind of information directly from the youngster. If communication is open and encouraged, coaches must be sure they are, in fact, truly "listening." This means that when the athlete is "leveling" with you about their feelings, you should not be working out your response in your mind while they are still speaking. If you are doing so, you are not really listening. Your goal is to try to understand how the gymnast makes sense to him or herself, not to negate their thinking. This does not mean you need to make decisions solely on this feedback from your athletes, but at the same time this information should not be ignored. Gymnasts who are not able for whatever reason to discuss their fears are candidates for injury and are safety risks. When your athlete is discussing this matter of fear, avoid saying, "What are you afraid of?" or worse, "No, you're not." Refer to the article "The Coach-Gymnast Conference: Listening and Leveling" as well as "Understanding, Overcoming, and Coping with Fear: An Overview" for a more in-depth discussion.

Physical Preparation and Safety

A third point for this discussion has to do with the important of physical preparation and safety. This may seem like a given to you, but the critical place that physical readiness plays from a psychological point of view in terms of safety is sometimes overlooked. All coaches know the excitement that a talented and quick-learning gymnast can bring to any program. We all have egos and the temptation with gifted children when we are anxious to show competitive results is to take a short cut and perhaps by-pass important building blocks. The psychological position that focuses on a "step at a time" learning model is, in the long run, the sensible way to go. Skipping steps in the didactic process cannot only result in a safety hazard but can mitigate against the gymnast realizing his or her full potential. It is much more difficult to go back to correct a missing link than it is to stay longer with the progressive basics until mastery is achieved. This results in a carry-over to the other skill learning, while the sin of omission often leads to a regression later in the athlete's career. Remember, overall,

 "Your physical preparation is your best mental preparation."

Summary

It is not possible in a brief article such as this to discuss the linkage between psychology and safety in an exhaustive manner. The points made here are designed to encourage beginning and even experienced coaches to pay greater attention to this more elusive aspect of coaching. The fundamental message is that not only is it crucial to keep the training setting physically safe but also to believe that a responsibility of a professional coach must include an effort to keep a budding gymnast mentally safe from harm and perhaps irreversible damage. Here are a few recommendations:

- Always attempt to maintain a positive learning model where gymnasts receive self-esteem-enhancing feedback.
- Be open and willing to accept feedback from your gymnast about their personal feelings concerning readiness and apprehension. Never invalidate these expressions of an inner psychological state.
- Load the deck in the favor of safety by adapting a psychological philosophy that guides the gymnast along a continuum which emphasizes progressive learning where safety is not compromised.

ETHICS
A PERSONAL CODE OF CONDUCT

In today's climate of politically correct responses, it is clear that ethics is a concept that is well known and discussed in considerable detail. Many professions have a strict and fairly well monitored code of ethics (lawyers, medical doctors, psychologists, etc.). Many of these directives were a direct consequence of years of planning and deliberation on the issue. Coaching sports as a profession should be no different and coaching young athletes should definitely have a strict code of ethics.

If we look in the past to an issue of "Olympic Coach" published by the U.S. Olympic Committee Division of Coaching Development, an article appeared that dealt with ethics in coaching. A challenge in sport was offered during a presentation at the USOC Coaching Symposium. In this presentation, it was stressed that the coach's highest priority should be in establishing relationships with athletes that help them develop in positive ways. The most important first step, in this regard, would be the development of a set of principles that would address expectations in the coach-athlete interactions—a code of conduct. In fact, that is the direction that USA Gymnastics took and this organization has made great progress in developing a Code of Ethics to better serve those who participate in gymnastics.

There are many obvious obstacles and resistances that interfere with the development and subsequent adoption of a code of ethics and behavior. One basic difficulty is that not many coaches like to talk about the subject. It is not just that they see it as an infringement on their autonomy and right to manage their own functioning, but also because some of the content is sensitive. Issues that present clear ethical dilemmas are touchy subjects for many coaches. They would prefer to deny the existence of such problems, even knowing that they are out there. A major contradiction concerning a code of ethics is that sport is often seen through a different set of moral lenses than those used in the rest of our lives.

Ethical Behavior

For example, in years past some of us have seen gymnastic coaches treat their athletes in ways that, outside of the training setting, would be grounds for dismissal if not a civil or criminal lawsuit. What to some is acceptable in the gym might not be outside of that setting. Does this mean the behavior in the training setting is above the law in terms of what is right and ethical? Many more athletes participating in sport today are sensitive to the issues of abusive, demeaning, humiliating, or degrading actions of their coaches. A larger than hoped for number of coaches uses the gym as a place to work out their own personal problems around authority and control. These personalized agendas usually involving themes of domination are used to abuse the power the coach has by virtue of their positions and role. A loss of objectivity can often occur and contribute directly to emotional damage in a young gymnast who sometimes holds the coach as a special person and even god-like figure. A code of conduct goes a long way in illuminating what can be expected and accepted by everyone.

Since many coach's livelihoods depend on production and performance of their athletes, it is understandable that they might tend, to some degree, to take advantage of their student's time and physical well-being. Safety has always been stressed in gymnastics, but we are all aware of the fact that far too many coaches go for the big "tricks" prematurely, without preparation, in order to produce a winning team. A code of ethics also addresses the issue of over-emphasis on winning to the long range detriment of the gymnast. When it is a question of keeping your job, some resistance to looking at this question is to be expected. Again, however, is that an ethical point of view?

Seven basic attributes have been identified that athletes between the ages of 12 and 20 look for in their coaches. It is suggested that priority by the coach should be in developing positive and helpful relationships with their athletes. Our own research over the years with competitive gymnasts here and abroad has revealed similar findings. These attributes will be discussed in this paper from the perspective of the sport of gymnastics.

Coaching Attributes

1. **Competence**. Research has clearly shown that most athletes want coaches who know their business. This not only means technical, biomechanically-based knowledge, but also the ability to communicate this information to them in a clear and useful manner. It is of interest, in this regard, to note that a questionnaire format survey, conducted by your authors involving hundreds of gymnasts, the less successful athletes felt that "technical ability" was the single most important attribute in a coach. The ability to provide "spotting" was also identified with the competence variable. More successful and experienced gymnasts as determined by actual competitive performance and record placed far less emphasis on this characteristic and indicated that the empathetic, emotionally supportive qualities of a coach were more highly valued. The question was raised, at that time, whether a partial key to outstanding coaching involves the coach's ability to grow and change in keeping with the changing needs structure of an athlete. Obviously rigid, set-in-their-way coaches might have difficulty when such flexibility is needed. This issue has not been adequately examined to date and remains an intriguing question, with many ramifications for professional coaches and program development.

2. **Approachability.** Another important identified attribute involves the gymnast's desire to have a coach who is open to what they think, say, and feel. They also look for coaches who can handle feedback about their coaching style, without becoming defensive, and who have the capacity to admit to mistakes. Many gymnasts have indicated that they often do not communicate with their coaches because they feel their concerns will be invalidated. Two of the most common examples involved the gymnast's reluctance to tell the coach that they are afraid of a skill and do not feel ready to execute it in the demanded way, or that they are hurting with some physical injury. Many have stated that the coach often denies the crucial emotional message in these kinds of statements and will respond with "What are you afraid of?," "so what," "that's foolish," "cut it out," or "you're faking it." Such a style, on the coach's part, makes it most difficult for a gymnast to "trust" that they will be heard, and many would rather not risk enduring the coach's anger. In terms of being able to admit to having made a mistake, a coach who says to an athlete, "Look, my behavior yesterday was out of line. I'm sorry," will gain returns in personal credibility and in establishing the human qualities of the coach that few other actions could achieve.

3. **Fairness and Consistency.** This dimension of the coaching interaction is one of the most difficult to maintain. Most coaches, although they may wish to deny it, have "favorite" athletes in the gym. Their preference may be subtle, but it is detectable in any training setting and sometimes is glaring. Gymnasts, as with other athletes, expect and should receive equal treatment. Rules should apply to everyone, and although individual differences need to be taken into account, athletes should expect that approaches to the unique needs and characteristics of each gymnast will be addressed in a timely fashion and does not automatically mean unfairness. All athletes should receive such sensitive and individually tailored management, not just a select few. A code of ethics would need to discuss this area in detail.

4. **Confidence.** Gymnasts want to know they can rely on the coach to set a positive example, both in and out of the training setting. Athletes look for a clear set of guiding principles that focus on the overall long and short term goals of the coach in relationship to the team as a whole, and its individual members. Many of the rules and disciplinary expectations that apply to the gymnast should also be evident in the coach's behavior and personal standards. Practice what you preach is associated with this kind of coaching characteristic and must be viewed as an ethical guideline.

5. **Motivation.** Another basic attribute sought by athletes in their coaches that has ethical implications involved motivation. There are basically two types of

motivation: extrinsic and intrinsic. External motivation concerns stimulation that comes from outside the gymnast. Pleasing the coach or family members, concrete rewards for success, etc. are examples of extrinsic motivation. Internally motivated athletes find their drive in more personal factors such as pride, the acquisition of skills, and demonstrated mastery. Rarely is a gymnast purely one or the other in terms of a motivating force, but as with most athletes, motivation is usually sustained by a combination of outside and inside factors. If it is the ethical responsibility of the coach to serve as a motivator, then it is crucial that he or she have a great deal of enthusiasm and love for the sport. This kind of dedication and excitement in the coach is contagious and serves as a very powerful and basic motivational technique. In this regard, passion for the sport is ethical.

6. **Personal Concern.** Most gymnasts and athletes, in general, want a coach who is genuinely concerned about their overall well-being as people, not just as motor wonders. Sometimes the coach serves as an adult friend and mentor as well as someone who directs the physical training of an athlete. Many young people want to be able to confide in their coach and ask questions without being treated as an inferior. Mutual respect, in this regard, is highly advantageous. At times of injury, this principle becomes very clear, and often young athletes are ignored or abandoned on some level when they can no longer "compete" and make an active contribution to a team. Such behavior on the part of a coach is not right and is, in fact, unethical.

7. **Support.** Gymnasts want coaches who encourage and also who demand that they go for the maximum realization of their individual potential. They are looking for coaches who instill security and confidence. All athletes want coaches who will recognize and praise their achievements and constructively deal with their weaknesses and areas for needed improvement. Coaching through the overt use of fear, intimidation, and domination is counterproductive and not ethical.

Adopting a "Personal" Code of Conduct

In summary, although progress has been made by several sport federations to develop a strict code of ethics, many do not involve the type of desired characteristics nor coach-athlete relationship issues just reviewed. The code of ethics for gymnastics addresses issues such as motivational or training methods which may be considered abusive, establishes guidelines for all registered coaches and gymnastics facilities, and continues to monitor and update their ethical code. However, based on the previous seven attributes of competence, approachability, fairness, confidence, motivation, personal concern, and support perhaps we, in the gymnastic community, should strive towards adopting these additional desired characteristics as our own "Personal Code of Conduct." For a more in-depth look at this important issue refer to the articles "Abuses of Anger in the Gym," "Male Coach-Female Gymnast," as well as "I Have a Problem with My Coach."

Chapter Three

COACH/GYMNAST
INTERPERSONAL RELATIONSHIPS

T he most important ingredient in an overall formula for success in gymnastics
or any sport, in our opinions, is the quality of the coach-athlete relationship.
This is the area which represents the most fruitful one for the coach working
with athletes. The special impact that a coach can have on an athlete has been
documented by many. Although there are some basic guidelines that have emerged
from research and experience, the essence of this interaction between coach and
athlete are totally individual and a matter of the chemistry of the people involved.
These papers scratch the surface of this human equation.

- The Art of Feedback: A Model for Coach-Gymnast Communication
- The Coach-Gymnast Conference: Listening and Leveling
- A Coach's Guide to Non-Verbal Communication
- "I Have a Problem with… My Coach"
- Abuses of Anger in the Gym
- Gender Differences in Dependency Conflicts
- Male Coach–Female Gymnast

THE ART OF FEEDBACK
A MODEL FOR COACH-GYMNAST COMMUNICATION

"Will you watch your form in the bottom of the giant," "That was a poor job from start to finish," "You need to be a little tighter, but it is coming nicely," "Not what we're looking for, but you haven't shown me much lately." All of the above comments are actual statements made by coaches to gymnasts. Some are positive, others rather negative, and still others a kind of mix. Ignoring the quality of the statements, they all represent verbal feedback from coach to gymnast.

Besides the kind of feedback that gives a gymnast technical information about physical performance, feedback can also be a communication which gives information about some aspect of personal, non-gymnastic behavior and its effect. In this article, we will focus on this particular type of feedback. We will think of such communication as part of a guided missile system where we help a gymnast know whether demonstrated attitude or personal behavior in the gym is on target or not. Feedback in this context is a way of helping "another person," for feedback always implies at least two people in touch with each other. This should not be confused with biofeedback systems, which are largely self-contained experiences, or reinforcement, which is primarily one-way modification directed at preselected objectives.

The giving and receiving of feedback as defined above is a skill that can be learned. It is an extremely important part of the coach-gymnast interaction and can go a long way to improve or destroy the atmosphere within which gymnastic training takes place. When behavioral feedback is attempted at the wrong time or given in an undesirable way, the results can be disastrous over the long haul. At best it will be useless.

Appropriate Feedback

The following are some criteria for useful and appropriate feedback:

1. **Feedback to the gymnast should be descriptive rather than purely evaluative.** It is most helpful to focus on what the gymnast did instead of attempting to translate the behavior into a statement about what he or she is. "You've distracted three teammates in the last half hour," is probably something that a gymnast doesn't want to hear, but it is more effective than, "You are a real pest."

2. **Feedback should focus on a feeling that a gymnast's behavior has caused in the coach or other gymnasts.** "When you don't work or you interrupt me, I feel frustrated and so do others," gives the gymnast clear information about

the effect of behavior, while at the same time leaving him or her free to decide what to do about that effect. The coach could always order or dictate a change ("Knock it off, now") and sometimes that is necessary, but this will not really contribute to the individual gymnast's learning in a constructive manner.

3. **Feedback should be offered in a specific way, rather than as a generalization.** For example, it is probably more useful to learn that you "talk too much," than to have someone say that you are "dominating." In this case as in others, verbal feedback can be accompanied by nonverbal action such as the universal gesture of putting a finger to the lips to indicate the need for less chatter.

4. **Coach-gymnasts communication in terms of feedback should be directed toward behavior that the gymnast can do something about.** An athlete's frustration and distress is increased when reminded of some shortcoming over which he or she has little or no control. "Don't be so scared" or "stop shaking" will not help a trait-anxious gymnast about to attempt a very difficult skill or sequence.

5. **Feedback about behavior is most effective when it is asked for, rather than imposed by a powerful other, such as the coach.** When a gymnast feels that he or she needs and wants feedback, the input will be more useful. Some coaches successfully trigger this by turning off or some other response that suggests a degree of alienation. "What am I doing wrong?" is a question that shows the coach that the gymnast may be receptive to feedback at a given moment. Gymnasts often ask this question about a missed skill, but it also can be cleverly solicited when some personal behavior has created a subtle, but clearly negative, response.

6. **To be most effective, feedback must be well-timed.** In general, as with other reinforcement techniques, feedback is most useful at the earliest opportunity after the given behavior. This, of course depends on the gymnast's readiness to hear it, and the amount of support available from others.

7. **Behavioral type of feedback should be checked to ensure that the communication is clear.** One way of doing this is for the coach to ask the gymnast to try to rephrase the individual feedback in question in their own words to see if their version goes along with what message the coach intended to send. In the rephrase effort, the feedback is often made even clearer to the gymnast.

8. **Feedback should never be given to "dump," "put down" or "unload" on the gymnast.** If a coach feels he has to say something very negative to the gymnast in order to "feel better," then the coach needs to ask him or herself who it is they are trying to really "assist."

9. **Feedback should avoid asking "why?"** To be effective it should stay within the bounds of a given behavior and the reactions to it. The coach who constantly asks the gymnast "why" they did or did not do something is in a world of theory about intrinsic motivation. Avoiding the "whys" will help the coach avoid the error of amateur "psychologizing" and losing the bottom line. Work on changing the behavior and getting on with gymnastics. It is tempting, and easy, to get buried in a therapeutic type discussion that leads nowhere.

We began our discussion by saying that feedback is a two way street although most of it is directed from coach to gymnast. If we accept the premise that properly given feedback can be a fine way to learn about oneself, it would make sense that the gymnast also provides this for the coach. This is easy to say but hard to accomplish. Coaches on ego power-trips will not tolerate such information. Much will depend on the maturity of both athlete and coach and on the degree of openness found in the basic relationship.

Resistance to Feedback

Even with all things being right, what are some reasons that feedback of the kind we are discussing is often resisted no matter what direction it is taking? Here are some reasons for resistance"

10. **Gymnast expects negative comments.** For one thing, it is hard to admit that we have difficulties not only to ourselves but surely to others. Gymnasts are often not sure that the coach can be trusted or that his or her observations about behavior are really valid. This, of course, is an individual matter and depends on the specific conditions found in the personalities and system within which people interact. It also depends on how close to the mark prior input from the coach has been and the outcome of efforts to change. Some gymnasts are afraid to learn what people truly think of them; this is true of not only gymnasts. It is amazing how many gymnasts we have spoken with who expect to hear primarily negative comment since the model for many coach-gymnast relationships is one of teacher-telling-student what they did incorrectly. With this expectation so common, it may be that coaches too often neglect to point out positive qualities in their non-technical feedback communications. A comment such as "I really like your attitude" may take a second to say, but can move a gymnast light years ahead in terms of motivation and self-esteem.

11. **Gymnasts are internal motivators.** Another problem, which our research with young competitive gymnasts confirms, as illustrated in the article "Psychological Characteristics of Jr. Elite Gymnasts," has to do with the fact that most high-level gymnasts are internal locus of control individuals who pride themselves on independence from others. The thought of depending on someone such as a coach in certain ways appears alien to something basic in their personalities. For some others, who have spent much of their lives relying on outside people or looking for someone on whom to depend, feedback interactions provide an opportunity to repeat or continue in this pattern through their relationship with the coach.

12. **Solving Behavioral Difficulties.** An additional source of resistance to nonphysical feedback is that the gymnast might be looking for support and sympathy rather than for direction in seeing the real difficulties in terms of behavior. When the coach tries to point out some of the ways that the gymnast is contributing to a problem, which might suggest that they gymnast will have to alter behavior, the gymnast may stop listening altogether. Solving a behavioral difficulty may mean revealing some side of ourselves which we have avoided or wished to avoid thinking about. Also, the gymnast may feel their problem is so unique that no one could possibly understand its true nature.

13. **Giving behavioral feedback.** On the coach's side of the interchange, it is not always easy to give feedback to gymnasts about their non-gymnastic behaviors or attitudes. Most of us like to give advice and surely this is one of the responsibilities of the coach from a technical point of view. Doing so suggests that we are competent and important and some coaches have an inordinately high need to come across that way. What happens, however, when it comes to behavioral feedback, is that they get caught up in a "telling" or "chewing out" role without testing whether the communication is appropriate to the total issue or to the capacities, fears or the powers of the gymnast we are trying to move back on target. Again, in this situation there is the danger of falling into the trap of playing amateur psychologist which can often have bad consequences for the youngster.

14. **Gymnast becomes defensive.** A further difficulty occurs if the gymnast we are trying to reach becomes defensive. The coach may, at this point, try to argue, debate the question or pressure the youngster. Defensiveness or denial on the part of the gymnast is usually an indication that the coach is going about trying to be helpful in the wrong way. It often means that the timing is off or that the coach is mistaken about the behavior. In any case, it is best to stop the feedback effort until the coach can reevaluate the situation. If

the coach responds to the gymnast's resistance with increased pressure, the resistance will only increase creating an even bigger communication gap in this important relationship. Further discussion can be found in "Defense Mechanisms and Gymnastics."

Feedback Requirements

To be most effective the feedback interaction as we have discussed in this article needs these characteristics:

- Mutual trust—this takes time and patience to develop.
- Careful listening by the coach, with the coach listening more than gymnast.
- Coach and gymnast must both see the feedback as joint venture.
- Supportive behavior from the coach is needed to make it easier for the gymnast to talk.

Feedback about non-gymnastic behavior in the gym that affects the quality of the effort takes into account the needs of both the gymnast and coach. Most gymnasts welcome such feedback, when it is genuine and given in a climate of warmth and respect. The art of feedback can become one of many primary means for a gymnast to learn about him or herself in a very specific situation and these insights will eventually show up in a more satisfying physical performance as well. Try it, you might like it!

THE COACH-GYMNAST CONFERENCE LISTENING AND LEVELING

It doesn't take a psychologist to recognize the importance of the coach-gymnast relationship. The personal communication between the athlete and coach has a very real effect on the outcome of training. This includes verbal and nonverbal communication, the giving of technical performance information and the feedback given the gymnast concerning overall behavior. All of these kinds of messages are critical in maintaining motivation and keeping gymnasts progressing towards their full potential as we illustrate in our article "A Key to Success: Part I." Since we are all human, it is natural that the coach-gymnast interaction comes under strain from time to time and this usually results in a breakdown of the teaching and learning process. At these times, the coach and gymnast often need to sit down together in an attempt to locate the problem and mutually develop a plan to deal with the issues.

This article will focus on the management of this important coach-gymnast conference itself rather than on any specific problems and their resolution. Two crucial ideas will be discussed: coaches listening and gymnasts leveling. The interplay between these two ideas will also be considered.

There is a general rule which should be kept in mind by both the coach and gymnast during these problem-solving conferences. When listening, the task is to discover how the other person makes sense to himself. When leveling, the task is to disclose to the other person how we make sense to ourselves. Of course, in any given conference the roles may be reversed, with the gymnast being the listener and the coach the leveler. In any event, the same principles apply to both participants no matter what role they are in at a given moment.

Coaches Listening

Listening and developing the ability to listen is one of the most difficult arts that coaches need to gradually master. In both the short and long run, this is the only way to really understand and hear the problems gymnasts present. This is made even more challenging for the coach who is usually an adult and is probably used to having his or her word go unquestioned. However, when the communication system with the gymnast has gone wrong, it is destructive to operate out of the "I'm the grown-up and boss" principle. This may result in a temporary solution, but can often make matters worse. For this reason, it is wise not to hold a conference if the problem involves a real incident or outburst and the coach and/or gymnast may be angry. It is better to schedule a meeting after things have cooled down, since there is a better chance of success when both people are rational. When that time comes, it is extremely important that the gymnast learn to resist the quick impulse to judge whether what the coach says is wrong or meaningful. The coach must assume that what the gymnasts says makes sense to him or her. Listening in this regard means working very hard to find out how what seems on or off to the coach makes perfect sense to the gymnast. When coaches refuse to listen or ignore much of what is being said, it means they are not giving the gymnast credit for making sense to him or her. No one likes to feel that what they have to say is considered unimportant or not sensible. This is exactly how a gymnast feels, however, when the coach does not appear to be listening. Such behavior on the coach's part implies disrespect for the athlete and even a certain degree of contempt.

There are some clear warning signs that the coach needs to be aware of during the coach-gymnast conference which indicate that the coach is not really listening:

- Thinking ahead to what you are going to say next to the gymnast suggests you are not really listening or trying to understand the gymnast's point of view.
- If you find that you are taking over the conference and more or less dominating the conversation with the gymnast having trouble getting a word in edgewise, you are probably not encouraging the gymnast's participation. In order to listen, the opportunity for the other person to speak must be made regularly available.
- If you change the subject under focus and ignore the specific topic on the table and the gymnast's remarks and questions concerning it, you are not listening.
- Playing head games is a real mistake and easy to make. If you find yourself trying to trip the gymnast up as a way to show his or her ways are foolish or inconsistent, listening for the purpose of understanding is missing from the conference.

Any or all of these behavior clues on the coach's part put the gymnast under unfair pressure. This makes it very difficult for youngsters to be open, to tell you why they feel the way they do and in what ways they make sense to themselves. This may protect the coach's ego from learning about the real concerns, but it will do nothing to resolve the problem and improve the necessary working relationship in the gym. In such negative conferences, both the coach and gymnast leave the meeting convinced that the other is unreasonable and end up further apart than ever from coming up with a mutually satisfactory resolution of the problem. In such cases, ill feelings continue to be destructive, although perhaps less obvious. It is a sure bet that the same issue will reappear only it will be even more difficult to solve the longer it goes "unheard" by either party.

Gymnasts Leveling

Young people feel that they are rarely understood completely or taken seriously. In fact many people of all ages often feel that way. It is a common experience for many and a simple test is to ask another person to repeat what they heard us say. They will almost never be able to restate what we think we have said to our total satisfaction unless it involves special situations. Each gymnast usually views their position as sensible, as based on real experiences and as an honest expression of what they believe to be the case, but others, including the coach, often behave as though none of this is true. They appear as if they do not see our good sense, or that they think we're making wild assumptions, or that they believe that we're speaking from hidden motives. One problem may be, of course, that they are not listening. Another may be that we are not leveling.

Leveling means to disclose fully as possible the concrete experiences, the thoughts and feelings that make our views sensible to us. Unless we do so we are asking others for an act of pure faith. We are expecting them to view us without real evidence and just as sensible, realistic and honest as we view ourselves and our position. Leveling with a coach who is not listening is very tough to accomplish so it is easy to see why the interaction can break down if that is the case. For a gymnast to level with a coach requires considerable courage on the gymnast's part, along with a coach who is open to really hear what is being said without becoming hostile or defensive. One would expect since they are adults that they would be able to handle this, but that is not always so. Despite the difficulties it is very important to get the issues out if any coach-gymnast conference is to be productive.

There are several factors that gymnasts need to be aware of that get in the way of or block efforts at leveling.

- Since the reasons for our views are clear and evident to us, we often assume that they should be equally evident to the coach. Even if not, we often can make the mistake of expecting the coach to simply trust in our good judgment.
- We are sometimes hesitant to assert our claim for the coaches' time in order to explain our views fully. This is especially true if the gymnast is a little frightened or feels that the coach is not prepared to listen.
- We often avoid exposing our true feelings by describing our concerns too matter-of-factly, or by attributing them to third parties. When we do this, we mislead others about the importance to us individually of what we are saying.

Gymnasts who do not level with the coach during a conference, no matter how difficult it sometimes is to do, will pay a price for holding back. Their concerns will either be ignored or misunderstood. In these cases, gymnasts will find themselves going around in circles or blaming others for being insensitive. If this should happen, the gymnast needs to ask him or herself if they are failing to level, to disclose the concrete experiences and feelings that underlie their personal concerns.

Coach-Gymnast Communication

With these basic guidelines understood and accepted, there are some additional skills that can be used by coaches and gymnasts to further improve communication during the coach-gymnast conference.

1. **Language**: Try to make your verbal and nonverbal (eye contact, note taking, etc.) behavior indicate your willingness to receive a message and to be attentive.
2. **Paraphrase**: A good thing for both the coach and gymnast to do is to restate in their own words what they think the other said so any mistakes can be identified right away.
3. **Perception checking**: State in your own way and words that you have received the emotional part of the message as well as the verbal content and that you are aware of the speaker's feelings as well as words ("you feel sad about this").
4. **Behavior description**: Exchange specific, observable actions which have a bearing on the issue being discussed without making accusation, putting the other person down, or generalizing about motives ("Tuesday you spent twenty minutes with one person and none with me").
5. **Feeling description**: Report your own feelings of the moment as they may have an effect on the communication process ("Right now I feel pretty nervous").
6. **Monitor the process by asking:**
    a. Does your nonverbal behavior match your verbal behavior (e.g. looking at the person, attentive posture)?
    b. Do you give feedback in a way that is helpful (e.g. "Maybe it would be better to...")?
    c. Do you recognize feedback from the other person (e.g. "That is a good observation")?
    d. Do you take responsibility for your own messages (e.g. "I've been thinking about this...")?
    e. Are you open about the intention of your messages?

If coaches and gymnasts make a genuine attempt to follow the recommendations made in this article, they will find that the coach-gymnast conference will be more successful and mutually rewarding. It takes time and effort, but every little step will make a difference in this important form of communication. Finally, it is worthwhile to note that all of the guidelines presented here are also useful in other related conferences between people such as parent-child and teacher-student.

A COACH'S GUIDE TO NON-VERBAL COMMUNICATION

Anyone watching a coach work with a gymnast will be aware of the communication that takes place between the teacher and student. In most cases, a verbal exchange will proceed in a particular physical action on the part of the gymnast. This is followed by another one-or-two way verbal exchange following the attempt. These conversations provide performance feedback and positive or negative reinforcement or a combination between the athlete and the coach is in the form of a verbalization of varying length, in other words, talking.

By virtue of much research and some accidental discoveries in the social sciences, our understanding of the process of communication has greatly expanded in recent years. At one time emphasis in communication studies was placed more or less exclusively on the spoken or written words. Currently, there has been increased interest in nonverbal forms of communication which have been neglected in the past.

The study of nonverbal communication and behavior probably dates back to 1872 when Darwin presented an account of the processes of emotional expression in animals and human beings. Freud was most likely the first systematic investigator of the field when he studied the hidden meanings of certain behaviors. Modern researchers in kinesics (facial expression, body language, etc.) have moved the study of nonverbal behavior into an era of legitimate scientific endeavor.

What does all this have to do with the gymnastic coach? If we agree to the principle that effective coaching designed to better the performance of the gymnasts under our charge is the major objective of coach-athlete interaction, it follows that all information be it technical, medical or psychological that serves to improve that relationship should be viewed as important by the serious gymnastic coach. There is much to learn from other fields and disciplines if we are open to see what might apply to our individual work and growth.

It is obvious that coaches do in fact use a considerable amount of nonverbal communication with their gymnasts as well as the more traditional and common verbal feedback discussed earlier. Usually, the non-verbal communication takes place in a rather spontaneous and unplanned for fashion. Examples such as the frown for a poor attempt, the grin for a good effort, the arm around the shoulder are numerous illustrations of nonverbal communication in the sport. Research has brought us to the point where some of these nonverbal expressions can now be incorporated into the coaching framework on a much more conscious and preplanned way. Observing a master coach utilize non-verbal communication occurred when watching Olga Korbut's trainer working with the famous gymnast.

During the observation period, Mr. Knesch rarely spoke a word yet there was clearly a great deal of "communication" going on which could be seen in Ms. Korbut's eye contact with her coach and her consequent behavior during training. The feedback was clearly there although very subtle. Obviously, arriving at such a communicative intimacy takes years of exposure between the athlete and the coach and it is unlikely that we will find many coaches approaching this kind of model. On the other hand, it is clear that as we move further into technology where video analysis of skill learning and execution is playing a larger role, the additional use of nonverbal communication in the actual coach-gymnast interaction may become more important as well as appropriate.

In addition, past research, such as found in the article entitled "The Gymnast's Perception of the Coach: Competence and Coaching Style," investigating the personal qualities most often named by top gymnasts as desirable in their coach has shown that one of the most predominant things sought was a coach who uses "minimum verbiage." In this context, the gymnasts were referring to the coach commenting only when he or she had something of value to say. Surely, nonverbal communication addresses the issue of too much talking and at the same time allows for important feedback to take place and messages to be sent and received.

Obviously verbal dialogue will always remain the primary means of communication between human beings. Surely in the teaching-learning model talking about problems and solutions has been successful for hundreds of years. At the same time, however, most people have experienced those moments when we are "at a loss for words" and where a nonverbal response "said" it all. Often these times are the most emotionally moving and have a longer lasting impact than any others we have known. With this potential evident, they are worth considering in a more than passing way.

Types of Non-verbal Behaviors

There are at least five types of nonverbal behaviors that people in general and coaches specifically use in communication.

1. **One type of behavior is called Emblems**. Emblems are movements that are communicative substitutes for words and are usually easily understood. Examples include such things as shaking a fist, waving as in a greeting, turning thumbs down or up, etc. The gymnast who sees his or her coach leap in the air following a successful attempt has little translating to do in order to get the message.

2. **A second type of non-verbal behavior is referred to as Illustrators.** Movements that accompany speech and accent, modify or punctuate it are called illustrators. Behaviors that illustrate what is verbalized are such things

as rapping on the horse while making a verbal point, touching the unevens or beam, etc.

3. **Regulators are a third type of non-verbal behavior.** These are movements that maintain or signal a change in the listening-speaking role. For example, small postural shifts or nodding the head indicating that the gymnast involved in the communication should now speak are nonverbal regulators.

4. **Affect displays primarily through facial expressions are a fourth type of basic non-verbal behavior.** These are distinguished from illustrators and emblems in terms of the amount of information they convey about the emotional state of the coach. Expressions on the face of a coach can obviously range from those designed to indicate joy, total elation or mild dissatisfaction to those that signal extreme displeasure, irritation or frustration. Part of it depends on just how forceful the non-verbal information is to be made. Unfortunately it is often the case that coaches wear their sour faces too much, as if the showing of happy feelings and affect is somehow unprofessional or will break down the "discipline" of the interaction. This is not, of course, the case. We know that positivity will win out over a negative approach as a motivator the majority of the time.

5. **A final type of non-verbal behavior is labeled Adapters.** Adapters are behaviors that involve self or object manipulations related to the individual's need or emotional state. This category is divided into self-adapters (head scratching, picking fingers, twirling thumbs, etc.), alter-adapters (folding the arms across the body, upward leg movements) and object-adapters (fondling jewelry, tossing a roll of tape from hand to hand, turning a wristwatch, etc.). Adapters are usually seen with other types of nonverbal behavior and tend to emphasize the feelings associated with the communication.

How can these kinds of observations about non-verbal communication be utilized in everyday gymnastic coaching? At the beginning of this article, we said that many coaches already do use nonverbal forms of communication, but that very often this is done in an unknowledgeable way by simply reacting naturally with whatever comes to mind. What is being recommended is that coaches make a more deliberate effort to try out some of the recognized and effective nonverbal types of behavior in combination with their spontaneous verbal exchanges with their gymnasts. Surely verbal language is necessary for the giving of performance information of a highly technical nature. However, research presented in the article "Right-Brained Gymnasts in Left-Brained Gyms" suggests that even this material is more easily processed by gymnasts when presented visually. A number of coaches can be very effective in "correcting" a move from a technical point of view by just manipulating the hands or some other large motor illustration. Combining this with video and minimum verbiage for clarification is an ideal package for learning.

Using some of the non-verbal behaviors discussed in this article makes it possible to get multiple messages across without taking the time or energy to put them all into words. For example, it would be quite effective for a coach to shake his head while punching one fist into the other open hand as a way of "saying" and emphasizing without words his frustration or disappointment. This approach avoids the necessity of verbally justifying the reaction or feeling. Likewise, a broad smile along with a pat on the back, a salute, clapping the hands together, or throwing the arms in the air can communicate a real mutuality of happiness about a successful attempt or pleasing effort. Again, no explanation is needed. In both of these illustrations in a brief instant the emotional message is clearly delivered to the gymnast with a saving in breath and time. This can be followed by giving technical correction without the morale risks implicit in stating how poor a previous effort was should that be the case. As with verbal reinforcement theory, the non-verbal feedback should be in approximately a ratio of four positive to one negative (4:1) statements.

We have all learned that often one picture is worth a thousand words. When it comes to gymnastic coaching, it is well worth the effort to practice that lesson on a regular basis.

"I HAVE A PROBLEM WITH ... MY COACH"

Over the years, we have received hundreds of letters from gymnasts, coaches and parents concerning issues raised in our articles or other concerns of a "psychological" nature regarding our sport. In the majority of cases we answer these letters one by one and that has proven to be satisfactory. It is always nice to hear from readers and feedback, whether positive or negative, keeps a person on his or her toes.

In any setting where people are striving for the kind of creative expression, as required in gymnastics, there are bound to be some problems. Since everyone is unique, with varied backgrounds and genetic dispositions, any given situation will be seen in a different way by each individual. It would be impossible to talk about all the various problems that might arise in a gym, and, because of our uniqueness, even more difficult to make suggestions that would always work for everyone. However, there are some basic issues that have continually been raised in our mail which many gymnasts apparently experience in common (individually or as a group) when it comes to their coaching situation.

On several occasions we have received a surprising number of letters, mostly from gymnasts, asking for help with a personal problem or with some special situation in their gym. The letters usually begin with "Doc, I have a problem with ..." Although all of your questions and our answers are of course confidential, enough letters have come in talking about similar difficulties in the gym of a general kind that we felt some type of larger response might be useful for more readers.

In this article, we felt it would be valuable to consider a few of the more often raised issues or problems that gymnasts have written to us about. And yes, we're talking about "The Coach." Here are a few examples which we'll call the "Super Coach," "Do It Coach," "Plays Favorites Coach," and the "Negative Coach."

The "Super" Coach

First, we need to say something about the notion of the coach as a "Superman/ Super person," an often assumed and stated myth. Coaches are, as a matter of fact, very human! They are subject to the same stresses and strains of all of us, and very often more so. This might seem like a very obvious and foolish thing to say, but it is amazing how many gymnasts apparently feel that their coach is superhuman in some way. Usually this attitude is found in the youngest gymnasts, older ones with more experience having learned that it is not the case.

Most coaches are dedicated, caring, hardworking people who have your best interest at heart. They love the sport and try to help their gymnasts achieve to the best of their ability. All of these are surely important characteristics. They do, like everyone else, make mistakes from time to time, but they learn and grow as the result of such errors just like you do. If the coach you are currently working with doesn't seem to have any of these qualities, then you're probably going to have to look for a new one soon. That is sometimes easy to say, but very hard to do. Maybe the gym you're working in is the only one to be found and in that case, you are pretty much stuck and will have to make the best of the situation to continue in the sport. Such a bleak situation is not common and fortunately, more options become available every year. In any event, if your coach has some of these characteristics, including the human capacity to make mistakes, you're most likely okay. Some gymnasts are looking for the ideal, dream world in which to do gymnastics and such athletes are probably going to be unhappy no matter where they are. Basically, it is a matter of finding the best match. Most gymnasts are looking for a setting where they feel pretty good most of the time, where they are learning slowly but surely, and where they have reasonable happy relationships with the other kids. Remember, whatever the combination you find for yourself – coaches are human with all the emotions, faults, and desires that condition implies. Respect the coach who has earned your trust and confidence, but don't expect miracles.

With that as a general background, let's turn to some of the specific situations gymnasts have written about concerning the coaching area:

The "Do It" Coach

Some gymnasts say they have a coach "who insists you do something you don't feel you can do or are ready to do." This is a big one! A real problem here is the question of who is right. Does your feeling of not being ready come out of expected, natural fear only? Is the coach correct but you are not willing to accept his or her judgment? On the other hand, are you quite right realizing that you really do not have a sense of near mastery or mastery, that gaps in your learning of a particularly difficult skill are truly there, and that you are being asked to do the impossible, both physically and mentally? These questions are very hard to answer since they are so very much dependent on the individual circumstances.

What is most important, and everyone can do in such a situation, is to let your coach know how you are feeling. In many cases, it will be apparent—you'll cringe, shake, cry or whatever. Most coaches will sense your discomfort and respond accordingly. Some gymnasts try to be brave beyond the call of duty, not wanting to betray a mutual trust or appear afraid. For some, that attitude will work, for others it will definitely get in the way of success if it is not you, or not really your style. In other cases, if you are a faker about these things, you might not receive any sympathy and will, depending upon past experience, be pressed very hard at these times. We have to assume that you do not behave in this doubtful way on all skills when the time has come to do them in the past. Therefore, although you have a responsibility to the coach, you also have one towards yourself.

Make your feelings known if they are not obvious in a non-emotional way and work out with your coach what additional steps need to be taken to get where you both want to be together. You may need to go back to some fundamentals to correct the current situation so see our articles entitled "My Goal is to... A Gymnast's Plan" and "Using Goal Setting as a Coaching Tool" for helpful tips and steps. If worse comes to worse and you are really so terrified of a coach's demands that you are incapable of thinking, you may have to just refuse and pay the consequences, whatever they might be. No sane coach wants you to get hurt and promising spotting is usually not the answer to your gut feeling. It will boil down to respect and openness in communication. Up to a point, you should expect this from your coach, especially if you are not a chronic psyche out person.

The coach's job, in part, is to direct your spirit, not break it. On the other hand, once you have decided to commit yourself to the sport of gymnastics, you have also agreed in principle to allowing and welcoming control from a professional coach. This often means that for much of the time you are not making decisions, but following directions. That is the way it has to be or there would be nothing but chaos in your gym. In the case under discussion here, we are talking about a very strong reaction that is not often felt by you and will get in the way of concentration. You may go ahead out of loyalty and, unfortunately, sometimes out of fear about the coach's response, but real learning will be hard to maintain under such circumstances. At the very least, you need to be straight with your coach and share your concerns. Coaches are not always right, but they should strive to always be sensitive.

The "Plays Favorites" Coach

Many gymnasts say they "are caught in a situation where their coach plays favorites and it is causing trouble for them and other team members." We have never met a coach, who is honest with him or herself, who has not had to struggle with this natural tendency to have favorites. In all human relationships, people form stronger attachments with certain individuals, rather than others. Why should it be any different in the gym? Of course, sometimes coaches pay more attention to the most talented gymnasts. In other cases, it is not always a situation that occurs based on talent but can come about because of some other factors that are not easily identified. Whatever the basis, it makes for a tough situation when a single gymnast or group of gymnasts who are part of a team clearly feel that certain individuals are getting preferred attention on a regular basis. Occasionally, a particular gymnast, because of special skills being attempted or competitive level, must have extra help and time from the coach. Most coaches make this clear beforehand and indicate that this may be the case from time to time, and that each gymnast in their turn, as appropriate, will receive the same special handling. Some coaches may ignore certain gymnasts at particular times—this may not have anything to do with "playing favorites," but may be intentional to encourage self-motivation and direction. This is perfectly acceptable and is usually temporary.

In the article, "Behavior Change: Part II–Self-Evaluation," we describe the benefits of having gymnasts work with and encourage each other, rather than always relying on the coach. This is not only good practice, but can reduce the effect of special attention given to a single person (one should also remember that the person receiving the special attention that is overdone is in a spot in their relationships with other kids). If the "playing favorites" condition happens continually with the same one or two gymnasts at the sacrifice of the others, nothing short of confrontation will help. What we mean is that the other members of the group, as a group, must bring this to the coach's awareness. If your coach is so domineering that he or she is too powerful, in your eyes, to be approached in this regard, then perhaps the only solution is to ask for adult assistance (e.g., parent). This is a suggestion we don't like to make, since, as we have stated in other articles, such as "My Daughter, the Competitive Gymnast," we have strong feelings that parents should stay out of the coaching interaction. On the other hand, the condition we are speaking of is in the extreme, and when it is out of hand, it will be obvious and clearly destructive to all, and must come to an end. We started this discussion by saying we never met a coach who has not had to struggle with this issue—struggle is the key word. Most coaches try very hard to be fair with their time and give equal attention to individual gymnasts as needed. In the majority of cases, they succeed in their efforts. But sometimes, the best intentions go off, and the further it goes, the worse it gets. Group action is the best solution.

We would be amiss to say that if a gymnast feels he or she is being neglected, they should also carefully think about their own behavior. Few people, not even saintly coaches, can only take a pain in the neck for so long. It is as natural to turn away from obnoxious behavior as it is to be attracted to favorable characteristics. Make sure you don't, in fact, bring about the so-called "neglect" out of your own "unpleasantness," before you launch a campaign to change things.

The Negative Coach

There are some coaches that talk a good game, but who just cannot seem to think "positively." They seem to always be putting the gymnast down with negative and/or sarcastic remarks. Often they yell a lot and even have temper tantrums from time to time. It surely is hard for a young gymnast to have a childish coach! The coach who operates out of a negative view of things often makes his or her gymnasts feel guilty for what they are doing or failing to do. In the worst of such conditions, gyms that have a negative atmosphere are very unhappy places to be. Some gymnasts adjust to it through willpower and personal drive—many, on the other hand, bow out of the sport with a bitter taste in their mouths. Some coaches seem to slip into a more negative mode close to meets when pressure is greatest—that is a different matter, but still a problem. When there are at least some positive things happening, most gymnasts can manage by accepting the negativism as part of the coach's "style" one has to live with over time. For more on this issue see "Abuses of Anger in the Gym."

Another method for coping with this type of situation is for the kids to pull together and provide the positive support to one another. Sometimes, this will give the coach a model for change which might rub off. Of course, doing this requires a kind of maturity among the gymnasts themselves and this is sometimes asking a lot. It may work for a few, and at least they will feel better in the setting. We are big believers in group influence and pressure—as in the case of the playing favorites coach, the ultimate action might be for the gymnasts to make a direct approach to the coach with the problem. Sometimes, this works and sometimes it doesn't. In any event, it will be difficult for the coach to claim he or she was unaware of the problem, once it has come into focus. Coaches can easily dismiss an individual's complaint, but it is a different matter when a group presents a case. Once this is out in the open, many coaches can alter their behavior. When they do, the results are usually so rewarding that they begin to modify how they operate on a more regular basis.

Summary

For the gymnast, bringing these issues to your coach is the first step in resolving them. In these situations we have looked at for openers, there is one other approach that can be made. If you are in a gym with several coaches, it may be possible to bring the message to the "head person" through one of the other coaches who are not part of the problem. Often in multiple-coach gyms, certain youngsters feel more comfortable with one coach than another when it comes to getting at certain problems. It is not disloyal or inappropriate to take advantage of this condition as a possible way to bring about change which will make things better for everyone. As a coach, you must be open to look carefully at your own behavior and the effects it is having on the team or individual gymnasts in your charge. Appropriate behavioral changes must be made to ensure the overall health of your gymnasts.

ABUSES OF ANGER
IN THE GYM

Most people find anger a very unpleasant emotion. It can cause dramatic physical changes such as increased heartbeat, sweating and even nausea. Gymnasts and coaches, being human, are subject to the same emotion. The coach-gymnast relationship is one where patience can often be stretched a little thin in both directions, resulting in feelings of anger. Research has clearly shown, however, that anger is a natural part of every healthy relationship.

Understanding Anger

To better understand the dynamics involved in dealing with these feelings, we first must know several things about anger as an emotion.

- Anger can often serve several psychological purposes. It is a mistake to always link anger to personal conflict. People use expressed anger in the wrong way to meet a variety of questionable emotional needs.
- Anger is usually developed as the result of other emotions. Fear and anxiety can quickly change into anger and be expressed as such in the gym during training. The angry gymnast may, in fact, be a frightened athlete. Sometimes these transfers from the emotion of anger can become habitual and the gymnast may lose awareness of the original situation from which the emotion has come. This can really spell trouble in the learning process.
- Anger is a form of energy that can be motivating. The experience of anger is usually so uncomfortable that most people are motivated to express it simply as a way of calming down. Once it is out, the relief is often immediate in most cases. Unfortunately, at times, this involves directing it against someone who may have nothing to do at all with the causes for the feeling.
- People are often unaware that personal needs are being met by their anger. Although it is relatively easy to recognize that we are angry, it is sometimes not as easy to identify the real emotional issues that have caused it. For example, the coach putting you down may be the surface issue, but the real reason for the resulting anger may have much more to do with your feelings of low self-esteem, in general, for which the put down serves as a stark reminder.

It is easy to misuse anger, and it is important to be aware of the possibility and to remember that this kind of response can really take its toll on a coach-gymnast relationship, limiting gymnastic progress. In such situations, there is a feeling generated that things can get out of control. One or the other party can become very defensive or even counterattack, and feelings of guilt often follow displays of irrational anger or loss of temper which can do further serious damage to the learning process so essential to gymnastics.

In learning to gain more insight into this emotion, it is important to first look for a pattern in your expression of anger. What were the specific conditions? Did it happen in the exact way before? Were you aware of any other feelings besides anger? What happened right before you lost control or had an outburst? Who else was involved? Any consistencies you can identify will help you narrow down your search to sort out those issues that are generating anger, which may be unfairly directed at others. Once you have clarified a pattern (if one exists) for your anger, you are ready to consider its emotional abuse/misuse and how to control it. Two related articles which provide more insight into this issue are "The Issue of Ethics" and "I Have a Problem with My Coach."

Below are some possibilities to consider; some are common, some are less so, some are subtle and others blatant. All are destructive to the working relationship in or out of the gym and to the overall sense of self. Although they apply to both athletes and coaches alike, abuses one through four are usually more often displayed by athletes, while abuses five and six are seen most often in the behavior of coaches.

Abuses of Anger /Corrective Behavior

Abuse Number One: Anger as a way of avoiding personal responsibility. This abuse often occurs when the gymnast is insecure or unable to admit fault for something going wrong. It is the "blame others" syndrome. We often see this type of anger displayed by very young children where responsibility for an act, or lack of one, is placed on other people or conditions. Translated to gymnastics, at a later time this would mean blaming the coach, judge, equipment, etc. when things don't go right. Such athletes often appear and cast themselves in the role of "victim." Over time, this usually leads to the development of a negative view of others. It is a very big sign of immaturity when seen in adolescents.

Corrective Behavior: The first job for this kind of gymnast is to accept the fact that no one is perfect. This is very difficult if the youngster is a perfectionist by nature and/or the parents are very demanding, expecting their child to be the tops of everything. The next task would be work on separating the self from mistakes or setbacks. An error on the apparatus does not make the individual gymnast a "bad" person. It will often become necessary to set aside false pride and learn to apologize or accept the situation. When this begins to occur, you will begin to learn from your mistakes rather than be blinded by them, and shut out information while you blame someone else for what happened.

Abuse Number Two: Directing anger at a scapegoat. This is a very bad habit, and is hard to control at times. This is when you become angry in a situation in which it would be very hard or inappropriate to express your feelings. For example, the coach has said something that has really gotten you agitated, but you can't let it out because he or she might explode, so you need to keep it inside. What usually happens is that you take it out on some unsuspecting safe target, such as a sibling, parent or even a fellow gymnast. Such innocent bystanders, so to speak, get the brunt of your anger just because they are handy and a little safer.

Corrective Behavior: The first step is to try to calm down and deal tactfully with the real source of your feelings. If you can't approach the head coach, for example, perhaps you can find a sensitive listener in the assistant or a fellow gymnast who is not directly involved. An objective listener can often help you think through the incident, and just letting it out will help. Eventually, when you are more relaxed, it is usually important to make your feelings known to the source itself. Hopefully, they will be open enough to give you the time and to also listen to your perspective. This kind of clearing of the air can help prevent future conflicts.

Abuse Number Three: Anger used to express and reduce anxiety or inside tension. This is by far one of the most common emotional abuses of anger, and is related to abuse number two. In gymnastics, tension and frustration can definitely build up. Although you may be able to keep it under control, that is not always the case. Often once out of the gym, these feelings get expressed in ways that are a real strain on relationships with others. Outbursts in the gym can also occur, and they don't win you any fans either.

Corrective Behavior: What is sometimes needed is a transitional time to emotionally downshift to a more relaxed state. This is one reason I often suggest to coaches that they give the athletes a cooling off period before they leave the gym for home. This can involve some additional stretching time, relaxation, or a mini conference. Besides the physical and mental benefits of this time, it is an opportunity to "burn off" any collected frustration that has gathered during the apparatus training.

Abuse Number Four: Using anger to get your own way. This is a most immature method sometimes used as a holdover from childhood. Many youngsters have learned in the past that if they create enough fuss, they will get what they want. Although this is usually not very successful in the gym, especially with a strong and secure coach, a less obvious, but more often seen method, which is related to anger, is sometimes substituted. Pouting and sulking are such forms, which can bring results. After a while, the coach will begin to sense the manipulation, and this entire abuse of the emotion of anger is surely not good for any working relationship.

Corrective Behavior: The first and most important thing is that those who have yielded to any display in the past must stop reinforcing the behavior. They have to hold the line and do what is right for the group, not for you. The gymnast needs to learn more crowd-pleasing ways to solve the problems that are making this behavior appear, and become more respectful and understanding of the needs of teammates.

Abuse Number 5: Using anger as a motivational technique. This misuse of the emotion of anger is a technique which is favored principally by those coaches who believe that the only real motive for good work is a sense of fear. Typically the fear is produced by outbursts of anger and threats of dire consequences. A by-product of this style of coaching is that an adversary relationship begins to develop between the youngsters and the coach. Growing resentment goes with any effort that is produced. Respect generated by fear is not respect at all. It may get results in the short run, but each time the task is approached, the situation will be the same. It will not be long, under these conditions, until the entire training-learning mode breaks down.

Corrective Behavior: Rewarding gymnasts in a positive way for the work they do well is at the core of all sound learning and is the only way to overcome this misuse of anger in the long haul. But first, the coach must be trained to see the good. This is easier said than done, and some coaches can't do it. They are not long for the sport! They and the kids who stick with them have our unending sympathy. Such a situation is always destructive and doomed to failure. Encouragement, support, and positive strokes encourage cooperation and instill ongoing motivation. At the very least, negative criticism should be done privately; sparing some team members and maintaining whatever morale might still exist.

Abuse Number 6: Anger that results from giving too much to others. By nature, many coaches are giving people of their time, energy, commitment, and knowledge, even if they are being paid to do so. But a problem occurs for such people when they have little ability or the time to give to themselves. Deep resentment can grow within and often results in unexpected outbursts that are the result of this personal frustration. The hidden message may be, "I'm giving so much to everyone else. Why isn't anyone giving anything back to me, not even hard work and results?"

Corrective Behavior: It is important for the coach to recognize that she/he has created a situation in which others probably take them for granted. Once this is done, the coach must decide what is needed from others, and to begin to give to him or herself as well. Beware, however, that you will have to break down some negative precedents that are already set in the minds of the gymnasts. If you are a coach struggling with these feelings, perhaps a modest beginning would be to let your gymnasts know that you expect a "thank you" from them at the end of each workout. With this as a start, maybe more and more personal rewards will be forthcoming that will help you with the anger associated with being unappreciated.

Summary

The above listed abuses of anger represent just a sampling. There are others that are too numerous to list, but that can be easily figured out by those who care to do so. In our sport today, everyone is interested in the achievement of excellence and we are hard driven with great energy towards that objective. That is fine and the way it should be. Too often, however, there is too much anger, frustration, impatience, and too little joy associated with our efforts.

Life is all too short and relationships too valuable to have them threatened by a lack of emotional control. Nowhere is this more relevant than in the coach-gymnast interaction, where the abuse and misuse of anger can readily occur. Maturing beyond the destructive uses of anger has benefits for all; more fulfilling relationships, rising self-esteem, and even the enhancement of health. As people grow within, in this regard, they find that anger is less of a factor. With a growing sense of control, people become more likeable to themselves and to others. A calmer self releases more emotional energy that can be used productively. Creating emotionally more healthy relationships is a most worthwhile personal goal for everyone.

GENDER DIFFERENCES IN DEPENDENCY CONFLICTS

It has always been of great interest to be in a training setting where both adolescent boy and girl gymnasts are working under separate coaching on relatively high level gymnastics. Even a casual observer will note "atmospheric" differences on both an emotional level and on a coach-gymnast communication level. The intensity of the training may be parallel, but the interaction is not. Although much depends on the individual coaches involved with the groups of youngsters, a significant amount of easily observed differences can be accounted for by gender. An awareness of these important sex differences in relation to the basic independence/dependence conflicts associated with normal adolescence may help facilitate the productiveness of the overall coaching effort.

Dependence vs. Independence

As part of this discussion, it seems necessary to provide some definitions. The dictionary defines the concept of "dependence" as the act of being determined by someone else who is in authority over one. Subordination and subjection are involved, and the dependent person looks to another for support or favor. "Independence" is defined as the act of not being subordinate or influenced by advice, control, or assistance from another. This notion involves freedom of action by an individual who exercises his/her own will and judgment in a separate and self-reliant manner. Obviously, being "independent," as defined above, in the gymnastic coaching situation would surely lead to much fireworks between the coach and the gymnast, particularly during the adolescent period when the struggle to achieve autonomy is at its peak.

In the American culture, females appear to experience fewer and less stressful conflicts over the development of personal independence than do boys. This seems to be particularly true during the earlier years of adolescence between the years of twelve through fourteen. Girls generally are more likely than boys to consider rules imposed by others to be reasonable, fair, and often even lenient. This includes "mandates" from parents, teachers, and gymnastic coaches. They seem also more likely to progress from the initial childlike acceptance of parental authority and authority figures in general to a more independent identification with that very authority. Females seem to avoid much of the in-between phase of defiant resistance and assertion of their own controls than are their male counterparts in and out of the gym.

The girls' lesser degree of conflict around authority and within themselves may be partially due to a greater presence of cultural reinforcement. This is especially true in the years prior to adolescence. During this time, dependency and compliance in females and more independence, self-assertiveness, and aggression in boys of a similar age is expected and accepted more readily by society at large. In addition, the onset of puberty may bring a greater, more sudden, and qualitatively somewhat different increase in the strength of both sexual and aggressive drives in boys. As a result, a greater need for establishing independent control of these impulses may lead to a greater likelihood of rebellion and conflict between boys and their parents as well as other authority figures, such as coaches.

It is important not to make too much out of and exaggerate these differences between boys and girls. Although it appears that adolescent girls may remain more dependent and therefore have fewer overt conflicts over the development of independence, any level of extreme or generalized dependence is not a good thing in either boys or girls. In modern society, such a high degree of dependence usually indicates a lack of real independent self-esteem.

Types of Dependency

As part of this discussion, it is necessary to realize that dependency takes on different forms. Not everyone who is showing "dependent" behavior demonstrates the same level or kind of involvement with the mentor figure or adult model. Anyone who has coached has seen these varying levels of dependent behavior in their gymnasts. One kind of dependency might be referred to as "focused learning" dependence. This involves the gymnast actively seeking help from a coach with the sole goal being to learn a skill. Here the gymnast is dependent on the trainer in order to learn the skill and seeks out the coach as the teacher for the purpose of skill mastery. This is a substantially different kind of dependence than when the coach is sought out as a provider of affection, support, and comfort. In this kind of what may be labeled "emotional" dependence, the coach is sought out in order to promote a feeling of personal well-being as the primary objective. In this situation, gymnastic learning is secondary insofar as the function of dependent behavior is concerned.

An additional form or type of dependence may be referred to as "aggressive." In this interaction, the goals are negative in character and are designed to be manipulative of the coaching relationship and related communication. In this case, dependency is used to act out a hostile struggle for control through the coaching format. Usually this dependence interaction is a carry-over of a conflict that is basically going on outside the gym. The coach who always feels that he or she is always fighting with a gymnast rather than "coaching" the athlete may, in fact, be a victim of this kind of dependency relationship.

Emotional dependence still remains fairly acceptable for young girls in modern United States society despite the feministic movement of recent years. This is far less the case for adolescent boys. This is primarily due to the stereotype of the male as a strong and independent individual. Male coaches working with boys will find that the "focused learning" dependency is more dominant than the "emotional" dependency among male athletes. This is not always true but surely is the most prevalent dependency relationship. This is the reason that the objective observer watching boys and girls groups training in the same setting may feel that the female situation involves more emotionalism than that of the opposite sex. In most cases, this observation will in fact be accurate as the coach-female situation does involve more "emotional" dependency than is usually present in the coach-male interaction.

Sex differences in "focused learning" dependency are smaller. Learning dependency (for example, dependence on a coach for obtaining objective help in skill mastery) is more acceptable in boys than is emotional dependency. Excessive learning dependency (for example, not being able to handle aspects of her training in a competent manner) is not seen as adaptive in girls, even though they may be more emotionally dependent on others. Indeed, if a girl is lacking in sufficient learning independence or is overly emotionally dependent, she may resort to using dependency as a means of controlling and manipulating others, and for avoiding responsibility for her own actions or lack of action.

Additionally, it is important to recognize that dependency is usually selective. A developmentally maturing, well-adjusted girl may be more emotionally dependent on a relatively small peer group of trusted friends than her male counterpart, but she in unlikely to behave in accordance with the misleading but common stereotype of a generalize dependency observable at all times. On the other hand, while adolescent males may be less dependent than girls on adult authority figures, such as parents or coaches, they may be very dependent on large male peer groups as a means of helping in the process of detachment from the family unit and the establishment of their own autonomy.

Coaching Implications

This brief discussion of sex differences in the development of conflict over dependence and independence holds some implications for coaches at a variety of levels. When working with young men, male coaches should appreciate that their charges may be very strong in their conflictual and rebellious attitude, not only because of the stereotypic expectation of men, but also because of the nature of puberty itself in males. The coach will find the training time more productive if he recognizes this fact and avoids the unnecessary power struggles. The technical demands for execution and the training load requirement can be enforced based on mutual objective setting, improvement in gymnastic prowess, and success. What needs to be prevented from happening, whenever possible, are debates which get side-tracked into a struggle about who is the boss. These become no-win situations and interfere dramatically with intensive task-oriented practices.

Strong coaches who boast about how compliant and disciplined their girl gymnasts are need to be sure that this pattern is again a matter of mutual commitment and goal setting, and not the result of a high degree of basically unhealthy conformity and dependency. These kinds of relationships are sometimes consciously, or even unconsciously, promoted by the coach to fulfill their needs for power or control. There are those coaches who cannot tolerate any challenge to their authority and vigorously discourage independent behavior in any form from their gymnasts. It may be more difficult to coach a group of early adolescent girls who from time to time feel able to express strong feelings about the authority situation they find themselves under, but a certain degree of rebellion may be healthier for the individual member of the group. In the long run, some opportunity to "rebel" will improve the overall training climate.

Finally, it is extremely important that male coaches working with girl gymnasts carefully monitor any "sexualization" that may be occurring in the interaction. Overt flirtations, an over amount of physical contact, verbal innuendos, etc. are behaviors that can terribly confuse the purpose of the coaching relationship and can do real damage to the psyches of youngsters. This is particularly true in light of the fact that emotional dependency, as discussed in this article, is often present to a greater degree with female gymnasts. The amount of physical contact with gymnasts is also somewhat determined by age, with little ones, and elementary school age children are less vulnerable to misunderstanding such forms of encouragement. During the latency age, contact and displays of affection should be reduced and carefully monitored. In adolescence, they should be few and far between and only at times of mutual celebration. Affection should be given following a great routine during a competition, for example, since coldness and aloofness is not being recommended, but caution is at all levels. Unfortunately, many coaches learn this lesson the hard way and surely an ounce of prevention is worth a pound of cure in this case. Additional insight can be found in the article "Male Coach-Female Gymnast."

MALE COACH–FEMALE GYMNAST

Establishing a positive relationship between coaches and their athletes is a necessary aspect of a healthy working partnership in the gym. However, the over-sexualization of the interaction between male coaches and the girls they work with in the gym are a serious matter. Over the years, a number of letters were received from interested readers asking to spell that point out in more detail. Here we will address the issue of male coaches working with female athletes in more detail as this topic provides for a more extensive article.

Many male coaches develop unique and supportive relationships with their gymnasts but others develop somewhat markedly neurotic, attitudes towards the girls they are working within the gymnastics program. In working with early adolescent and adolescent girls, there is always the danger that the relationship, which is heterosexual by fact, will become too intense (in fantasy or otherwise) for the youngsters to handle. This is particularly true if the coach is somewhat unstable in his own right when it comes to male-female relationships. It should be remembered that growing sexuality (menstruation, development of secondary sex characteristics and other biological phenomenon) reach their peak during the years of 12-18. This is also the time for classic "crushes," the need to sever the natural "sexual" connection with the father, and to formulate attitudes that go into the future value system of young people.

Gymnastics is one vehicle for the expression of this kind of growth as well as an avenue for the development of other things, such as individual competence, a sense of mastery and personal recognition, social comradeship, refinement of poise and a positive body image and general self-identification. Competitive gymnastics by its very nature and physical demands is an intensive sport. The thousands of hours that a coach and gymnast spend together, in the various aspects of the struggle for perfection, almost automatically results in closeness at several levels. This happens whether working in a group or individually. It can be a most rewarding experience for everyone; however, it is a most vulnerable time for many teenagers.

Coaching Concerns

Here are a few areas which need to be addressed, assessed, and monitored in the gym:

1. **Coaching Style**. If the coach has a style that includes a continual amount of "flirtation" with the girls he is working with, he is most likely going to have problems. Needless to say, one must not be afraid of genuine warmth and demonstrated concern, but there is a difference between these qualities and overt behavior beyond the limits of professionalism. Most girls, as well as their mothers, will instinctively, if not consciously, retreat from such "sexualized"

situations. Such a climate contaminates objectivity and creates too much anxiety for the young gymnast. Of course, there are exceptions to a point, and some girls thrive on intense personal relationships with a male coach, but these situations are relatively rare and questionable, and usually involve special circumstances. Probably the best rule of thumb, as discussed in "Coaching the Team: Part II," is to establish an atmosphere of mutual respect and affection which is task oriented and free of any elements of "hanky-panky" at any level. In other word, all seductiveness must be avoided. At this age, the line between "kidding around" and threatening behavior is very thin. Sometimes, this can occur with perfectly good intentions as the motivating force.

2. **Physical Contact/ Spotting.** Another area where these concerns come about has to do with spotting by male coaches. This may seem like something that is of little significance and does not need to be addressed, but on many occasions youngsters, in talking about their gymnastics with me, have spoken about the fact the Coach X or Y makes physical contact with them in a way not called for by nature of the gymnastic skill being executed. We have seen this in action, and it can be a real issue which raises serious questions about the motivation of the coach in his work with young females he is responsible for in the gym.

3. **Dominance Issues**. There are also a number of male coaches who use the coach-gymnast relationship as a way of exerting their sexual dominance over females in general (or their wish to dominate and control). Obviously, this type of behavior has its roots in earlier life experiences of the male coach and the gym, and coaching interaction is used to act out unresolved problems in this area. Such an attitude usually results in a domineering, dictatorial atmosphere where productivity is built on fear, blind submission and obedience. The strain in such a situation can become unbearable. Quite often, such a hidden agenda is disguised as "discipline." Gymnasts usually cannot survive in such a climate for very long.

4. **Male Ego.** It should also be remembered that for many male coaches the activity is a real "ego trip." He is the hero figure in and out of the gym, the knight in a warm-up who will make the little gal a star. It is easy to fall into this trap. Everyone wants to be likeable, but there is a difference between that position and the need to be "worshiped" or "loved."

The attraction between males and females is historically and biologically natural and creative. In the male-female gymnastic coaching situation, this same attraction can be over-determined on a psychological level by both the coach and the gymnast creating major difficulties. The coach is the adult, however, and this must be kept in mind. It requires careful self-monitoring and a willingness to ask one's self, besides the obvious ego gratifications, why one is coaching in the way one does. The answer can sometimes be most alarming, but the inquiry should be made, followed by the necessary modifications in behavior. The coach/ gymnast relationship is one of the most important aspects of coaching but the well-being of the young female athlete is paramount. For more information on this and related matters we have established several guidelines and addressed this issue in the articles, "The Psychologists' View of Coaching: Part II" as well as the "Coaching Commandments."

Chapter Four

UNDERSTANDING MOTIVATION

The papers in this section represent an attempt to bring the elusive notion of motivation into perspective. Some are slightly technical in nature but provide valuable information. Suggestions are made for both coaches and athletes to enhance an understanding of motivational forces at a basic level and some ideas are presented for applying this awareness in the training setting.

- A Key to Success: Part I: Motivation Sources
- A Key to Success: Part II: Extrinsic Motivation
- Behavior Change: Part I: Reinforcement
- Behavior Change: Part II: Self-Evaluation
- Locus of Control and Coach Effectiveness

A KEY TO SUCCESS
PART I: MOTIVATION SOURCES

One of the major difficulties in both learning and teaching, whether it be in the home, the school, or the gym, and hence in the methods of training, is that of inducing and utilizing the "will to learn." For purposes of this series, we will equate the will to learn with motivation. Without motivation, learning is ephemeral at best. Research has clearly indicated that the more profound and total the motivation, the more lasting and assimilated is the learning. In gymnastics, motivation can arise from the felt needs of the athlete, but often such needs can, and sometimes necessarily must, be initially prepared by the coach. Motivation cannot exist in and by itself, in a vacuum. The deepest motivation can fail to result in success if training methods are so ineffectual that they dull the spirit, the will to learn, or prove to be overwhelming barriers to it.

It should be clear to even the layman that motivation is significant in all aspects of life. Both the quality and quantity of work and play are to the fundamental reasons for working and playing. Satisfaction, gratification, and the basic need to see results are all factors in motivation. These can come about from many sources, such as fear of not succeeding, pure pleasure in approbation, or the general agreeableness and elation which accompanies success and victory.

Intrinsic vs. Extrinsic Motivation

The sources of motivation are so numerous that no one list could be exhaustive. In order that this article can be of some practical use to gymnasts and coaches, we will limit our discussion to an examination of what psychologists call intrinsic and extrinsic motivations for skill learning and the relationship between these two as it relates to the gymnastic performance.

We define intrinsic motivations for learning in the gym as those which come about from the satisfying fulfillment of needs felt by the gymnast. Extrinsic motivations are those which arise from satisfying needs and requirements which the gymnast has, more or less, imposed upon him by the coach. Obviously, parental expectation might fall into this category, but for the most part extrinsic motivation in gymnastics finds its major source in the coach-gymnast interaction.

We offer the following examples as a means of translating these definitions into actual practice in the gym:

- A skill is learned as a consequence of intrinsic motivation when a gymnast recognizes either the pleasure or the usefulness of the end product of the learning.

- An athlete learns from extrinsic motivations when he or she feels he "ought to" because of demands made on him by the coach or peers or because of a usefulness which he is told will result from his learning.

Some gymnasts get a real "rush" or excited feeling when they master a new skill. How many times have you seen a smile on the face of a gymnast which not only is the result of the pleasure of learning, but is a product of the feeling associated with the actual physical experience? We have heard gymnasts talk about the super sensation of being in air, executing a full twist, and planting the feet solidly on the mat once again. Trying for this sensation is a form of intrinsic motivation. Recognizing the usefulness of the end product is easiest of all in skill-acquisition since it improves the routine and, hence, raises the objective score one may receive from a panel of judges. Again, this is an intrinsic motivation for continued skill mastery.

The degree of extrinsic (coach as source) motivation and its effectiveness is in direct relationship to the degree of authority, respect, and personal impact that the coach has with the gymnast or team. Many gymnasts will "work for" the coach as well as themselves, realizing from experience that following his or her mandates results in success. Obviously, the coach who constantly makes the "wrong" decision or whose input does not result in a positive outcome will eventually lose all of his or her ability to motivate the gymnasts. An occasional error is forgivable but continual "goofs" spell doom for the incompetent coach. The only exception is when the intrinsic motivation is so great that the athlete persists despite the stupidity of the trainer. This is a rare situation indeed, and don't count on it.

The line of demarcation between intrinsic and extrinsic motivation is not always clear and a relationship exists between the two which should be understood. Ideally, in gym situations youngsters learn skills because of the excitement they find in the learning. They learn to perform better because of the stimulation they derive from the exercises they are demonstrating. However, these motivations are not always available in short order or apparent to the young gymnast. The beginner may see conditioning and stretching primarily as drudgery Daily intensive repetitions, which may lead, eventually, to the mastery of a new skill, can quickly become boring and an ordeal to the novice, even when a certain degree of intrinsic motivation is present. It is here that the coach finds the most difficult challenge in discovering the key and providing the needed extrinsic motivation which will sustain the gymnast's interest and will to learn on a day by day basis and which satisfy creative needs. So if you're having problems with conditioning, see our article entitled "Conditioning... It's So Frustrating!" for more help in this area.

It is our contention that extrinsic motivations must be used in our gym schools more often than they currently are, because not all learning situations are such that gymnasts would choose them of their own accord. Many children will want to come to the gym because of the parent's aspirations or as the result of what they have seen on TV or videos, such as we illuminated on in "My Daughter, the Competitive Gymnast," but the reality of the task can quickly turn them off. It is good that there is a natural selection process mounted in this way but often times some real talent with fundamental degree of intrinsic motivation may be lost. The heroic illusions created by the glamour of the sport may bring a youngster to the training center for the wrong reasons, but nevertheless it is the small step that may be the beginning of a promising career. Perhaps it is worth the careful investment of some time.

Coaching Management

Until such time when potent intrinsic motivations "take over," if they ever do, the extrinsic forces need to be created by the coach and staff to keep the striving young gymnast going in the face of numerous frustrations and disappointment, the least of which is the realization that a dream is not easily achieved. This is, of course, easier said than done. Additional information on this topic can be found in "Behavior Change: Part I & II."

To create the external conditions needed to maintain enthusiasm for hard work and a manifest system of encouragement and overall "atmosphere," management is a big challenge and requires much thoughtful planning. Anyone who has worked with young people in gymnastics knows that it doesn't take long to run out of ideas. Some programs are dull indeed and although highly motivated gymnasts may hang in, the level of interest is bound to eventually decline. It is unusual for such efforts to prove productive over the long haul and many potentially successful gymnasts drop by the wayside.

There are coaches and gym school directors who feel that if the intrinsic motivation is not strong enough to sustain the gymnast then he or she shouldn't be in the sport. Obviously, the coach should not have to provide twenty-four hour a day motivation. The reliance solely on a personal drive resident in the youngster, however, without a consideration of the ongoing need to provide external stimulation is an unfortunate position to adopt. Even a coach who feels he or she is only interested with the top, elite gymnast with great motivation will find it necessary in time to provide extrinsic stimulation. Very often the intensive work and competition at this level will, given good conditions in the gym, encourage continued effort. However, the success of such endeavors can be increased with some conscious attention given to the development and provision of extrinsic motivational factors in an organized manner which will be explored further in "A Key to Success: Part II."

A KEY TO SUCCESS
PART II: EXTRINSIC MOTIVATION

The notion of motivation was defined as the "will to learn" and some differentiation between intrinsic and extrinsic motivation was discussed in "A Key to Success: Part I." It should be remembered that the ultimate objective is to minimize the need for external motivation (although it must always be present to some degree) and to maximize the intrinsic motivations of pleasure in the need-satisfying experience and the recognized usefulness of learning. It should also be acknowledged that motivation is related to maturation (physical, emotional, and intellectual readiness), and that one does not motivate a six year old the same way one approaches a teenager. This may seem like an obvious fact but it is striking how many coaches ignore the rather subtle developmental issues involved in working with young people and talk either "up" or "down" to their students.

For purposes of our discussion we will focus on providing the proper extrinsic motivations needed in every gym. We will also focus on the preadolescent, adolescent, and young adult since the issues concerning young children and motivation fall more into the area of basic movement education and should be reserved for a separate paper.

Conditions in the Gym

First and foremost, it should be recognized that the conditions in the training facility—physical as well as nonphysical— provide the greatest source for extrinsic motivation. A pleasant, colorful, well thought out, pragmatic arrangement can encourage concentration and hard work. Large corporations, for example, have long been aware of the use of music to stimulate productiveness. This is not a random idea, but is based on the knowledge we have about the psycho-neurological system of human beings. Not only the type of music, but the volume has been shown to have an effect on the motivational level of people. Unfortunately, the kind of music conducive to gymnastics is not always the type that bubbling adolescents enjoy. As in most situations, compromise is the best solution. It is also interesting to note how many gyms are improperly lighted. Good lighting is important for safety reasons, but research has also shown that it can effect an individual's motivation to do certain kinds of tasks.

Needless to say, the coaches' and staff's overall attitude, enthusiasm, expectations, personal commitment, and dedicated hard work all serve as a major source of extrinsic motivation. It is important to remember that any specific conditions that are manufactured to increase motivation must take place in an atmosphere where the emotional climate is positive and conducive to disciplined training.

Praise

Everyone enjoys praise. Earned praise, like punishment, is a form of discipline. Both praise and punishment are at both ends of a continuum which is designed to modify and place a value judgment on manifest behavior. The source of these responses in the gym again rests primarily with the coach. Encouragement, coupled with supportive, positive technical input, is the best overall way of motivating the gymnast from an extrinsic point of view. This is one reason why the coach-gymnast relationship is so important and why I have emphasized in past papers the wisdom in the coach understanding the individual communication and need system of each gymnast. Most gymnasts, alas, most people, generally thrive on positive input which says "You did a good job," "You are coming along just fine," and "I am pleased with your effort." It is amazing how many coaches will start a critique by focusing on the negative, with perhaps something positive stated as an afterthought, rather than beginning with an encouraging statement follow by "but you must..." etc.

The absence of praise or the reflection of disapproval can also successfully motivate the gymnast, especially in the correct doses. For some it is devastating. If negative input does occur in a constructive way, it can also encourage (extrinsically) the gymnast to try harder to do better. Usually, disapproval ranging from a frown to an outright condemnation is about all it takes, on the "punishment" end of the continuum, to bring about a modification in behavior. After all, the coach cannot physically inflict punishment on the athlete, although we have known coaches who have hit their gymnasts. There is a time perhaps when a crack on the back of the thigh of a gymnast working uneven bars might emphasize the need for more careful attention to form, but that is about as far as it should ever go. We have seen coaches and gymnasts who do best when they are in constant "battle." In any event, it is a matter of personal style and individual communication. If it works and is not destructive to the youngster, by all means use it!

Goals and Objectives

Along with the calculated use of praise to motivate the gymnast, the establishment by the coach and gymnast of task-oriented objectives can also be effective. This is a relatively easy thing to initiate and carry out. Each gymnast has a folder of his or her own. In it, by event, is a list of objectives with a timetable for their acquisition which is developed with the coach. Primary input comes from the gymnast.

An example might be: every week, or whatever time frame makes sense for the pace and level of the gymnast, the coach and athletes take the time to sit together and review the progress being made in relation to the objective. Appropriate revisions are made. When a skill is mastered a check is made on the paper and a new task is decided upon. In some gyms, these sheets can be posted. This is risky and depends on the climate and sociology of the group. Seeing how others are doing is obvious in a gym—they are progressing, making their exercises or they're not. It is relatively clear. Posting individual objective sheets (or it can be done by team) can be stimulating, depending once again, on the coach and the gymnasts. This type of activity should not be used to humiliate an athlete. There are variations on this form of extrinsic motivation that coaches can figure out as they experiment with it. Our article "Using Goal Setting as a Coaching Tool" provides more examples of tracking objectives and the gymnasts will want to look at "My Goal is to… A Gymnast's Plan" for examples on how they can track their personal objectives.

Variations in Motivation

In the many gyms we have been in here and abroad, one constantly sees an endless variety of extrinsic motivations— encouragement of team spirit (cheering when a teammate gets a new skill, "Gymnast of the Week" award etc.), stimulating posters, slogans, special schedules (play time, wild trick day etc.), and challenging events. All of these things are important areas of external motivation and need to be continually reviewed and revised. We have only touched on the concept of extrinsic motivation in this paper and everything that is done, from handstand contests and mini-meets to cake sales and special exhibitions, serve this purpose. One is limited only by their own imagination when it comes to "inventing" forms of this kind of motivation.

Most important in this regard, however, is a gym where "positive thinking" predominates, learning is encouraged, and where mutual respect and hard work are key elements of the overt philosophy. Hard work, in and of itself, can be an extremely powerful motivating force, and sometimes the only reliable one, if it is task oriented and carefully planned. It takes time, but is surely worth it in the end.

Summary

The most successful program, although always maintaining extrinsic motivation, is one where an ever increasing number of participants operate out of an internalized drive. Sensitive extrinsic motivation will gradually lead to more highly intrinsically motivated gymnasts. The individual's felt need will be recognized; the usefulness and pleasure associated with the end product, and the gymnastic performance, will become a primary force for continued participation.

Our major concern in these basic articles on motivation has been to emphasize:

- That the will and need to learn is basic to all gymnastic learning.
- That the more deeply embedded is this will in the individual, the more and lasting will be the learning.
- That superficial motivation is often necessary to induce deeper motivations.
- That effective training does not remain at the superficial level of motivation but continually seeks in various ways to bring about more self-motivation.

BEHAVIOR CHANGE
PART I: REINFORCEMENT

It should be clear that motivation is significant in nearly all aspects of life. Both the quality and quantity of work and play are related to the fundamental reasons for working and playing. Satisfaction, gratification, and the basic need to see results are all factors in motivation. These can come about from many sources, such as the fear of not succeeding, the pure pleasure of receiving recognition, or the general agreeableness and elation which accompanies success and victory.

In two previous articles, "A Key to Success: Part I & II," we had a general discussion of motivation in gymnastics. It was pointed out in these articles that one of the major difficulties in both learning and teaching, whether it is in school or in the gym, is that of inducing and using the will to learn. In the earlier papers it was emphasized that the more profound and total the will to learn, the more lasting and assimilated is the learning. It was also observed in that series that the most ardent personal striving to excel can fail to result in success if the training methods are ineffectual and consistently dull the spirit or will to learn. We often encounter the terms "extrinsic" and "intrinsic" in the literature dealing with motivational theory. Translating these definitions into gymnastics:

- Intrinsic motivations for learning come about from the satisfying fulfillment of needs felt by the individual. A behavior is shown (skill is learned) as a consequence of intrinsic motivational forces when the gymnast recognizes either the pleasure or usefulness of the end result of the learning,
- Extrinsic motivations are those that arise from satisfying needs and requirements imposed by the environment. A gymnast learns from extrinsic motivations when he or she feels and "ought" to because of demands made on them by the coach or because of a usefulness which he or she is told will result from the particular learning.

For purposes of this current discussion, we will again equate this elusive will to learn with the notion of motivation. We will focus on the development and alteration of behaviors through a use of the potential for control found in the external environment, that is, by capitalizing on the opportunities for extrinsic motivation.

Positive Reinforcement

The most common applied technique for gradually gaining control of behavior in this mode involves the use of positive reinforcement. Simply put, this involves rewarding the individual for a display of the desirable behavior—the gymnast for the proper completion of the desired skill. In practice, positive reinforcement increases the response rate of the desired behavior. The number of such positive reinforcers that may work for any one individual usually far exceeds those identified by the coach.

Methods for measuring and reporting on those conditions in the environment that serves as positive enforcers for individual athletes have been developed over the years. Of course, most coaches continually experiment with various techniques for encouraging the desired behavior, but the more we avail ourselves of research, the more effective we will become in the development of our gymnast's full potential.

When coaches utilize positive reinforcement theory, they should keep a couple of points in mind. Contrary to some popular opinion, it is necessary to produce negative reinforcement from time to time, rather than rely only on positive reinforcement. The standard ratio of 1:4 or 1:5 provides an acceptable guide for the frequency of the two. Another principle to remember is not to assign negative and positive qualities to the same action. For example, doing more sit-ups, push-ups, or sprints, is desirable behavior for conditioning, but if used as punishment for not executing a particular skill or exhibiting correct behavior, these activities decrease the potential for achieving effective control, because of the introduction of an inconsistency factor.

Frequency of Reinforcement

Another important principle affecting behavior by gaining control over it is the need to increase the frequency of positive reinforcement. This usually can come from two major sources: the coach and other gymnasts. First, let us look at the coach as a primary motivator. If a coach considers him or herself to be an important source of reinforcement, he/she should attempt to maximize efforts in this direction.

Obviously, the logistics involved when the coach to gymnast ratio is large can severely limit the coach's opportunity to concentrate on this important, and often underemphasized activity (we will address this and other related problems in "Behavior Change: Part II" of this series). Research has shown that group rewards have no permanent effect on the individual performance of gymnasts within the team. The key to success appears to lie in the provision of individualized positive reinforcement. The coach can be more effective by increasing the quantity and quality of positive reinforcement.

Increasing the quantity of positive reinforcement means that when the desired skill is properly executed or related behavior displayed (e.g. determined attitude), a positive reinforcer is applied. This is often referred to as taking advantage of the "teachable moment." The point is to provide the reinforcement immediately after the desired behavior has occurred. The theoretical model suggests that the greater the number of reinforcers provided, the more effective the control becomes over the behavior. Some of the techniques that can be used involve voice modulation, arm gestures, and varying proximity to your athlete or group. Coaches need to be aware of this fact and facilitate it as much as possible.

Feedback

It is important, at this point in our discussion, to consider another related aspect of communication between coach and gymnast which we discussed in "The Art of Feedback: A Model for Coach-Gymnast Communication." This has to do with the provision of technical correction and other performance information. While rewards indicate an approval of the behavior, performance information provides feedback about the actual merits of the behavior itself. Such performance information does not always involve an analysis of an isolated skill or an entire routine, but may also address such factors as total execution, level of effort, work volume, etc. Reward and performance information should be combined whenever possible since performance information alone has no motivational benefit. When these inputs are combined, the gymnast is motivated (by the reward) to do the behavior once again, but this time in accordance with the new information provided through the skill critique (performance information).

Summary

To sum up our discussion so far, coaches should strive to:

- Individualize rewarding or reinforcement responses as much as possible.
- Increase the number of rewarding behaviors.
- Improve and vary the quality of verbal and nonverbal rewards.
- Increase the number and quality of rewards in combination with performance information of a technical nature.

In our next article, "Behavior Change: Part II," we will take a detailed further look at various research efforts in this area and at methods for increasing the sources of reinforcement beyond the coach, i.e. the gymnasts themselves. We will also consider some possible program organizational changes that can promote continuous positive reinforcement and look at methods for stretching rewarding behavior so as to get more performance mileage, while at the same time reducing the consumption of reinforcement fuel.

BEHAVIOR CHANGE
PART II: SELF-EVALUATION

A discussion of motivation both in general and specific terms involves such notions as; "the will to learn," "intrinsic and extrinsic," "positive and negative reinforcement," "teachable moment," and "performance information." In "Behavior Change: Part I," we focused on the alteration of behaviors through the use of the potential for control found in the external environment, that is, by capitalizing on the opportunities for extrinsic motivation. We emphasized that the most common technique for gradually gaining control of behavior and bringing about behavioral change involves the use of positive reinforcement on an individualized basis. We also discussed at some length both the quantity and quality of reinforcement and how to maximize theoretical positions in actual day to day work in gymnastics.

It was pointed out that while rewards indicate an approval of behavior, performance information provides feedback about the actual merits of the behavior itself (skill analysis). Rewards and performance information should be combined whenever possible since performance information alone has no motivational benefit in most cases. When these inputs are combined, the gymnast is motivated by the rewards to do the skill once again, but this time in accordance with the new technical base provided through the performance information.

In this article, we will move further into the area motivation and examine methods for increasing the sources of reinforcement beyond the coach, i.e. the gymnasts themselves. We will also consider some possible program changes of an organizational nature that can promote the benefits of this approach on a larger scale within the training setting.

Sources of Reinforcement

We have pointed out in the past that coaches can definitely influence the quantity and quality of reinforcement in their gyms. Research suggests that gyms that are primarily coach oriented, in so far as reinforcement is concerned, generally appear to have relatively low motivational effects. Motivation in such situations seems to be maintained by trial and error response to the environment, and is weak in reinforcing strength over the long haul.

A previous study in sport psychology can give an illustration of motivational effects. A comparison was made between coach-controlled and athlete-controlled organization effects on the behavior of swimmers. Three conditions were compared; 1) normal training circumstances, 2) training sessions where two coaches provide reinforcement to the exclusion of other behaviors and 3) training session where the swimmer used a behavior game and provided consequences for each other's behavior.

When the coach concentrated solely on positive and negative reinforcement there was, in fact, a noticeable effect. However, when the swimmers, using a behavior game, were responsible for controlling each other's behavior, the effect was most striking and far more effective than the other two conditions. The point is that when the consequences of behavior (reinforcement) are frequent, as would be the case in athlete-controlled condition, behavioral control is much more effective.

Such results suggest that coaches increase the amount of reinforcement in the gym by using sources other than themselves. Coaches with the well-known "ego" problems too often encountered in gymnastics will have some trouble with this since it implies a willingness to let go of some personal control which might be associated with prestige.

Following the trend indicated by such research, gymnasts should be taught how and why to provide reinforcement for each other. They should also be taught how to reinforce themselves through self-evaluation of their performance. Also, the more the gymnasts are aware of the technical "tasks" involved in skill training, the greater will be the amount of performance information that can be gotten from the coach and, most importantly, the gymnasts themselves. Finally, the coach will be more successful in behavior control when he or she can provide more frequent quality reinforcers to small, skill-matched (homogeneous) individuals, rather than to a larger group.

The motivation can be increased if the coach can alter the training situation, as much as possible, from coach-oriented control to gymnast/coach-oriented control. Obviously, the quantity and even quality of positive reinforcers will increase in this situation and the training will provide more behaviorally-based motivation than could possibly be managed in the more common restrictive coach-centered approach.

Continuous Positive Reinforcement

We have already indicated that increasing the number of positive reinforcements is initially very important for bringing about the desired behavioral change. To get the most out of this, every occurrence of the desired behavior should be reinforced, in other words, reinforcement should be continuous. In running a comprehensive competitive gymnast program, it is clear that this approach to one's teams would become overwhelming by logistics alone. If this, however, makes the most sense from a psychological point of view, is there some way to provide continuous positive reinforcement (+CRe)? It is a difficult task indeed, but not impossible by any means, particularly in a training environment which is enriched through the utilization of gymnasts themselves, as well as coaches, for the provision of positive reinforcement. Another aspect of the solution involves the provision of +CRe in the initial stages and then to gradually stretch the impact of the reinforcement schedule over multiple behaviors.

In order to facilitate the provision of continuous positive reinforcement (+CRe), some organizational changes are appropriate. For example:

- The coach as the source of +CRe would devote specific blocks of time to individual or compact homogeneous groups of gymnasts to the exclusion of others on the team. This can be managed particularly when positive reinforcement comes from other sources (gymnasts) than the coach for controlling the ongoing work of the gymnast not being attended at that moment by the coach.
- Gymnasts themselves have to be helped to evaluate and reinforce their own behaviors. In addition to increasing their "technical" awareness about the specific gymnastic skill, this requires some training in self-analysis.
- Training sessions must be coordinated and organized so as to have every member gymnast evaluating each other on similar behavior content, as in a behavioral game.
- Whenever possible, use modern technologies which provide continuous evaluative information.

Coaches must make a real attempt to generate +CRe by removing as much of the organizational inertia often found in our gyms. This can be promoted by developing a systematic program over a period of time. It takes big thinking, small steps and guts. The provision of +CRe will gradually increase the occurrence of the desired behavior in the gym. The next problem is that of persistent response once the behavior wanted is frequently shown. The procedure for accomplishing this has been called "stretching the schedule of reinforcement." What is required for stretching the schedule is the intermittent missing of reinforcements until the gymnast performs many desired behaviors (skills) for a single reinforcement.

Your authors have actually seen gymnasts with slightly bewildered expressions on their faces when, for the first time, the expected reinforcing stroke associated with a given behavior is not forthcoming. Do they refuse to go on? Clearly the answer is no, they continue their work and after the successful completion of several desired behaviors a single positive reinforcer is given. The gymnast is still motivated and is operantly conditioned to stretch their expectations, as it were. The implementation of this kind of stretching in gymnastic coaching is a real art. If the schedule is stretched too quickly, the response rate may decrease as the desired behavior is partly abandoned. Coaches should be very careful and conservative in this phase and plan things out in advance.

As in most experiences in life, a reliance on a contrived or artificial set of circumstances can produce problems. The same holds true for contrived positive reinforcement. If the program's success hinged exclusively on certain devices or the presence of a certain individual, one can easily imagine what would happen should these conditions be terminated. Therefore, for attaining the most total control, it is very important in the final stages of this kind of effort that the sources of reinforcement occur naturally in the environment.

Self-Evaluation

The most readily available and easiest source of reinforcement to use in producing persistent responding is found in self-evaluation. When a gymnast is able to evaluate his or her behavior (skill performance, work load, etc.) and to determine how adequate they have been then the source of reinforcement will always be available, no matter what the circumstances. It appears clear that when +CRe is self-generated and based on objective measurements (successful completions of skill), the desired response is very enduring. The final principle for altering the state of motivation is the relinquishing of control to naturally occurring reinforcements in the environment of the individual gymnast. The implication for our coaches is that gymnasts need to be taught how and when to evaluate behavior and to solidify standards for decision making. Ideally, during this phase, circumstances would be engineered by the coach so that both self-reinforcement and external reinforcement would be available independently, but also simultaneously when needed. But that is the ideal model of some future world. Two articles which discuss self-evaluation and performance in more detail can be found in "My Goal is to…A Gymnast's Plan" and "Using Goal Setting as a Coaching Tool."

Summary

In summation, the promotion of behavior change (motivation) requires the following:

1. Identify the specific gymnastic behaviors to be motivated.
2. Carefully develop a schedule for the implementation of desired change.
3. Work to enrich the quantity and sources of positive reinforcement.
4. Continuously reinforce the target behavior to obtain the desired rate.
5. Stretch the schedule of reinforcement so that multiple responses are required for reinforcement to occur.
6. Transfer the reinforcement to naturally occurring consequences (self-evaluation).
7. Repeat as necessary. It's worth it!

LOCUS OF CONTROL
AND COACH EFFECTIVENESS

Motivation, or what moves people to act or not act, has been the topic of several articles. "Stroking" is a concept often associated with the area of motivation. The dictionary defines stroking as gently rubbing in one direction. In this article, stroking will be further defined as the feedback and rewards gymnasts receive for their efforts. Defined in this way, strokes are already connected to positive or negative motivation that influences the gymnast's mental attitude towards work. The coach-gymnast relationship is very much involved in this whole idea as is the effectiveness of various styles of coaching.

Every individual is different, and the kinds of strokes that influence their behavior are equally different. However, there are two common ways in which gymnasts get motivated. One is from outside influences, and the other is from factors that originate within the individual person. In many cases, of course, athletes respond to a combination of the two, rather than relying on pure external or internal strokes for motivation. Each gymnast develops a personal belief about what types of motivations work best for them.

Locus of Control

Recent work into something called "locus of control" has a direct connection to the idea of stroking as defined here, and has some crucial implications when it comes to motivation and effective coaching with gymnasts. Locus of control is a label given to a psychological notion regarding people's beliefs about how they gain control of strokes or reinforcements they receive as the result of their personal striving. Reinforcements are those things that happen to an individual, positive or negative, verbal or nonverbal, that encourage or discourage particular behavior. The general idea is that there are two types of locus of control: internal and external. Gymnasts who exhibit an internal locus of control tend to believe that their actual, real behavior is what influences and determines what rewards they get. That is, what they do well in their opinion has a built in payoff and reinforcement of its own. External locus of control gymnasts believe that their strokes or reinforcements are controlled more or less by fate, chance or powerful others, such as the coach. The interconnection between the ideas of stroking, motivation, reinforcement and locus of control is obvious on a level of definition. What is not as obvious; however, are the coaching implications on an applied level. These implications become clearer when seen in the light of various studies that have examined locus of control in more detail.

Over a span of six years, your authors consulted with the National Jr. Elite Development Program of the United States Association of Independent Gymnastic

Clubs. This was a highly selective effort with the gymnast's entry and participation carefully controlled and monitored. The resulting groups of young athletes were truly quite remarkable, and represented a high level of gymnastic proficiency and involvement. Part of our role as a member and assistant to the sports medicine staff was to collect information about this population related to motivation, attitude, personality and other psychological factors. One of the areas evaluated in an effort to establish a profile of these gifted athletes was locus of control using a Directed Self-Inventory Locus of Control Scale. Of over 400 gymnasts assessed with this instrument, 86.87 percent, measured as clearly "internals!" These interesting findings have important implications for coaches working with identified gifted gymnasts. Further details can be found in "Psychological Characteristics of Jr. Elite Gymnasts."

More formal research conducted in the past concerning locus of control provides other findings that have direct application when it comes to the motivational nature of the coach-gymnast relationship. Studies have found that externally oriented people are more easily influenced by attempted coercion of conditioning than are internals. It was found that externals responded as expected to subtle verbal influences. On the other hand, internals showed no change in response to similar attempts. Translated to gymnastics, internal locus of control gymnasts (like the USAIGC Jr. Elite) would not react to such subtle conditioning influences on the verbal level since they would be seeking the reward or stroke primarily from actually executing a skill successfully. This fact should partially, at least, determine the coaching approach to such gymnasts when maximum motivation is being sought.

Other studies into this same variable have shown that overt and less subtle attempts to more forcefully coerce external locus of control individuals, such as the coach becoming angry and threatening, worked surprisingly well. With internals, however, the same approach not only did not work, but in most cases caused the individual to change their behavior in the opposite direction of that of the overt coercion. These internals basically dig in and resist this influence with their behavior often described as "frustrating" and "negative." Another most interesting and related piece of research in this general area involved gymnastics judges, whom researchers identified in terms of their locus of control. The results of this study clearly showed that external locus of control judge's scores went up as the so-called "better gymnasts," by order of competition, appeared, even when actual performance did not support this higher score. In this study, it appeared that some judges were affected by an expectation phenomenon, which is, expecting the fifth gymnast to do better than the first one. External locus of control judges appeared to be influenced more by their expectations, however, this was found not to be true in the case of the internal locus of control judges. Since this was the case, the researchers suggested that it is possible that outside factors could influence judgments made by external locus of control officials, for example, negative crowd response and intimidating comments from a coach.

Most of the research in locus of control indicates that internals are resistant and externals are conforming to attempts to influence them. The applied challenge here would be, once identified, how to best motivate the internally oriented locus of control gymnasts who tend to resist subtle verbal influence and surely turn away from an overt coercion from powerful others such as the coach. Perhaps the coach who has a "tough kid to reach" is dealing with an internal locus of control gymnast. Such a frustrating gymnast might be a strong individual personality who looks inwardly for his or her strokes and reinforcements and less so to the coach. The coach's approach in such a case might be more successful if it was purely task-oriented with skill acquisition, the source of reward, rather than relying to any degree on outside schemes of influence. Feedback to this gymnast would avoid much "personal" content and would be, strictly in technical terms, focusing on what must be mechanically accomplished in order to gain mastery of the movement. The article "Using Goal Setting as a Coaching Tool" provides more understanding of this issue.

Effective Coaching

The above discussion of internal-external locus of control strongly suggests that the most effective coaching will utilize different approaches depending on the primary motivational system of an individual gymnast. To stroke or not to stroke and when and how are all connected to a true recognition and appreciation of the uniqueness of each athlete. Given this degree of complexity, the following general ideas appear to make sense in terms of learning and motivation regardless of how strokes are provided and processed by individual gymnasts.

Probably the most significant guideline that can be drawn from all motivation behavioral, educational and psychological literature and/or theories is that a positive approach to interpersonal relations and learning is the most appropriate. There is little doubt that a strong correlation exists between a positive coaching approach and effectiveness. This may appear like a terribly simple idea, but it is amazing how many coaches, even those who believe they have a positive approach to the teaching-learning model, do not, in fact, operate in a positive manner, although they give lip service to the soundness of the concept. This is not always a matter of intentionally failing to practice what one preaches, but often is simply a matter of forgetting under the pressure to produce. Having a positive approach to the coach-gymnast interaction does not mean it is how it is done that counts. Commenting on the technical merits or faults of skill execution is a mandatory part of relationship, but such analysis should be accomplished in a psychological climate which is supportive and positive in nature and built on a foundation of respect for the individual involved. In such a setting, critique is a healthy condition for learning. Comments on improper behavior can be approached in the same way under this positive umbrella.

Establishing this favorable climate is a matter of emotional attitude and not easy to come by. As a matter of fact, some coaches simply cannot think or function "positively." Such coaches may also get results but it is doubtful progress can be sustained over the long haul, or, if it is, the issue of the price paid by the athlete is a serious one.

Coaching Suggestions

There are several ways to enhance positive thinking and the kind of climate which is preferred:

1. One thing to remember is to "reward" or reinforce immediately when the desired action occurs. Reward effort as well as results; verbally "good job" or nonverbally, a pat on the back, a smile, etc.

2. An equally important aspect of this same approach is to encourage the gymnast (another form of reinforcement) immediately following a big, obvious error. What went wrong at one level is usually obvious, it is not necessary to go into a long detailed technical explanation of the mechanics involved in falling flat on one's back. Once it is clear that no injury has occurred, give a caring, warm, positive stroke and get back to the task with a minimum amount of fuss. Again, encourage the effort, don't demand results.

3. When you offer constructive suggestions (criticism), first point out something that was done correctly. There must have been at least one part of the body that was close to correct; emphasize that initially and then go on to discuss things that must be altered. This method fosters self-motivation to correct the mistake, rather than negative motivation to avoid failure or coach disapproval.

4. Never take your gymnast's efforts for granted. Letting them know individually or as a group that you appreciate their striving is a good idea and will help establish the positive work climate which is so conducive to learning.

5. Use encouragement selectively so that it is meaningful. Be supportive, but also avoid becoming a glorified cheerleader. This can really irritate your gymnasts and will have the opposite affect you wish to achieve (this is especially true of internal locus of control gymnasts as discussed earlier).

6. Never use sarcasm. Sometimes it can work used in a "joking" manner, but in most cases should be dutifully avoided.

7. Stay away from punishment—this is also a negative reinforcement. Don't require kids to run laps, do push-ups or use the piling on of gymnastic skill

repetitions in this manner. Also, this can promote a negative association with conditioning.

8. Fear of failure is reduced if you work to reduce the fear of punishment or negative disapproval, verbal, physical or otherwise.

9. Use positive reinforcement whenever desirable group behavior occurs, such as the verbal stroke, "you really pull together well," etc. In other words, prevent negative behaviors from occurring by using the positive approach to reward and strengthen their opposites.

10. Avoid getting in the position of constantly hassling or nagging a gymnast like a drill sergeant. If one gymnast just can't hack it, remove him or her from the scene in a non-punitive manner, indicating that it would appear that they can't manage things at this time. Don't stop everything and go into a complicated analysis of what is going on.

11. Avoid applying a disciplinary action to the team for the behavior of one individual. Reserve any deep discussion for a private time.

Conclusion

The same positive approach suggested above with individual members of a team obviously applies to the overall management of the group as a unit. It is extremely important to maintain an external order which will facilitate the kind of psychic calm that enhances learning. Generally, in order to make training more effective, coaches should remember:

- Each athlete responds differently to motivation strategies. Usually, this response involves both external and internal sources of inspiration.
- Each coach should try to determine if an individual gymnast is primarily an internal or external locus of control athlete. Elaborate testing is not needed. Careful observation of responses to motivational efforts over time will help identify the "style" most effective with each gymnast.
- Whatever the motivational preference is with a given gymnast, a positive approach is best for consistent and maximum learning.
- Although it takes much time and effort for the coach to figure out what strokes are best for what folks, the effort will not only improve the interpersonal relationship, but, in the long run, will increase productivity.

Chapter Five

OVERCOMING AND MANAGING FEAR

I t is clear that one of the most important variables above and beyond sheer talent that affects the outcome of training at any level in high risk sports such as gymnastics is the management of fear. In fact, the single most asked question we receive from gymnasts has to do with handling fear. This section opens with a summary of surveys which were collected in the past but still contain powerful truths for today. In addition, the papers in this area are designed to: 1) give the coach and athlete a basic orientation to the concept of fear, 2) provide very practical approaches to dealing with fear, and 3) share with the young gymnasts themselves the problems that they presented and some recommended solutions.

- Fear Survey and Coaching Implications
- Fear in Gymnastics "I'm Afraid!"
- "I'm Afraid to..." Coaching Strategies
- "Dear Doc" Fears and Falls
- Understanding, Overcoming, and Coping With Fear: An Overview

FEAR SURVEY
AND COACHING IMPLICATIONS

Over the course of decades, we have collected data on the psychological aspects of gymnastics through the form of surveys, psychological instruments, and performed more rigorous research as well. For the most part, the findings vary little year to year, gymnast to gymnast. However, the data received and the implications for the coaches and gymnasts in general are noteworthy.

This article represents an informal survey and report of information concerning fear and gymnastics. The surveys were conducted with groups of relatively high level young female gymnasts, between the ages of eight and thirteen, who attended week long national development training camps representing private gymnastic clubs throughout the United States. The following provides the survey questions and results of these findings:

Fear Survey Questions

The questions asked on the survey and the results are as follows:

What are you most afraid of in gymnastics, if anything?

Beam Routines and Beam Flight Series got fifty-six percent (56%) of the "votes" as being the most feared event in the survey.

Has being scared ever been fun for you?

Fifty-four percent (54%) of the gymnasts indicated that this was the case. Specific things such as roller coasters, fun houses, etc. were named.

Have you ever been so fearful that you thought about quitting gymnastics?

Seventy-eight percent (78%) filling out the survey indicated that they had felt like quitting gymnastics because of their fears. Many indicated that this feeling had come about more than once.

Do you feel that way right now?

Feel like quitting now: Six percent of the gymnasts at one training camp indicated that they felt very fearful and felt like stopping at that very time. Each of these youngsters was seen individually to discuss the issue.

What helps you the most in overcoming your fears?

Specific mental strategies such as imagery, visualization, and self-talk were mentioned most often.

Who do you talk to about your fear?

Only sixteen percent (16%) of the gymnasts talk with their coach about their fears. However, fifty percent (50%) talk to their parents about fear.

Survey Results

The results of this survey are not only interesting and informative, but they present some significant implications for gymnasts, parents, and coaches.

1. First of all, gymnasts should take heart in the fact that having feelings of fear is very common indeed and is a universally experienced phenomenon.

2. Gymnasts should also take from this survey an awareness that those in the sport have felt like quitting from time to time, because of their feelings of fear. Considering that 78 % of the gymnasts at this camp felt that way, but in fact were attending the camp and had not quit, are encouraging. It means that these feelings can be strong but are not necessarily terminal, insofar as doing gymnastics is concerned.

3. The area of mental strategies used for overcoming fear named by a majority of gymnasts in the survey involved techniques that can be taught and learned. Visualization (seeing skill in your head,) positive thinking (I'm ready,) concentrating (what I have to do here and now,) cueing (counting,) as well as plain old courage (just go without fuss) are important methods for managing fear. This suggests that coaches and gymnasts should make a real effort to train the mind with the same degree of dedication that they train the body. Mental "strength conditioning" and "flexibility training" should be faithfully pursued as an additional "event."

4. The fact that Balance Beam got such a high "mark" as being an event where considerable fear is present for many female gymnasts has some implications in its own right. For the gymnast, it again confirms that this is a common experience, and the presence of fear does not necessarily mean they will be "bad" performers in this event. It is the most psychological of the four events for women and is the only one that presents the special challenge of two "ground" levels—the one you walk on (beam itself,) and the one 49 inches below that surface, the floor. This creates a really unique situation in all sports and taxes the central nervous system to the maximum, particularly since balancing is also involved which is a neurophysiological task. Coaches need to remember this and allow ample time for skill mastery and confidence development in this event where individual differences and tolerances will be substantial. This ample time may require more actual clock hours than is devoted to the other events and surely will require lots of patience on everyone's part.

5. The implications of the finding that only 16 % of the gymnasts indicated that they would talk to their coaches about their fear are disturbing. Your author

asked the gymnasts as a group why so few would discuss their fears with their coach, and their response is indeed revealing. Basically three reasons were given for their reluctance:

    a. Gymnasts reported that the primary reason they did not want to share their feelings of fear with their coaches were that they were certain that their coaches would invalidate their feelings. That is, they would be told "no, you're not" or "there is no reason to be afraid" etc. They would rather live with the feelings of fear than hear such comments. In some cases, the coach's reaction was described as being more sensitive, but the general consensus was that their concerns would basically be ignored or made to seem "dumb."

    b. A second reason most often given by the gymnasts for keeping their feelings of fear to themselves and not sharing them with the coach was that they did not want to appear weak to the coach or teammates and risk being called a "chicken" or "wimp." This is different than having your feelings invalidated. In this case, they felt, although they were not being told that their feelings were unreal, they were being told that having them was a sign of a personal lack of courage.

    c. Thirdly, and of somewhat less significance, was the gymnast's desire not to admit any weakness to themselves. It would appear that athletes have egos too!

6. It is very important indeed for coaches to realize how crucial it is that they, in fact, try to establish a training environment wherein their gymnasts believe that their feelings will at least be heard, respected, and validated, rather than shut off and denied as being real. This is further support for a "democratic" model in coaching. This not only makes a great deal of sense in terms of the psychological management of individual team members but can also play a role in reducing the chance of unnecessary injury and the development of more sustained and irrational fear in the future. See the article "Coaching the Team" for more insight in this area.

7. Finally, a somewhat surprising outcome of this informal survey was finding that out of these gymnasts only one reported that "lots of encouragement" was helpful in dealing with feelings of fear. This suggests that the experience of anxiety associated with the execution of certain gymnastics skills cannot be reduced simply by a "pep rally" mentality and approach. The physical symptoms of fear that go with the emotional state need to be addressed in a more knowledgeable and sensitive way. Pretending that these feelings do not exist or cheering the athlete on, despite them, may be helpful for some in the

short run, but lasting assistance to the athlete will require more sophistication and effort.

Conclusion

It would appear, from this survey, that external type solutions are not effective, and that ultimately the management of fear comes from within the gymnast in the form of an individual mental strategy. Coaches need to strive to expand their awareness of the problem and modify their response patterns for helping gymnasts cope with fear, recognizing that it is the number one psychological issue that keeps youngsters in the sport from realizing their full physical potential. A further investigation into this issue can be found in several articles concerning the management of fear such as "Fear in Gymnastics" and "Understanding, Overcoming, and Coping with Fear."

FEAR IN GYMNASTICS
"I'M AFRAID!"

How many times have we heard the familiar phrase "I'm afraid!"? How often have gymnasts of equal physical ability arrived at a point when they part ways because one will and the other will not, go for a particular skill? Other than fundamental talent, the most important variable in success or failure in this sport is probably the management of fear. Learning how to cope with this experience requires practice very much like the attainment of new gymnastic skills. A good starting point would be to look at the concept in more detail, as there are a number of related "states of mind" that need to be understood.

Fear, the state of being afraid, in the most general sense, is always connected with something called anxiety. Every human being has run into the rather strong feelings associated with this experience. Physically, there are changes at these times in the body's chemistry: a discharge of adrenaline, increase in the heartbeat rate, a stiffening particularly of the neck muscles, an urge to urinate, unusual degree of perspiration, a ringing in the ears, trembling, an increase in the yawning response, etc. Accompanying these reactions on the positive side is a marked increase in alertness and an overall tuning-up of the sensory modalities, such as visual acuity and perception, auditory discrimination, etc. It is important to be aware of the physical reactions people experience in relationship to this emotional condition of fear and being afraid. More detail on this can be found in "The Performance Connection: Part II."

Fear and Related Concepts

It appears appropriate to look at what the standard dictionaries as well as psychiatric texts have to say about fear and related concepts:

- **Fear.** Fear is defined in most sources as "an unpleasant and often strong emotion caused by the anticipation or awareness of a dangerous situation."
- **Dread.** Dread, which often accompanies the more general notion of fear, is represented by a very intense reluctance to face a situation, a turning away, an aversion. Dreading a move and the entire notion of "going for it" is surely not uncommon among most gymnasts at one time or another in their careers.
- **Phobia.** A phobia or phobic reaction is an exaggerated fearfulness and is usually irrational and an over-determined psychological state, which usually cannot be dealt with except through prolonged therapeutic intervention. Phobic reactions are not common among gymnasts, although the unrelenting fear, let's say, of going backwards, borders on such a state.

- **Panic.** In the most extreme form of fear, namely panic, all reasoning disappears and the person is often emotionally and physically crippled or out of control. Again, most gymnasts, surely successful ones, don't panic. We have seen athletes prior to the moment of truth become so anxious that they near panic; some even throw up and have other extreme reactions. Many coaches have had the experience of the gymnast who is able to approach the particular skill right to the brink of execution who then suddenly loses control and seems to go physically berserk! At these times so has the mind. In many cases that is all it takes and the next attempt is more successful, since that first terrible moment of initiation has been physically passed. Generally speaking, however, few gymnasts reach this degree of anxiety.

For purposes of our discussion, we will utilize the narrower dictionary definition and consider the emotion experienced by gymnasts in coming to terms with the felt anticipation and awareness of an acute or potentially "dangerous situation." However, if a gymnast is dynamite in the gym during practice, but turns to jelly during the competitive meet, we are not dealing with fear in the sense addressed so far. In these situations we are seeing a reaction to the psychosocial dimensions of competing: being evaluated, exposure to others, anxiety in proportion to the degree of fear of failure, and the ego damaging potential of competitive pressure rather than with a fundamental apprehension of possible danger implicit in the specific skills of the activity. For now we are looking at the emotion of fear in the learning-training phase.

Triggers and Fear Responses

Everyone experiences fear and fearful reactions sometime in their lives. It is natural and very human. The level and degree of fear present in any given gymnast is a very individual matter. Basically timid individuals tend to be more fearful than those who operate out of a more aggressive stance. This is not always the case of course. We have known such gymnasts who are absolute tigers when the screws are down, while their more aggressive contemporaries turn out to be windbags! Being timid and being quiet is not the same thing. Only by getting to know an individual gymnast over time in a variety of situations can the coach begin to understand their unique personal temperaments and what kind of communication and support is appropriate insofar as the management of fear and its effect on performance are concerned.

The things that trigger and set up the state of "danger" which results in being afraid, is different for everyone. What appears hazardous and death-defying to one gymnast, another takes in stride. These variations are present within a single gymnast; you know the type, the girl who easily handles a back tuck on beam, but struggles to execute a simple back walkover on the same apparatus. The differences are mind-boggling at times. There are some gymnasts who appear fearful about almost everything or at least their verbal comments suggest that is the case, but, despite this kind of diffuse anxiety, they somehow plug it through in a manner that is awe-inspiring to those who just can't quite handle it. Others may appear relatively calm and cool until the moment of decision and action when one discovers they are actually very afraid. There are some signs to watch for, but there is no infallible system of prediction other than experience over time. It is important to identify early the particular set of circumstances that create the most fear behavior for any given gymnast in order to minimize its impact during training. These observations are important and helpful as they can partially determine what selected skills should be pursued and on what kind of timetable, under what conditions.

The individual gymnast's fear response as discussed above is the product of very personal experiences, as well as the basic child-rearing practices of the parents. The child whose mother or father continually remind them of the implicit danger in certain activities ("be careful on the jungle-gym; you could hurt yourself") has most likely built into the child some hypersensitivity to the signs of potential danger in the world around, particularly with reference to physical action. It is interesting to note here that some research suggests that firstborn children tend to avoid high risk sports such as gymnastics. The reason being that new parents are often over-anxious and over-protective of their first child. The youngster who has fallen on his or her head doing a particular skill will naturally shy away from that and related movements in most cases especially if the original fall resulted in some real physical trauma. These kinds of experiences coupled with early life rearing practices and our instinctive drive for self-preservation can produce caution in many and some very fearful people indeed. In any event, these individuals ordinarily do not tend to gravitate toward gymnastics as avocation. This is a general rule and those of us who have encountered the exceptions often have our faith in the human spirit renewed.

As stated earlier, no one is without fear, although many appear rock-like in the light of known risk. We have often heard people speak of a gymnast as being "without fear," but this is not accurate in the literal sense. What is really being indicated and observed in such cases are individual gymnasts who have developed a defensive system which enables them to manage this natural emotion and to face dangerous situations with a high degree of success.

Coping with Fear

Your authors have spoken to many accomplished gymnasts (here and abroad) about fear and how they deal with it. Refer to the article "Fear Survey and Coaching Implications" for more insight. It is amazing how some gymnasts can clearly articulate their coping mechanisms. The most common general position encountered can be referred to as the "fate" or "determinism" philosophy. Simply put, the gymnast takes the position "If I am going to get hurt, it will happen no matter what I do (karma), so I will prepare well and just won't waste energy and concern myself with it." This kind of gymnast is usually able to concentrate very well, and although overtly fearful from time to time, will most likely attempt the skill being approached with minimum support. Past interviews have suggested that this is a most popular general stance for successful gymnasts when it comes to the control of fear. The problem is dealt with by placing the occurrence of any mishap beyond the control of the physical world. The prerequisite is confidence in one's physical preparation and readiness. It is not that fear is denied as a reality, but it is relegated to a kind of predetermined destiny. Obviously, this is easier said than done, but its prevalence among top performers suggests a high degree of effectiveness. Of course, many gymnasts have developed highly personal methods for coping with the anxiety associated with fear and with being afraid. They are too numerous to list but they range from religious ritual to the anxiety management involving controlled breathing exercises, relaxation techniques and even self-hypnosis. Our advice to aspiring gymnasts is: If it works, use it!

We would be remiss if we did not indicate that many gymnasts overcome fear on the basis of plain old fortitude and guts. They recognize the potential danger, but go after the skill despite this because of a high degree of motivation and old fashioned courage. Such athletes make few excuses and are usually characterized as "taking the bull by the horns" when the challenge is on. They are not oblivious to danger, but are determined to overcome their fear and not be "afraid to do..." For some gymnasts, simply acknowledging their fear and letting you know about it is enough to get them moving. Each is different. It should be noted this approach is a far different attitude from the gymnast who will try anything seemingly totally unconcerned about risk. A complete lack of any visible apprehension is usually not a healthy sign in the extreme. Eventually such spurious bravado will most likely prove rather foolish, if not fatal! Beware this one.

Basic Guidelines

In the coaching situation, the trainer deals with fear every day. Assisting the gymnast to overcome and/or cope with being afraid is a most difficult, but challenging, task. Here are some general guidelines which should be stressed and considered:

1. **Progression**. First of all, as in all good coaching, the concept of progression should be used in approaching a new skill. A step by step method is necessary where each element needed for completion of the final skill is mastered in an orderly and planned fashion. This building block technique reduces the amount of fear which accumulates around the learning of a difficult

movement. This is a basic preventive technique which can virtually eliminate fear behavior difficulties later in the training process.

2. **Physical and Mental Readiness**. Related to the idea of progressive learning is the notion, often mentioned in this column, of physical and emotional readiness. Proper conditioning not only facilitates the learning of a new skill but promotes a positive mental attitude, which is the by-product of feeling good about your physical condition and preparation. The coach who emphasizes this kind of readiness along with progressive teaching will automatically be assisting the gymnast with the management of related fear around the new "dangerous" move, routine, etc.

3. **Spotting.** A third basic guideline has to do with spotting and its role in the entire process. It isn't necessary to dwell on the importance of selective safety procedures with our readers, but it should be pointed out that it is through good spotting that many gymnasts are helped to deal with specific fear behavior as they approach aspects of a risky skill. There are some coaches who feel that no spotting should ever be necessary if the building block, progressive-readiness system is devotedly adhered to. Perhaps this is true, and surely over-spotting is to be avoided. However, reasonable spotting can facilitate learning and not set up a dependency reaction. Besides the actual spotting to be provided, it is often of considerable help if the gymnast understands the method to be used and how it relates to the acquisition of the particular movement. For some gymnasts, the only thing they want to know is that you will get them and no further explanation is needed. Generally speaking, the more clearly the athlete understands the entire movement (technical, spotting, etc.) the less fear will be associated with its performance.

In another paper, "I'm Afraid to…-Coaching Strategies," we will make some very specific, concrete procedural suggestions that coaches may wish to use to help their gymnasts cope with being afraid.

"I'M AFRAID TO..."
COACHING STRATEGIES

In the first article on this topic, "Fear in Gymnastics: I'm Afraid!," we defined being afraid or having fear as a strong and very often unpleasant emotion associated in one's psychic structure with an awareness or anticipation of danger. We confined our discussion of this issue to the management of the emotion in the learning-training phase of gymnastics, separating it from the kind of more generalized anxiety that some gymnasts experience in relation to the entire competitive situation. We also stressed that being afraid to one degree or another is a perfectly natural response to the implicit danger residing in gymnastic efforts. It was also pointed out that, besides basic talent, the gymnast's ability to cope with fear is probably the most significant factor separating good gymnasts from more competent performers, or at least more successful ones.

Three basic guidelines designed to assist the coach reduce fear behavior as it pertains to acquiring difficult skills during the training phase were emphasized. These were:

- Progressive learning of skills of increasing difficulty in a "building block" fashion.
- Physical and mental readiness in skill development.
- Attention to some artificial support system seen in spotting procedures.

In this follow-up article, we will discuss some specific, concrete procedures that a coach may wish to utilize in helping the gymnast manage fear as it relates to the execution of particular skills. It should be remembered that the coach, in most cases, has developed a strong working relationship with the athlete over time and has an awareness of the general psychological style of a gymnast when it comes to learning and to fear-behavior. Such acquired knowledge, often painfully gathered, is indispensable and the best teacher for it will dictate to a large degree how the coach approaches any given individual gymnast. Obviously, the following suggestion must be modified to fit the communication system of the actual people involved but it does serve as a frame of reference that is both practical and psychologically sound.

Procedural Steps
The sequence goes something like the following:

1. **Step I.** Discuss with the gymnast that the time has come to attempt a particular skill unaided. Emphasize that the skill has been well developed and that any fear expressed during this period has been addressed and mastered. Note: At

times, the gymnast will indicate that they feel ready to go for the skill before you make the overture. Do not stifle this enthusiasm, but be sure you are in agreement.

2. **Step II.** Review the progression that has occurred in the learning phase (low beam mastery of a skill, for example), the gradual improvement in the overall execution that has been observed and the increasing physical and mental readiness to perform the move. If overt fear is expressed, try to pinpoint it in reality. Try to eliminate as many "unanswered" issues as possible.

3. **Step III.** Reflect the attitude that the gymnast will be successful in the attempt and that the skill is ready, if you are in fact sure that this is the case.

4. **Step IV.** Begin any warm-up progression that has been used in relation to the skill under attack. It is very important that the coach remain low-key. Excitement about the challenge is fine, but not anxious quivers.

5. **Step V.** Run the skill through with the usual spot used in learning. The gymnast should be assured that you will in fact provide the spot if necessary during the first attempt.

6. **Step VI.** Perform the move a second time (in sequence if appropriate) with a reduced spot. Physical contact is often helpful at this time—a pat on the back, etc. Talking through it can also facilitate the effort. Auditory cluing is useful depending on the individual gymnast and the teaching-learning style.

7. **Step VII.** Without further adieu—go for it. Note: It should be said that many gymnasts prefer the "cold turkey" method. That is, no hocus pocus, no chit chat, and no instruction— just going. If this is the case, and obviously it is in many situations, then the classic approach of steps 5, 6, and 7 above are useless and not needed. If you as the coach can tolerate the cold turkey method then step aside and let it happen!

8. **Note about freezing.** If the gymnast "freezes" at this point one should remain patient and encourage a second attempt with greater effort. Run through the warm-up procedures (do it on the floor, low beam, whatever) and then perform once more with the usual spot. In the majority of cases, if all other things are equal, the gymnast will probably push at this point to get past that "first one" we are all familiar with in the sport. If freezing occurs with the same gymnast over and over again on numerous skills, the fear-behavior is over determined and the coach needs to review the entire training strategy being used with this athlete.

Coaching Considerations

Here are some areas to explore and consider in the management of fear in the gym:

Peer support can often be very helpful to the acquisition of the new skill and in getting over the fear associated with the first attempt. This is particularly true if another member of the group already has mastered the skill under focus. Coaches will find that utilizing that same gymnast in the training phase can speed up the learning of a skill since the coach cannot often relate to the skill along the same dimensions that the gymnast who performs it can. Of course, this depends on the individual gymnasts involved and the nature of their relationship as well as upon the emotional climate of the gym.

The same holds true for **group encouragement** and its effective use as part of the training atmosphere in the facility. Some gymnasts do not want any audience when they first go for a skill and prefer to struggle it through without any witnesses. Generally speaking, however, verbal and spiritual support (even applause) from teammates is a beneficial motivational technique. In fact, we use a strategy where the entire practice is paused for a gymnast to perform to the entire gym and even parents when they have performed a pre-determined number of skills successfully. This has been hugely successful as a personal motivator and a way for the gymnasts to reach their goals. The article "My Goal is to…" deals with some of these strategies.

Once this skill has been performed, **praise** should be forthcoming in modest amounts (don't make too big a deal out of it, rather an expected result) and genuine joy over the mutual satisfaction can be expressed. This can go a long way in the learning reinforcement model. With no further discussion repetitions should follow in somewhat rapid order. The skill should be drilled independently and with moves in and out of it progressively added depending on the routine construction. Successful repetitions should mitigate any residual fear of the skill.

Should a mishap occur during this time, it is usually a good idea to move back (depending on the individual) to a repeat of the progression and performance with a **light spot**. This problem should not continue for long and the gymnast will usually get back into the swing of the execution with relative ease. Again, it is an individual matter; for some gymnasts a break at this point will lead to a total regression, for others its impact will be minimal or nonexistent.

Mental imagery or **visualization** can be utilized for re-enforcement purposes. Simply encourage this gymnast to think about the movement before making attempts. They can also practice before going to sleep at night and to picture it in the "mind's eye" being executed flawlessly. Again, in this drill they should try to feel the skill as they picture themselves doing it. See "Mental Gymnastics Training" for further explanation.

Despite much preparation some skills and gymnasts do not mix at a particular time in space. Very often simply **"letting it go"** and returning several weeks or months later may result in some success. For some, certain skills should be abandoned. All of this depends on how much fear and strain is associated with it and how neurotic the coach and/or gymnast are in reference to training philosophy!

Very often it is helpful to have a **timeline** for the acquisition of a new skill. The coach and gymnast decide when they feel the skill should be ready for execution and they work for that date. This must remain somewhat flexible so no one gets uptight. However, some outside limit and goal-time can help consolidate mutual effort. "Using Goal Setting as a Coaching Tool" provides steps for developing a timeline and "My Goal is to…" is useful for the gymnast in setting their goals.

The question is often asked, **"What do you do when the gymnast who is ready simply won't go for the skill?"** There are several options at this point and once again much depends on the individual situation and past history. One option is to continue encouragement and gentle coaxing. Another is to raise appropriate questions. Overall the best approach is to restate the issues, set a termination date (i.e. two more workouts), and stick to it. Beyond that point the coach should indicate that the skill is kissed good-bye and that no more energy, physically or psychologically, should be expended on a single skill. A return to the skill should not occur unless the impetus comes from the gymnast, and then only with definite limits established. This usually does it. If fear of execution is beyond all proportions in the skill learning it should be remembered that the additional tension of a compulsory skill or a meet situation probably spells a poor prognosis for success with the move. It is important that the coach not rub the gymnast's face in this minor failure. There are many skills available; after all not all gymnasts can do everything, otherwise they would all be world champions!

Remember, overcoming fear-behavior in the training-learning phase of gymnasts is not easy. To do so, besides a supportive working relationship, there needs to be focus on progression, physical and mental readiness, and scientific assist. Follow the outlined procedural steps and pay attention to other considerations as the gymnast works through their fears. Have patience, persistence and faith. Above all, do not become afraid of fear but try to understand it. In a very real sense, acknowledging this human emotion and struggling to master it can be a source of lifelong inspiration.

"DEAR DOC"
FEARS & FALLS

The single most often asked question that we have received over the years has to do with fear and the gymnast's attempts to deal with it. A wide range of problems concerning fear and its control are presented and this paper is an attempt to address these and to provide some guidelines to gymnasts in dealing with the problem both generally and specifically.

Gymnasts often talk to us about the fact that they chicken out and become quite frightened when it comes to performing certain skills that they feel they are ready to do. An example often given is that they can do something pretty well on the "baby beam" but can't go for it "up high." Similarly, there is the gymnast who can go for it on the single bar over a pit but can't get their psychological act together when it comes to executing the same movement on the unevens or high bar with regular mats. They often report being immobilized by fear. In one case, everyone was chickening out everywhere as if it was a contagious disease affecting the entire team to the point where progress was paralyzed. The fear seemed to spread from one gymnast to another. In most situations, however, the letters concerned one or two athletes who were fearful of specific skills like back handsprings or series on beam and releases on bars.

It should be pointed out here that the kind of fear we are talking about is different from the anxious feeling we often experience before and during a meet. Those feelings can be positive, getting us up, keeping us on our toes and moving us to do our best. You can find more information on this topic in "Butterflies and Pre-Meet Anxiety." However, what we are talking about here is the kind of fear that works against us, rather than improving our performance.

The vast majority of inquiries received wanted our recommendations at a point a bit past the basic training phase, that is, at a place where the gymnast was actually executing the skill under special circumstances (spotted, low beam, over pit, etc.), but would not attempt it when these conditions were changed despite repeated efforts.

An Illustration: Fear of a skill your coach believes you are ready to attempt on your own.

Perhaps the best way to illustrate our opinion on what to do when you arrive at this kind of situation as described in personal correspondence is to reproduce a copy of an answer sent to a gymnast who was struggling with this very problem.

Dear Ann,

Thank you for your letter about your gymnastics. I appreciated your writing and hope that the article will help you. Let me know how you're doing.

Now, Ann, let me try to help you with your specific problem with the back handspring on low beam. One thing you did not tell me is whether or not you are fearful of all skills that go backward or just the handspring on a beam. If you are afraid of all backward moves, then you have a very special problem. I will assume in my letter that it is just that skill on the beam. First of all, from what you said in your letter, you can do the move. As you have said your coach just stands by you and does not help and it goes fine, but when she leaves you can't do it. If this is really the case and your coach has told you that you are physically capable of performing the skill correctly, then you are truly ready to move on. When this kind of block is reached there is really only one thing to do. You must have the kind of conversation that follows with yourself several times and then act on it. It goes like this:

"Ann, this has got to come to an end. You have worked hard on this trick and inside you know you can do it. You are letting yourself down and probably others as well. You're afraid, well, so are many gymnasts with some of the skills that they try but you can no longer wait for that feeling to go away because it isn't going to. The only way to master it now is to do it no matter what because you can and you really want it."

At this point, Ann, you need to have some faith in your ability and some courage. Once you do that first few on your own steam then, all things being equal, you should be on your way. If it is not something you can overcome then the only choice you have is to drop the movement from your thinking and go on to something else. No one likes to give up, but sometimes this will help and you can return to it at a later date with more success. You must realize, of course, that bypassing this skill probably will make it harder to do other difficult skills because of the self-confidence factor. This is not always the case and it may be worth a try.

I do not know your coach or how tough she is but she surely is patient. At three months, trying to get on the floor beam is not acceptable at this time in your career. One other approach may help. Decide with your coach on a deadline date, a specific day you will attempt the skill, first with her standing by as usual and then with her moving away. If you do not keep that agreement then she and you should abandon the move for now at least. She should be definite about this and not allow herself to back down on this contract or target date. No way should she assist you again unless and until you are really going to do it. Also remember, Ann, that if you are going to compete with this movement in your routine you will have to perform it on your own during the stress of competition. If you are having so much difficulty with it now, how do you expect to perfect it for the meet situation?

Well that is about all I can say at this point. I hope my response will be of some assistance. You might want to share it with your coach. Again, thanks for writing.

Sincerely,

Doc

This answer leaves little margin for doubt. At this point for Ann, and many gymnasts who wrote with a similar problem, it is a matter of "fishing or cutting bait." Positive thinking is obviously very important in all learning, but there comes a moment when specific, task-oriented demands must be made if the gymnast is to make progress beyond this junction.

Fears Following a Fall

A related additional problem a number of gymnasts and coaches wrote about concerned the heightening of anxiety over an event following a bad fall. Sometimes the fear is around the specific skill a gymnast felt, while in other cases the emotion is generalized to the entire event. This latter condition is particularly common in falls from the balance beam. One gymnast put it very clearly in her letter when she indicated "I am worried that the beam is not going to be under me." This athlete had a fall while doing a tumbling movement and missed her foot resulting in a crash and a mighty sore coccyx. She continues to describe her dilemma with optional routines; "now whenever I do a trick it seems like I try to get off the beam, such as when I'm upside down in the middle of the trick I'm scare to land my feet..." In essence, she is trying to get off, not stay on. It is clear that this situation is different from the gymnast who is afraid to do a learned skill for the first time as in our previous case since this girl was doing the skills and as a result of fall has found "a newly developed fear of the beam."

As with so much of gymnastics, mental recovery from a fall is a highly individualistic matter. Some kids think nothing of it and just go back to business as usual once physically able. Others never quite fully recover and this is simply a reality of this unique sport. Assuming the gymnast in our current example is somewhere between these extremes, what needs to happen now is a confidence rebuilding. It is very important that this be tackled quickly; otherwise the gymnast's irrational anxiety about the skill or event will only get worse. The longer she practices "getting off" the beam, the more rooted the responses and motor behavior will become. It has to be solved before it becomes a fixation and coach-gymnast energy all goes into the wrong struggle. This rebuilding process is going to require some extra, supportive time and help from the coach and lots of encouragement without making a big deal of the whole affair.

During this period the gymnast is going to need a certain amount of faith in her ability as demonstrated in the past. The coach should assist her to call upon this reserve, however, positive stroking can go just so far and the rest is up to the youngster. The gymnast knows that the beam isn't going to go anywhere and she must concentrate with all her strength on completing the skill to her feet thinking of proper execution rather than of a potential fall. We would wager that every coach in the country has seen the gymnast who appears to be anticipating a fall rather than expecting a completed skill. The mental focus is in the wrong place, she needs help redirecting her attention. Usually with patience and some extra fortitude on the gymnast's part, things will return to normal in a relatively short time. If recovery drags on and on then perhaps, as this same gymnast suggests, "My coach…is losing patience," a firm position may be the best psychological medicine. For some kids, the coach's reaction is all it takes; it allows them to displace their fear with an anger of their own freeing them to be more aggressive about doing the skill. If it works, use it, for once the skill is being done again, no matter how arrived at, the gymnast's confidence will grow. However, losing patience or getting angry on the part of the athlete or coach is not the ideal way to deal with fear. See the article "Abuse of Anger in the Gym" to make sure you are not adding to an already difficult situation.

Another matter is worth mentioning here. Remember everyone falls from time to time. The coach has got to watch his or her reaction to this happening. An overreaction can create an exaggerated fear in the young gymnast that might not have otherwise been there. On the other hand, the coach is responsible for that youngster and falls should not be treated like a joke when, in fact, they are serious and an injury may be involved. It is not always easy to tell since some kids shriek and carry on over a stubbed toe as if they were about to perish. Others underplay a mishap or injury and try to block it out, although they are in severe pain. Neither extreme is good. Again, knowledge of the gymnast's personality is so critical. All falls are going to be scary to some degree; trying to accept this with good humor and applied guts is most sensible.

UNDERSTANDING, OVERCOMING, AND COPING WITH FEAR

This paper is designed to be an overview of material concerning the management of fear. Some general observations about understanding the problem, overcoming and coping with fears are presented as well as specific recommendations for coaches and gymnasts. Special guidelines for the individual gymnasts are also provided.

Understanding Fear for Coaches and Gymnasts

1. **The amount of the "feeling of being afraid" that someone experiences will vary with every single individual.** Past experience, such as bad falls, anxious parents, etc., can contribute to the individual response. With some gymnasts the fear is predictable but with others only becomes apparent when stress is real and present. What is gravy to one will appear life-threatening to another.

2. **Fear can be very specific in nature.** For example, fear of going backward but not forward, fear of feeling the hands and feet off the ground at the same time, fear of height, fear of not being able to "see" it, fear of imagined pain that will result from a fall, etc. Identifying the specifics of the emotion of fear is important in understanding it and working at beating it.

3. **The longer a person puts off dealing with the fear the more acute it can become.** A point may be reached where the main task is lost and all focus is on the negative aspects of the feeling. "What happens if I go early?" etc., rather than, "What should I do and when?" to get the move.

4. **Sometimes the fear is at a secondary level.** That is, the gymnast is not reportedly afraid of the skill itself but is afraid that his or her body will get out of control and go berserk when the moment of truth finally comes. This concern, however, is very often a smoke screen hiding a more basic issue.

5. **Fear is possibly the number one factor that can get in the way of progress.** This appears obvious but some talented gymnasts never quite recognize that it is this unstated problem that is keeping them in a lock step and not realizing their potential. Some people are ashamed to admit that they are afraid; it is equated with being weak in their eyes. They can't admit it—what would the coach etc. think?

6. **Some people feel that daring gymnasts are born and you either have guts or you don't.** To a degree this may be true. We are all genetic composites of a variety of traits, which, when combined with our experiences, make us unique individuals. It surely is true that you can't go to a supermarket and purchase courage. On the other hand, you can surely learn to cope better with this threatening feeling and make improvement in your own domain

with your own personal emotional equipment. Doing so successfully builds confidence.

Once we have established and considered the above observations, plus a few more facts about fear depending on what the individual gymnast has provided the coach concerning his or her specific problem, attention can be given to potential solutions.

Coach/Gymnast Solutions

1. **Part of the solution rests outside of the gymnast.** That is, how he or she is coached and the sensitivity of the trainer to the issues associated with fear. If you are faced with a coach who says, "I don't want to hear about it" when you suggest you are afraid or who makes too light of it when it is eating you alive, then you have a difficult kettle of fish to swim in. Our experience has been that most coaches are not this way. If yours is, let me know and we will try another approach! We also make the point that the earlier the entire idea of fear is recognized and addressed in our gymnastics training the less dramatic will be its impact in the gymnast's later career.

2. **There is no substitute for the progressive, building block type of learning.** The gymnast and coach should be sure that there is an intellectual understanding of the demand of the skill and a physical awareness of what is required for success. Step by step input facilitates learning that lasts. An interesting point here is that some gymnasts tell us they have lost a move they once had and are now terrified of attempting it. A careful look at this usually reveals that somewhere a critical step was skipped and the gymnast made it originally through some kind of compensation. In time, through body changes, additional stress, etc., the gap makes itself known. One step at a time building towards the ultimate execution of a skill is a very important way to solidify learning and reduce fear behavior.

3. **Careful attention has to be given to the gymnast's physical and mental readiness in this same sequence.** It is amazing how human beings somehow "know," at a physical level, when they are not anatomically ready for something to occur. For example, doing a front salto between the bars for a gymnast whose leg and lower trunk flexibility is poor becomes an enormously scary experience and darn near impossible to do. No wonder someone would be afraid under such circumstances. What has to happen is the coach and gymnast should determine what is required in terms of body readiness and

develop a program of conditioning and drills that will maximize that aspect of the needed work.

4. **Although some people believe that spotting should never be provided, we are not an advocate of that position.** However, we do believe that minimum spotting should be provided and removed as soon as possible but that the systematic, planned provision of physical assistance can, along with progressive learning and physical readiness; greatly reduce the gymnast's fear. The procedures should be clearly understood by the gymnast and consistently applied with a gradually reducing amount of force. Suddenly taking away an anticipated spot without telling the gymnast in order to "prove you could do it" is a sure way to increase fear, not reduce it, in the majority of gymnasts. This can even be true when the gymnast makes the move. What often enters the youngster's mind is, "Is he or isn't he going to spot this time?" "Will he or she be there if I miss?" etc. There is no substitute for predictability to enhance the gymnast's movement towards the mastery of a skill. Should the gymnast him or herself request that the physical assist be removed or the coach indicate that the time has come for the removal of this support, and then we have a different matter. We know there are people who disagree with this approach and feel that the surprise of discovering, "Wow, I can do it," will promote learning. In some cases, of course, this can be true, but it has not been our observation in the majority of situations we have seen.

However, there is so much to accomplish in the sport, that it is inappropriate to spend thirty workouts trying to get a gymnast who can perfectly well execute a back walkover or back handspring, depending on their level, on the baby beam to perform the same movement on the high beam. To hang-in beyond reason is not helpful to the gymnast or the coach. We should mention while talking about the beam that tries on the floor level beam should be restricted once near mastery is apparent. Each new height presents a physiological figure adjustment as well as a mental shift in attitude and "babybeamitis" can be an endless excuse. Piling mats under the high beam so they come just below the beam can be a waste of time if used too long. Removing them will be like starting from scratch. The feeling of being up high that this method may promote is far outweighed by the artificial nature of the arrangement and does not address the basic issues; "What that heck happens to me if I miss or fall off?" Mat stacking won't help that one. Eventually, it comes down to whether you are fishing or cutting bait. All gymnasts face that moment at some point in their training.

Some Special Guidelines for Gymnasts

The following points represent a summation of some important points athletes should remember as they attempt to overcome and cope with fear.

1. **Fear is natural.** All gymnasts experience it, so don't become overly concerned about this uncomfortable feeling. If you tell your coach, "I'm afraid" and he or she says "No you're not," make sure you talk that out together and that you carefully explain what the issues are for you. In learning, good relationships and communication are important.

2. **Learn your skills step by step.** Make certain that any unknowns about the move you are working on are cleared up as you go along. Ask technical questions—how, why, where, etc. Also be sure you listen well so that you pick up the answers.

3. **Don't shortchange your conditioning.** Follow faithfully your program of strength building and stretching. Cheating on this is cheating on yourself. It is not the "fun" part of gymnastics, but in the long run will make your progress much easier, quicker, and less fearful and that is fun! Remember, for example, a stalder on the high bar is quite awesome indeed if your hamstrings are tight and you can barely straddle. On the other hand, if you have worked hard on your flexibility and have a great range of motion in that position the trick becomes relatively easy. Hence, there is little fear associated with it. See the article "Conditioning…It's so Frustrating" for help with this issue.

4. **Use the idea of spotting to help you move along.** Nothing can increase your fear faster than falling on your head a couple of times. However, only use spotting on tricks you really need it for, or pretty soon you'll need help just walking! Seriously, although this is the coach's job, know about it and cooperate in this regard.

5. **Ask a fellow gymnast for help.** If you are working on a skill that they already do, find out how they managed it in terms of any fear they had. Sometimes another athlete will have a much better "feel" for a skill than the coach, including the secrets that may go along with the movement.

6. **Develop a timeline for skill acquisition.** Once it is agreed that "you're ready," an ultimate date for doing the move can be established. If you are still freezing or messing around at that point, it's bye-bye to the skill for the time being. "One more chance" is just game playing and should not be allowed. It is a tough decision to make.

7. **When your coach says you are ready and in your heart you know he or she is right, then go for it.** Avoid making excuses unless you really still have questions and concerns. The longer you put off doing a skill that you are

clearly ready for, the harder it will become to face. Warm it up, think through it in your mind and picture yourself doing it successfully, check to see that your coach is ready too. Then get on with the job at hand. Be courageous! Celebrate your success and repeat the move slowly adding moves that go before and come after the one in focus if appropriate.

8. **Take a look at yourself.** Eventually along the way the gymnast, him or herself, must take a look at where they are coming from. Given progressive teaching, physical readiness, and planned spotting, the next move belongs with you the gymnast. That will be the bottom line and in it you are alone. A personal confrontation with yourself may have to take place; "What is this—I'm ready, I know it, so does my coach, so why won't I do it?" How to get over this hump again is an individual matter. There is a limit as to what can be done from the outside at this point. It is important not to overlook plain old guts and fortitude as a solution. Some gymnasts chew themselves out and with support from the coach and/or peers, go on and get the job done. Others fret for weeks, endlessly discussing technical issues and driving themselves and the coach up a wall.

Always remember that you are in the very difficult and demanding sport of gymnastics to grow and develop a degree of personal excellence. It is not "crazy" or "mental" to be afraid but it is less than productive to pretend to yourself that you can go on to higher goals without dealing with and overcoming your fear to some degree whatever the level at which it affects you. You may also be interested in the following articles: "Fear in Gymnastics... I'm Afraid!," "I'm Afraid to... Coaching Strategies," and "Dear Doc... Fears and Falls" as well as results from "Fear Survey and Coaching Implications."

Chapter Six

Psychological Health and Well-Being

In many of our articles we have stressed the connection between the mind and body. It seems very obvious at this point that when the body "feels" right and the gymnast has a sense of well-being about his or her physical condition, the mental attitude needed to do one's best is definitely enhanced. Conversely, when the athlete feels like they "can do nothing" the resulting psychological frustration and learning blockage has a direct physiological impact on performance ability. Several of the following articles look specifically at some of these issues such as self-esteem and "slumps" along with defensive behavior and provide guidelines for both the coach and gymnast in overcoming them. The paper on anorexia is a scientific, as well as a personal look at a very serious problem and recommends specific behaviors for coaches, parents, and others involved with such young athletes. Another article is written primarily for coaches and addresses an important issue concerning injuries which can affect training and the athlete's future in the sport. Lastly, the reasons an athlete leaves or "drops-out" of gymnastics prematurely are discussed.

- Promoting Self-Esteem
- "Help, I'm in a Slump"
- Defense Mechanisms and Gymnastics
- Anorexia Nervosa: A Psychosomatic Illness
- Psychological Recovery from Injury
- Reasons for Dropping-Out Prematurely

PROMOTING SELF-ESTEEM

Esteem is defined in standard dictionaries as a feeling a person has about themselves that is basically favorable and based on a sense of merit, self-worth, and personal value. These estimations about oneself are confirmed in reality by significant others who treat the individual as a person of excellence. Obviously, in gymnastics, the coaches' responses to a gymnast as well as the actual gymnastic performance are related to the level of self-esteem experienced by the athlete. In fact, the coach can have a very critical impact on the development of esteem in young people and this places considerable responsibility on professional coaches that goes beyond pure technical training in the sport.

In this article, the idea of esteem will be examined more closely and this exploration may provide some guidance for coaches who are interested in the development of the whole child, and not just in producing a top level performing gymnast. In addition, parents may find some helpful suggestions on the promotion of self-esteem that will supplement their efforts to enhance the growth of the child in all areas.

Research and Myths

An examination of the factors that lead to the emergence of high self-esteem, produce a number of surprises that may contradict some of the popular myths about this notion. There are several factors, for example, that appear to have little or nothing to do with self-esteem. Classic research into self-esteem in young people, strongly suggests that there is no consistent relationship between self-esteem and physical attractiveness, sibling order in the family, or overall social position of the family. Young people gauge their individual worth primarily by their achievements and treatment by others in their own interpersonal environment, such as the gym rather than by more general and abstract measures of success. Success, when it comes to self-esteem, is related to day-to-day personal relationships. Surely the daily contact with a coach in the training setting is one very important variable in this regard.

Research also shows that an examination of the backgrounds of youngsters with high self-esteem usually reveals a close relationship exists between the child and his or her parents. The degree of interest shown in an accomplishment of such children by their parents, however, is based on support and sharing of success, not on controlling the child's experiences. This fact is one reason parents need to carefully and continually monitor their involvement in their child's gymnastics as a way of keeping things in proper perspective. More insight can be gathered in the article entitled, "My Daughter, the Competitive Gymnast."

The parents of high-esteem children, in addition, **tend to be much less permissive** than those of children with lower self-esteem. Parents of high self-esteem children, demand high standards of behavior and are strict and consistent in the enforcement of rules and limits. Their discipline, however, is not harsh and, as a matter of fact, the parents of these youngsters are less punitive than parents whose children are lacking in positive self-esteem. Children with high self-esteem are reinforced with positive feedback and rewards, rather than negative punishment and the withdrawal of approval. Very often, the parents of low self-esteem children are very permissive, but, and this is crucial, inflict and demonstrate extremely harsh responses when behavior is not within expectations. Such youngsters often feel that the lack of clearly stated limits and guidelines for behavior is evidence of disinterest on the part of their parents.

The backgrounds of children with high self-esteem not only reveals the existence of well-defined behavioral limits, but also the presence of what might be described as a "democratic" environment, as opposed to one that functions under dictatorial control. Permissiveness and the presence of a democratic spirit are not the same. These children thrive in situations where the principles are clear, power is defined, and privileges and responsibilities understood, but also where the setting is presided over by a benevolent authority in the form of an important adult. This leader figure is an individual **who is respectful of dissent within reason, open to some persuasion, and generally willing to allow youngsters some voice in making certain decisions.**

It seems safe to conclude that all of these factors that is, deep non-controlling interest in the child and his/her activities, guidance provided by well-defined rules of expected behavior, non-punitive treatment, and respect for the youngster's view and feelings contribute greatly to the development of high self-esteem. Coaches need to incorporate these factors into the coach-gymnast interaction. Of course, there are those coaches who believe that a strict dictatorship works best and perhaps such a position will produce acceptable gymnastic performance, but it is doubtful that it will also maximize the enhancement of self-esteem over the long run. Check out the articles on 'Coaching the Team" for more information on the dictatorship style of coaching.

Goals and Self-Esteem

The issue of the level of aspiration or goals and its relationship to the achievement of self-esteem, needs also to be considered. It might be supposed through abstract theory, that it is easy to attain success and consequent high self-esteem simply by setting goals at a lower level. The psychological facts refute this idea. Low aspirations do not promote self-esteem, and, on the contrary, they are usually found in youngsters with lower self-esteem. Research has demonstrated that athletes with measured high self-esteem have significantly higher goals than those with only medium or low self-esteem. Not only do youngsters with high self-esteem have higher goals, but they are usually more successful in achieving their objectives. Those individuals with low self-esteem usually perform at a lower level and have lower ambitions as well. In addition, they tend to fall short in attaining their lower goals.

Coaches who utilize goal setting as an aspect of the mental preparation of their athletes, need to set up definite standards of performance that enable the gymnast to know whether or not he or she has succeeded in a task, how far they have fallen short when they have failed, and what efforts would be required in order to achieve the desired success in the future. It is very important to present the gymnast with challenges within his or her own capacity, so that they can learn and begin to appreciate the potential of their strengths. Two good articles are recommended here including "Using Goal Setting as a Coaching Tool" and "My Goal is to… A Gymnast's Plan"

It is generally assumed that outstanding competence in gymnastics would automatically result in a higher level of self-esteem. Again, an examination of the facts raises questions about this common belief. In theory, one would think that the especially talented gymnast, placing a high value on the behavior at which he or she excels and "putting down" performance which is inferior, might develop a high degree of self-confidence. However, it should be remembered that youngsters are subject to many influences that effect self-evaluation. Parents, school, friends, and other gymnasts, generally lead an individual to accept group norms and values. We know, for example, that children who do relatively poorly in school, nevertheless, place just as high a value on academic performance and basic intelligence as do more able students. The same is true of gymnasts.

Therefore, although athletes with special capacities obtain considerable gratification from their real achievements, they are unlikely to accept this special competence alone as the principal basis for evaluating their worth as people. As a matter of fact, they often become negatively focused and dwell on their deficiencies and shortcomings as a function of their need for perfection. They often are lower in overall self-esteem than might be suspected from their overt performances. Most coaches have had gymnasts who are their own worst critics. Such youngsters may appear very psychologically strong and overtly successful, yet they have a lower opinion of themselves as a result of a measure of worth that is influenced in a powerful way by sources outside of the observable training or competitive situation. It is important that coaches have at least some awareness of these various outside pressures, which are more common than is usually realized, in order to plan their strategy in motivating and training an individual gymnast.

Coaching Implications

In this article, several factors that contribute to the formation of high self-esteem have been briefly discussed. These are not exhaustive in scope, but are the most important variables demonstrated to influence the gradual emergence and promotion of positive self-esteem. They have important implications for coaches and parents as well, and these can be summarized as follows:

- Youngsters develop self-trust, self-assuredness, and the ability to cope with difficult times if they are treated with respect, provided clear standards, specific demands for competence, and help in problem solving.
- Self-reliance and positive self-esteem is promoted by a well structured environment, rather than by largely unlimited permissiveness and an absence of focus.
- Positive reinforcement is always more effective in developing higher self-esteem than is a punitive atmosphere and approach.
- Although the coach needs to be clearly in charge, the development of self-esteem is enhanced when the gymnast's views and feelings are understood and respected.
- Self-esteem can be promoted by goal setting as a mental preparation activity. Goals should be realistic, but high. They should be evaluated regularly in terms of successes, shortcomings, and measures needed to be taken to achieve more success.
- Actual performance competence is not always an indicator of the existence of positive self-esteem. Pressures and expectations from other sources, outside of the gymnastic experiences, need to be considered as important influences that are carried into the gym. These need to be taken into account when planning individual coaching strategies.

The promotion of self-esteem, although not the major objective of the competitive coach, is a process in which the professional trainer plays a key role. It should be a welcome responsibility which can contribute to the overall development of a youngster, and one which can eventually be measured by increased positiveness in actual performance.

"HELP, I'M IN A SLUMP"

If you consult standard dictionaries to define the word "slump," you will find all definitions refer to "slump" as being a marked or sustained decline, a falling, sinking, or sudden collapse, a downward slide, or a period of poor team or individual play. All of the definitions have in common the idea that a "slump" is something that comes on rather quickly, and that it represents a level of performance below that which was previously demonstrated. Another idea that is implicitly suggested by the notion of "slump" is that the condition may be thought of as time-limited and temporary.

The ideas of staleness and burnout are two additional concepts that need to be mentioned at this point as they are related to, but not synonymous with the notion of "slump." Staleness is considered to be an overall state that the gymnast experiences, which is the result of monotonous repetitions in a rigid schedule of hundreds of movements or set of movements leading to a general condition of workout doldrums. As we see from the definition of "slump" given earlier, "being in a slump" refers to an actual curtailment of performance, rather than simply a bored, attitudinal state. Getting stale can influence the onset of a "slump" and both can eventually result in burnout. Burnout is the final end product of overtraining and/or a number of other high level gymnastic antecedent/consequent interactions over time such as competitive stress, injury status, etc. All three notions—staleness, slump, and burnout— have some overlap on a psychological level as well as similarities insofar as prevention and remediation are concerned. For the purpose of this article, however, focus will specifically be on "slump" as a temporary period of poor individual performance, which can be successfully reversed if skillfully managed.

All coaches have known gymnasts who have had a "slump" and most athletes are painfully familiar with this dreadful event. "Slumps" on a physical level are very often accompanied by a similar feeling and experience on an emotional level. One of the difficulties and challenges in dealing with "slumps," has to do with identifying which came first. That is, has the gymnast's performance suddenly begun to deteriorate because of psychological issues, or has the physical decline triggered an accompanying slide in the athlete's mental state highlighted by apathy, irritability, discouragement, or even depression?

Identifying the Slump

Most sensitive coaches are aware when a youngster is having acute physical difficulties with the learning or performing of a particular skill. In most cases it is fairly obvious. Less apparent, on the other hand, is when the gymnast is having some emotional problems which are affecting concentration and effort in negative ways ultimately reflected in a decline in acceptable physical output and a prolonged "slump."

It is relatively easy to determine which came first, the chicken or the egg, the emotional problem or the physical learning difficulty, when the coach and gymnast have a good relationship, which has been built over time on principles of mutual respect and communication, rather than a model that involves servitude and order giving. When a positive relationship exists, it is important for the coach to approach the athlete directly and up front, in an effort to find out if non-gymnastic factors may be at the root of an apparent "slump." There are a host of outside influences which could be casual in this regard. Troubles in school of an academic nature, problems with friends, family conflicts, personal health issues, and others are just a few examples of such influences. More insight may be gained in our article, "School and Gymnastics." It is also an important to consider that something closer to home that is, within the atmosphere of the training setting itself of a non-physical nature, may be involved and contributing to a "slump." Examples of these factors would include difficulties with fellow gymnasts on the team, problems with the coaching interaction, training stress, or competitive pressure.

If the "slump" is identified as being the result of factors and events outside the gym, it is clear that remediation is going to involve dealing with these issues to one degree or another. The coach cannot get immersed in the problems of his/her athlete outside of the gym in an intense way. This is not the business of coaching. On the other hand, it does fall within the coach's prerogative to assist in any reasonable manner, to alleviate the problems, or help guide the individuals involved towards a solution. Usually this takes the form of cooperating and working with the parents and gymnast once the areas of difficulty are known, in an effort to assist the youngster get back into training without the outside baggage being carried into the gym, and exerting a negative effect on progress. This is not only important to break out of the "slump," but also to prevent a serious injury that might occur if the gymnast's mind is somewhere else, and not on the task at hand.

In cases where something is amiss in the actual training situation of a non-physical nature, the coach can and should be more actively involved. The best starting point is again an open dialogue with the gymnast to identify the issues, and plan a remedial strategy. In most cases, once the non-gymnastic matters are addressed, recovery from the "slump" can begin as quickly as was the observed decline. It is usually a matter of the severity of the outside difficulties, or in-house problems, and the individual resilience of the athlete and coach.

If no outside variables are identified by the coach and gymnast, then what is most likely occurring is the more classical gymnastic "slump," that is a slowing down of the learning process, resulting in a dedicated gymnast becoming disheartened and progressively concerned about the apparent collapse in performance. Very often in such situations, a negative vicious circle begins to develop, where poorer results leads to more worry on a psychological level, resulting in ever poorer output, followed by even greater concern. Obviously action has to be taken rapidly, so that a real block to progress does not set in over time. When the "slump" is of the more traditional nature involving an arrestment of the learning process, it is clearly appropriate for the coach to take an extremely active role in helping to develop a solution.

Coaching Solutions

Here are a few steps which the coach can take to help their gymnasts who are experiencing "slumps:"

1. **Take a careful look at the specific skill difficulties involved in the learning block or slowing down process.** That way both members of the teaching-learning model are on the same wave length. In this regard, it is critical that the coach be sure that the technical communication being transmitted to the gymnast is being accurately processed.

2. **The coach should solicit direct feedback from the athlete to be certain the proper message is coming across.** Asking the gymnast to repeat what the expectations and technical demands are for a given skill is one method for checking to see if performance information is being understood. It is also very important to consider varying the props used at this point, for example increasing the use of video review, using more non-verbal communication, reducing or increasing chalk talk time etc. It is also very important to consider readiness factors such as flexibility, strength etc. to determine if they have been adequately addressed. It is very frustrating indeed to make repeated attempts that fail, not because the demands are not understood, but because the gymnast is simply not ready on a physical level for a particular skill. This can surely contribute to a "slump" response.

3. **It is crucial during these times, that the gymnast be helped to see that such "slumps" are not uncommon.** Plus, they do not predict a doomsday insofar as the athlete's long term progress is concerned. The coach needs to remain very positive during this time and provide as much encouragement and individual strokes to the gymnast as possible. Losing one's cool or increasing pressure or demands for appropriate performance, in line with talent, invariably will lead to a further deterioration in output. "Slumps" are difficult times for everyone;

coaches, gymnasts, parents and all parties need to practice sustained patience with a capital "P." During "slumps," mutual support is a must, although major motivational responsibility rests with the coach. Coaches and gymnasts need to approach "slumps" as allies not adversaries. A positive attitude cannot be overstressed at these times.

4. **Additional individual attention during this period of time is also often helpful.** Most other team members will understand this coach behavior and not resent it, especially if the coach has responded in a similar way when other team members have experienced "slumps." It is also important to remember that a good sense of humor, while not making a joke out of the individual athlete's concern and distress about a "slump," can go a long way in reducing the tension for everyone involved. Humor can also communicate once more that "slumps" are not terminal and life-threatening in nature and that life, as well as gymnastics, will mostly go on.

5. **The psychological tool of goal setting can be most helpful during "slumps."** The coach and athlete can develop a flexible time set for helping to break out of a "slump." Such goals should not be poured in concrete. Productive goal setting can only take place when a majority of factors that have contributed to the decline have been identified. This is one reason that the careful analysis by coach/gymnast referred to earlier is so important. Positive goals can be developed that involve realistic performance objectives directly related to the overt symptoms of the "slump." These goals should be on paper, not just carried in the head. Of course, goal setting is always important, but during these times it can be modified in such a way as to assist the athlete recover from the "slump." Refer to our articles "Coaching through Goal Setting" and "My Goal is to…" for assistance in developing these goals.

6. **An increase in the use of mental imagery training can also be assistance at these difficult times.** Although the gymnast may not be able to physically recover from a "slump" in a rapid manner, he/she can imagine recovery through positive visual-motor rehearsal activity, "seeing" themselves in successful performance. This kind of psychological effort can make a real contribution to the gymnast's attempt to reverse a "slump" period. Such imagery will enable the gymnast to experience the emotional high that can accompany this mental activity.

7. **It is very useful, during "slumps," to hold periodic "state of the slump" discussions with the gymnast.** These need not be often and certainly should not be long winded. They should involve a non-gymnastic, private moment of

feedback and communication designed to monitor the situation, and provide the athlete some sound-off time, if needed. As always, the nature and extent of these meetings will be an individual matter, depending on the specifics of the "slump." Open dialogue is almost always more productive than a closed monologue delivered by a coach.

8. **Even when serious gymnastics training is concerned, it may be necessary to alter the workout schedule.** Obviously this might help alleviate a "stale" feeling, but it may also be necessary to help break out of a "slump." Although most dedicated coaches will not like hearing it, it may be necessary during a severe "slump," to give the gymnast some extended time simply to be, that is, time off from coming to the gym and training. This might involve anything from a couple of days to a week, or even more depending on the individual issues, and how clearly the origins of the "slump" have been examined and identified. Prolonged "slumps" can lead to burn-out and quitting primarily as a result of inordinate frustration. Surely some time off is better than permanent absence from the beloved gymnastics. Less drastic variations might be attempted by mutual consent, such as varying days, hours, rotation schedule etc. for the given gymnast. Again, it is a matter of considering the individual situation and responding appropriately.

9. **It is strongly recommended that coaches stay as relaxed as possible about this phenomenon, and avoid triggering a situation that could have easily been avoided altogether through simple patience, and we might add, silence!** A word of warning is warranted at this point. There are coaches who see the slightest variation in performance as the beginning of a dreaded "slump." They become convinced, based on one poor workout that their athlete is on the dawn of total regression. It is extremely important not to make a mountain out of a mole hill. Putting a negative idea in the mind of a gymnast, particularly a highly sensitive one can result in a self-fulfilling prophecy.

10. **It is a sad fact that not all storms can be weathered and recovery from a severe "slump" is not always possible.** Although this state of affairs is not the rule, it is a painful exception that does take place. Some athletes, despite every type of intervention and modification, will not be able to return to a state of competence seen prior to the "slump." There is a limit to patience and understanding, and the time may arrive, when for the good of the individual, and his or her safety, and in best interest of the team, the effort must come to an end. Obviously, this is the action of last recourse, but it is a reality.

Summary

In summary, "slumps" are not uncommon in gymnastics. When they do occur, it is important to:

- Identify any non-gymnastic variables that might be involved, such as home, school, personal issues, etc.
- Carefully analyze the actual performance difficulties to identify physical factors that might be causal in nature, i.e. strength and flexibility.
- Maintain patience, a sense of humor, and a very positive attitude.
- Approach a "slump" as the gymnast's ally, not with the boss/worker model.
- Utilize modified goal setting and positive mental imagery training.
- Consider periodic conference checks to monitor the "slump" recovery.
- Make sure the issue is potentially chronic, not just a one shot acute behavior.
- Provide for additional individualized attention as needed.
- Give careful consideration to modifying the overall training schedule for the gymnast involved.
- Maintain an optimistic attitude.

DEFENSE MECHANISMS AND GYMNASTICS

Defense mechanism is a concept familiar to most people. Sometimes the term is used loosely and literally, e.g. a method for defending oneself. The origin of the notion rests in the area of clinical psychiatry. Theoretically, a defense mechanism is a psychic construct presented in verbal or non-verbal behavior, which is adapted by a human being as a means of protecting the individual from acute anxiety. The source of the anxiety can be internal (coming from our impulses) or the result of external pressure (relationships with others). The major objective of the defense is to avoid psychological pain. The ego (sense of self), and its frustration and vulnerability is involved in this concept.

Understanding Defenses

Defenses may be understood through example. When we are very much hurt by something someone has said, we might respond with "Let's just say it didn't happen." This represents a denial of the impact of what was said and is a rather primitive defense mechanism. In addition, we might add "I'm better off without their support anyway," which is a rationalization (sour grape syndrome)—a most common defensive mechanism maneuver. Both denial and rationalization are two defense mechanisms out of many that we develop and use over the years in our interpersonal relationships and life experiences.

Some defense mechanisms are simple, such as "avoidance" (leaving the scene), while others are more complex, such as "identification with the aggressor" (you have all seen this in action at boxing matches when the audience joins in). Others are extremely complicated, such as "reaction formation" where one sees excessive trends in one direction—"virtue to a fault"—which is the buttressing of the repression of unacceptable impulses of a very different nature. In other words, take an overly nice individual in appearance who may really be a terrible person underneath it all. Sound familiar?

Some defenses are more complicated. There are two defenses which are often confused—projection and rationalization. Projection is referred to as a "primitive," low level defense. It involves the basic question—will I keep or throw out? When the ego (self) can or will not tolerate a blow to self-esteem, the source of the irritation is referred to as "ego alien." "I am sad, therefore the trees are sad." The qualities of oneself spill over to other things. In projection the alien concept is repressed and then projected to another. This defense is not the same as rationalization referred to earlier. Obviously there is a relationship between the two concepts, but strictly speaking, they are different defensive stances.

At one time, defense mechanisms were thought of as totally bad and psychopathic. We now know that they are relatively normal psychological constructs which can help us cope with daily life and remain productive. Most so called "healthy" individuals have a wide variety of defenses that are brought into play in psychological emergencies, while others have a limited repertoire and usually related adjustment problems.

Since the utilization of defense mechanisms is part of being alive, we find them in all human beings—including gymnasts and their coaches! The gym is a rich laboratory for observing ourselves under stress (in anxiety states of various degrees) and therefore provides a stage where multiple defense postures strut forth often in a blatant manner!

Defenses in the Gym and Competition Arena

For this discussion, we will briefly look at a kind of behavior which perhaps is best described as rationalization combined with a kind of watered-down, non-classical projection.

How often have you heard coaches, gymnasts and/or parents say the following?:

- "The gym was too cold."
- "I didn't get enough warm up time."
- "The judges were unfair."
- "My gymnast/daughter/son really got robbed!"
- "I'm not used to those kinds of bars."
- "I had a poor spot in the lineup."
- "That coach is a buddy of that judge."

This behavior, unfortunately, is as common in the gym as to be near comical to say nothing of embarrassing. What is clearly happening here is the search for a scapegoat—something or someone to identify as the cause of our personal suffering and frustration. As in so many cases where this kind of quasi-projection is involved, there may be a fragment of truth involved in the observations or accusations. This is why the technique is perpetuated and utilized defensively so often. It can be most difficult to deal with, except when it reaches the absurd, and it does (e.g. a girl falls off the beam three times, while all other competitors stay on, but the coach claims that the beam was "slippery").

Anyone who has ever coached has, at one time or another, had such feelings, and in most cases, has expressed them— sometimes in a not-too-subtle fashion. An occasional such lapse of judgment and fall into infantilism can easily develop into a habitual pattern or style. When this occurs, we are looking at a process that is very destructive. Slowly but surely, all motivation to succeed begins to vanish.

We have all known coaches who have assumed this position in the extreme. Through the process of identification, the youngsters respond to competitive setbacks with the same mechanism. The entire group in action can become rather pathetic, and it is sometimes difficult to remain even in the same physical proximity with such individuals when this kind of degrading behavior is taking place. Needless to say, these coaches and eventually the gymnasts who have become ingrained with this response are disliked and usually not held in respect within the gymnastic community.

At another level, the energy expanded in this kind of negative behavior is no longer available to be used where it is really called for; the motivation for a good hard look at improper coaching and poor training which results in constantly inept performances. Herein lays the real shame in such coach and gymnast behavior. The youngsters who have picked up this "technique" are being deprived of an opportunity to grow as individuals, learning how to cope with justified failure, as well as not receiving the kind of rational input from a coach designed to improve their efforts from a technical point of view.

In past years, we have studied world-class gymnasts looking at personality characteristics that were evidenced by international caliber gymnasts. One of the three major factors present in the vast majority of profiles of these athletes is referred to as abasement. This concept is defined as the tendency to accept personal responsibility for outcome, not to blame others for inadequate performance or motivation, and to feel guilty when met with defeat. Since this appears to be a characteristic of top gymnasts, perhaps the corollary behavior, that is, to project blame (to look to external conditions and individuals as the cause of frustration), is characteristic of generally poor performers. These individuals spend an inordinate amount of time looking outside of themselves for excuses, rather than more painful, but productive time, reviewing their own shortcomings. Our articles "The Gymnast's Perception of the Coach" and "Locus of Control and Coach Effectiveness" provides more insight into these behaviors.

Coaches should be acutely aware of this problem and their influence on the youngsters they are training. They should make a conscious effort to avoid slipping into this easy trap. Naturally, one should protest where there is legitimate cause, for that is an acceptable part of the sport, but a coach must carefully monitor such action, lest it become a blind type of personal defense.

ANOREXIA NERVOSA
A PSYCHOSOMATIC ILLNESS

Anorexia nervosa, a disease primarily found in single females between the ages of twelve and twenty-one, is becoming of increasing concern among members of the psychiatric and psychological professions as a result of high numbers of young people exhibiting symptoms associated with the condition. Most medical dictionaries define the condition in brief as "A persistent lack of appetite, a refusal of food and an obsession with loss of weight resulting from emotional conflicts." The anorexic youngster develops an active disgust for food, loses an alarming amount of weight, and may become emaciated to the point where life itself is threatened. It is often accompanied by severe menstrual disturbance, slow heart rate, low metabolism and constipation. In speaking of anorexia nervosa we are not talking about the youngster who would like to lose some weight to be more attractive or physically adept. Such a young person goes about it in a systematic way, maintains reasonably good health, and is in control of her effort monitoring the weight loss and taking appropriate action when the goal is achieved.

It is clear that anorexia is more than a preoccupation with thinness promoted by a cultural bias that states thin is beautiful. It is, in fact, a very serious disease with lasting and profound consequences which is out of the individual's control. Bulimia (Hyperorexia), a pathological drive to overeat often followed by vomiting, is often associated with anorexic behavior. However, Bulimia is a separate clinical syndrome and will not be examined in this article.

It should be obvious to all of us involved in the sport of gymnastics that the very nature of the activity and its technical demands strongly encourage a stance which emphasizes lightness. Some gymnastics programs often refer to "weight problems," "dieting to get to competitive weight," "losing unwanted pounds," etc. Clearly an absence of extra bulk will facilitate graceful movement and help contend with the forces of gravity gymnasts are always trying to defy.

Based on our observations and on the amount of inquiries we have received over the years from parents and coaches, the line between being healthy, remaining "skinny" and becoming anorexic in the sport is becoming less clear. It would be a mistake to think gymnastics promotes anorexia nervosa, for it does not. Participation in the sport does, however, provide a socially approved setting where weight loss is sometimes valued and approved and, if you will, an excellent excuse for the emergence of the illness. If we remember that this condition is seen most often in the 12-21 age group, we can easily understand how this would be the case since it is usually during this same time period that girls are usually attracted to the sport. The young person who works at controlling her weight during her competitive experience usually returns to a more balanced lifestyle once out of the sport; for anorexic youth the struggle remains without recourse to the rationalization, "I don't eat because of my gymnastics." Of course in severest cases, the youngster deteriorates during her gymnastic career and there is little doubt that the problem is not connected with training or the sport in a general causative relationship.

Young people suffering from this illness are not just concerned about their weight; they are totally preoccupied with it in a very obsessive manner. The youngster is constantly weighing herself and the slightest one pound gain is often responded to with anger and panic and immediate further starvation. Far from the adolescent who gets upset about being somewhat overweight, the anorexic pursues a clearly self-destructive course that defies intellectual argument or logical appeal.

Understanding Anorexia

Because of the serious nature of this illness, it seems important that coaches have some familiarity with the condition and an understanding of some of the dynamics associated with it. This understanding should not be construed to mean coaches should attempt to remediate or address the problem. It is definitely a situation requiring professional medical and psychological intervention which should not be undertaken by the coach. On the other hand, some more than surface knowledge will assist the coach in recognizing and coping with attendant problems. In addition, there are some specific things the coach can do to assist with the overall management of the anorexic gymnast under the guidance of the treating physician. We will discuss this aspect a bit later in the article.

The first formal identification of anorexia nervosa is generally credited to an English physician, Richard Morton, who reported two cases as early as 1689. It was not until over a century and a half later in 1868 that a more elaborate description of the disease was provided by William Gull. Both of these men were physicians and the condition was primarily viewed therefore under a medical model, which is, attributed to a diffuse "nervousness." The treatment of choice emphasized organic responses without any attempt to address the psychological factors involved. Even today, some research is conducted into possible etiology involving cerebral, pituitary and hypothalamic factors. Drug therapy with amitrptyline, dilantin and others is utilized in treatment efforts. The medical model, however, often ignores the interrelationship between mind and body.

Anorexia nervosa is probably the single most important clinical syndrome responsible for bringing the medical profession in the 1930s to believe that there may very well be a psychological background for certain physical diseases. In other words, expanding understanding of this disorder led to psychodynamic model. In this psychologically based model, the loss of appetite is seen as serving an unconscious purpose such as escape from problems or defense against dangerous impulses. Youngsters show some history of early emotional problems often involving conflict between mother and daughter. Such children tend to be selfish, overly sensitive and perfectionist in personality.

The psychodynamic model suggests that the motivation behind this condition is an unconscious expression of resentment against a mother who has overprotected the youngster or who has rejected her by giving too little affection in growing or by showing favoritism to another child. Refusal to eat is seen as an ideal weapon, especially when the mother has made a great deal of fuss about eating in the past. The anorexic condition not only causes great anxiety in parents but brings secondary gains to the youngster in the form of attention, solicitude and a control over others. Also in this model the refusal to eat is often seen as a response to a determined urge to make one unattractive. This motivation is due largely to inner anxieties about emerging sexuality and feeling threatened by problems that go along with growing up and assuming a feminine role. In some cases it appears the resistance to food is a form of self-punishment inflicted by the youngster on herself for feelings of guilt associated with certain forbidden impulses.

In the past a behavioral model involving operant conditioning has been added to the conceptualization and treatment of anorexia. In a nutshell, this school of thought looks at what people are doing, not why they are doing it. From an examination of actual behaviors a program is designed in this model that will reinforce behavioral change through operant conditioning and result in a termination of pathological actions. In most recent years investigators are beginning to view the biologically and psychologically dynamic human being more and more within the context of his or her social world including the family. This approach is referred to as the systems model. This approach, to many, makes the most sense and holds the greatest potential for a reasonable theoretical framework as well as a sound program of remediation.

The Systems Model

Based on the popularity of the systems model, it seems appropriate to summarize the basic premise behind the orientation and view of the disease. Researchers in this area have identified four characteristics of the overall family functioning of anorexic youngsters. None of these characteristics alone seemed strong enough to ignite and reinforce psychosomatic symptoms. Rather a cluster of such factors in the family process appear necessary to encourage somatization.

The four family characteristics are intense involvement, over protectiveness, rigidity, and lack of conflict resolution. They are as follows:

1. Intense involvement refers to an extreme closeness in family interactions. In this highly enmeshed, over-involved family, changes within one family member can have severe consequences among all other members of the family system. There may be a shift in the chain of alliances within the family; as other members get involved direct communication may break down. Often the boundaries that define individual autonomy in an enmeshed family are weak and individuals get lost in the system. Parental control of children is often ineffective. Excessive togetherness and sharing bring about a lack of privacy. Family members intrude on each other's space, thoughts, and feelings.

2. A second characteristic of the family system of anorexia is the omnipresence of constant nurturing and protective responses. Family members are highly sensitive to signs of distress, tension, or potential conflict. In such families, the parents' over protectiveness retards the youngster's development of a sense of self-control and competence.

3. Rigidity, a third characteristic of these families, refers to a heavy commitment to maintaining things as they are. In periods of growth when change is necessary they experience considerable difficulty. For example, when a youngster in a typical family reaches adolescence, the family can change its rules that allow for increased age-appropriate independence on the part of the teenager while still preserving a degree of family harmony. The family of a psychosomatically ill youngster, however, insists on maintaining accustomed methods of interacting. Issues that threaten change are not allowed to surface.

4. The overprotective and rigid nature of the psychosomatic family, combined with the constant intrusion elements of intense involvement make such families ability to cope with conflict very low. Often strong ethical or religious codes are used as a rationale for avoiding conflict. As a result, unresolved difficulties remain, continually encouraging the families' avoidance behavior.

The four structural characteristics outlined above have been identified as typical of families with psychosomatic youngsters. The adolescent's symptom acquires new significance as a regulating influence in the family system. Research has made it appear that the pervading factor supporting this symptom (anorexia) is the youngster's overall transactional involvement in parental conflict. Therefore, this involvement can be viewed as the unifying characteristic of a psychosomatic family system.

Overview

This brief theoretical discussion of psychosomatic illness, specifically anorexia nervosa, clearly enforces our original observation; that is, anorexia is a complicated illness requiring highly professional and controlled intervention. As indicated earlier there are some things the coach can do when there is a suspicion that one of his or her gymnasts may be suffering from this disorder. First and foremost is to vigorously encourage the family to seek professional help. Often a coach can have considerable influence in this regard and should surely attempt to exercise it when appropriate. Sometimes, based on a family systems model, resistance will be encountered since there may be a need to avoid conflict in such a family and deny the existence of any problem. The coach should persist in the effort utilizing a team physician if one is available and, if necessary, prohibiting further participation in the sport until such a consultation has taken place. This may mean temporarily "losing" a top performer, but it is a matter of responsibility toward the gymnast that should determine the coach's behavior. Once the youngster and family are involved in some kind of a treatment program the coach should cooperate with the ongoing effort in any way that is recommended (e.g. designing a behavior-modification schedule in the gym designed to provide positive rewards for weight gain when suggested by the physician).

Finally, the coach should remember that the reinforcing applause and recognition that a gymnast receives for good performance, if the athlete is suffering from this disease, does not justify the long range damage that can occur. Responsible action on the part of the coach is not only ethically suggested, but morally mandated. Related material can be found in "Behavior Change: Part I" and "My Daughter, the Competitive Gymnast."

PSYCHOLOGICAL RECOVERY FROM INJURY

In a sport such as gymnastics or other relatively high risk activity, injuries are bound to happen. If the gymnast and coach have followed the golden rules in so far as training is concerned, such as proper physical readiness, progressive learning, and planned spotting as well as basic safety precautions, these injuries should be minimal in number and moderate in severity. Despite everyone's best efforts, however, young athletes will get hurt from time to time during their careers in the sport. The physical impact of such events are clear, the psychological issues are often less evident. Much has been written concerning recovery from injuries, especially from a medical and physiological point of view. Prescriptions for rehabilitation often include the physical activity recommended to strengthen the joint, rebuild muscle tissue, etc., but a few go on to specify what to do to help the gymnast recover emotionally.

With the exception of severe trauma, the mental recovery process can begin at the very onset of the mishap. The coach's and gym staff's response to the mishap is critical beyond what is actually done physically to address the injury. Overreaction is a most common and potentially destructive response that can be communicated to the gymnast when the accident occurs. Obviously, ignoring the event is not only ill advised because it is a reflection of personal insensitivity but also may provide grounds for a negligence lawsuit. Much depends on the nature of the injury itself. A dislocated elbow is quite another matter than having the wind knocked out of you, a simple bruise, or a torn hand. There should clearly be a differentiated response in each case. The coach and staff must respond with the procedure that has been adopted as policy by the program director and the dictates of common sense. Experience has shown that athletes read signs sent by coaches at these times very well, and at a deeper level than might be expected. Therefore the selected response must be considered in terms of potential long range impact. The choice of psychological "first aid" is more subtle than the physical counterpart!

Psychological First Aid

A calm, concerned and positive attitude is usually the best in cases of minor concern. Youngsters respond to a sense of confidence in their coach just as they will to a sense of a panic reaction. An attitude on the coach's part that communicates, "Relax, everything is under control," will help the gymnast manage their own fear about the accident. The athlete's own attitude toward the injury can often be influenced by what is seen in the coach's initial behavior. Playing doctor is not part of the job but demonstrating knowledgeable action or inaction, whichever is appropriate based on an evaluation of the incident, is a responsibility that rest with the coach and sets a tone about injuries that can affect the entire training program.

In clearly unremarkable incidents, a sense of humor can go a long way. This can also be overdone and should only be used after some genuine concern has been shown and an "A-Okay" status established. Tears can quickly be turned into smiles under such selected circumstances. Coaches need to be caring and supportive, but on guard against making mountains out of molehills. To do otherwise can have a long lasting and surprising negative effect on your gymnast's rate of mental recovery. There are a number of concrete things a coach can do to help a gymnast recover from a more serious injury from a psychological point of view.

Case Study

Assuming that the medical issues have been completely addressed and are being monitored, here are a number of suggested guidelines you may wish to consider to assist your athlete through the difficult recovery period. To make these more vivid, a real case illustration will be utilized.

> Karen was a Class I (Level 10) gymnast who also competed with her local high school team. She trained primarily in a private club. As a high school junior she was the state champion in one event and scored respectively in the All-Around category. For some months Karen had been experiencing lower back pain, an often chronic complaint among gymnasts. After rest periods of short duration (one or two days without working out), Karen's pain would cease, but reappeared when she returned to a vigorous schedule of training. She was an extremely flexible girl, including her lower back and many movements in her exercises were designed to capitalize on this extraordinary ability. These same movements, however, also put maximum strain on her lower back.
>
> Finally, after many months of off-again on-again training, it was decided that Karen should have a comprehensive physical appraisal made of her persistent difficulty. Although she had been under the care of her family physician it was determined that a thorough examination be carried out using hospital facilities. This prolonged and extensive evaluation revealed the presence of a small but significant fracture of the fifth lumbar vertebrae of her back. The physical prescription called for Karen to wear a plastic body brace from beneath the shoulders to just below her lower back. This brace was to be worn for twenty-three hours a day. The prognosis was good, but she would not be able to train strenuously or compete for over six months. For a youngster in love

with gymnastics, this was devastating news and such a prolonged restriction was psychologically very painful, as well as frustrating.

Coaching Intervention

Using this case as an example, what was done by the coach and others to help Karen begin to recover emotionally from this bad news and the mental heart-felt anguish that such a forced inactivity brought her?

1. The first response of the coach was a sincere expression of empathy. The athlete needs to know that you recognize what an important part of their life the physical activity of gymnastics represents and that you realize how maddening it is not to be able to participate. Being a senior made this especially difficult for Karen, as it was her last year of high school competition and she was interested in participating in college gymnastics. At this point in time a big hug of understanding and feeling is very much in order.

2. It is extremely important, along with an expression of empathy, that you assist the gymnast in coming to an intellectual position concerning her injury and recovery. The youngster needs to clearly recognize that the inactivity now will result in her eventually being able to return to some level of training free of the pain she tolerated for so long. The gymnast must be helped to believe that the restriction on the short term is certainly better than ever present pain or even possible permanent damage. There is something, in fact, beyond gymnastics! See the "Decision to Quit" for more insight.

3. The third thing the coach did was to consult with Karen's parents and the treating physician to determine what, if anything, she could do without aggravating the condition in any way. In Karen's case, the doctor indicated that she could do some modest stretching and strength training. Once a gymnast is injured, some coaches behave as if they have vanished from the planet. This behavior is not only unprofessional, but downright cruel. Karen's coach demonstrated to her that she was still important and was wanted. Such an action can go a long way in healing a mind and heart. The excuse that she can no longer contribute to the team as a competitor and can't be afforded the time is totally unacceptable.

4. Following an analysis of what was still permitted, the coach and gymnast worked out a specific program of gymnastics related activities above and beyond any other physical therapy that had been recommended. Again, this was accomplished with the consent of the treating doctor. The coach and Karen went together to a local department store and purchased a set of

dumbbells which would be used in her strength building and maintenance regime. Ordinarily, it is not wise to become involved with your gymnasts on an individual basis outside of the gym, but in these cases the extra tender loving care is appropriate as part of the psychological prescription. Special attention in modest doses can go a long way. Other team members fully understand it, within limits, and it should create no morale difficulties.

5. Karen was encouraged to come to the gym whenever she could. She did so, on a regular basis, and as the weeks passed by she was able to expand the degree of participation always with the advice and consent of her parents. The body brace was part of her life at this point, and she began to accept it making jokes such as, "This might help me stay tight on clear hips," or "How would you like to put your arm around my waist and discover this thing?" All of her comments were good natured and reflected a healthy adjustment and the beginnings of emotional recovery. Except in cases of extreme injury, it is important that the athlete be allowed access to the gym and encouraged to come of their free will. Karen often brought her dumbbells in with her and this activity helped her maintain and even improve her peer relationships within the gym. Without embarrassing her or overdoing it, the coach held her up as a model of courage and fortitude. The boost to her ego helped Karen feel valued.

6. Karen provided some extra assistance in the office and participated in related activities that made her feel she was emotionally and physically still productively involved in the gym program with her contemporaries. A major step was taken when the coach arranged with the program director for Karen to assist a regular instructor with a preschool class. Again, this was done in consultation with the treating physician. She even assisted another coach with one of the developmental competitive teams which elevated her status and positive feelings about herself. It was clear from her growing enthusiasm that Karen was making a successful emotional recovery from her long term injury. She was also gaining prestige among the up-and-comers and the experience of actually coaching, including technical input, put her in touch with her sport at an exciting and different level.

7. After four and a half months, Karen was allowed to begin to swing a bit on bars and increase her beam walking with some skills added. The fruits of her continued stretching and related strength building began to show themselves, and this gave Karen terrific motivation at a critical time. She realized she was not as far behind as she thought she would be. Prior to the final removal of the brace, time was spent carefully planning a special training schedule for Karen. It is often tempting to go full blast, not only out of joy to be able to

do gymnastics once again, but in an effort to make up lost time and catch up. This temptation needs to be carefully avoided in such cases as Karen's and cannot be left to chance. The coach, working with the parents and doctor when appropriate, needs to take responsibility for guiding the gymnast back into a full workout program in a systematic way. It takes patience on the part of the coach, as well as the athlete. Included in this process was a review of the routine content and overall composition to determine what movements needed to be removed or altered in order to minimize the taxation on Karen's lower back during her initial return period. Needless to say, everyone in the gym celebrated with this young gymnast when she came to the gym and announced with great pride and happiness, "It's gone!"

Case Study Results

Fortunately, Karen eventually made it back in full swing again. It appeared that she not only "caught up," but had gone beyond where she was before the injury. It is clear that her concentrated weight training program increased her strength and ability to manage related challenges. Most strikingly, her mental attitude greatly improved, most likely, to the fact that pain or the expectation of pain on the horizon had been eliminated. She was a happier young athlete. In this gymnast's case, the injury contributed to the positive nature of her career. The sensitive management of the situation by her program and coach was a real factor in her recovery. Finally, and most revealing, was the fact that Karen decided on a college program in sports medicine, an interest that came into clear focus during her recuperation period.

Summary

In summary, it should be remembered that the psychological recovery of the athlete is influenced significantly at the moment the accident occurs by the coach's and staff's behavior. Subsequent behaviors are important, but the initial response can often set the stage for a positive and quicker mental rehabilitation. The coach/gymnast/physician relationship becomes critical as rehabilitation progresses and the gymnast transitions back into the training arena.

REASONS FOR DROPPING-OUT PREMATURELY

Does it appear that talented athletes are leaving the sport of gymnastics prematurely? Some say yes, but others disagree. Over the years, coaches have been worried about this phenomenon as professionals charged with the responsibility of helping to develop young talent and bring it to full potential. We are equally concerned about the potential "drop-out" rate for the same reason, but also because of its mental health implications for youngsters who leave. This exodus is not because of injury, training burnout, or frustration from competitive failures, although these are related, but appears to be more frequently a result of the **"fun being extracted"** from the experience. Surveys have clearly demonstrated that the major reason for leaving or remaining in athletic activity is the **degree of pleasure** accrued through participation.

The word "extracted" has been deliberately used to describe the end of the joy in participation in gymnastics. The definition of this word in Webster is "taking away forcibly," "to remove by effort from someone unwilling," and to "withdraw through a process." When a young gymnast experiences the end of the "fun" in doing gymnastics, it is often the result of having had the fun taken away, not the result of some implicit characteristic of gymnastics itself. This event is often accompanied by some emotional damage for the youngster. In many conversations we have had with gymnasts and concerned parents about leaving the sport, this fact have been made movingly clear. It was felt that perhaps an article might help draw some increased attention to this problem and serve to stimulate some thinking and discussion among those more directly involved in the management and development of talent: namely, dedicated and creative coaches.

Here are some factors which lead to the sense of discontentment and the "fun" being extracted from gymnastics and possible reasons for leaving or dropping-out prematurely:

1. **Level of Training.** First of all it is important to recognize that this problem occurs at all levels, not just the Elite. Although the training and performance demands at this highest level are extraordinary, it would be a mistake to think that such intensity in and of itself automatically means there will be no fun associated with the hard work. It is true that at the Elite level there is greater attrition expected. This is not, however, necessarily because the passion for participation has been systematically demolished. In most cases it occurs because time has run out, or the physical and psychological demands

of the sport simply outstripped what the gymnast had available to them for continued commitment.

2. **Intensity of Training.** There are those who would attempt to equate or find a correlation between leaving the sport and the level of hard training, but this is often a spurious connection. It is only valid if the training experience is essentially negative and built on the destruction of self-esteem and individuality, rather than on the enhancement of these important aspects of personal development. The fact of the matter is that consistent hard work that is directed toward goal attainment can be most rewarding to youngsters and provide a great deal of fun at the same time. The joy comes through the learning process and is measured in terms of skills acquired and appropriate competitive success. Most athletes thrive on disciplined hard work and are more comfortable in this kind of predictable and productive environment than in one that is less demanding or even haphazard in quality. It is not the amount of work that is the issue—it is the nature of the re-enforcement system for motivation and emotional climate within which the work takes place.

3. **School Issues.** The reality of greatest concern is probably not at the Elite level, but in the feeder ranks where gymnasts are leaving at an alarming rate because they are no longer happy. There are a number of factors involved in this phenomenon that should be considered. One of the most critical out-of-gym influences that contribute to an athlete leaving the sport has to do with pressures associated with school. It is obvious that serious gymnastic training requires a very big time commitment. Most athletes go to the gym three or more hours a day, five or six days a week. Organizing one's life around this schedule and maintaining your academic expectations is a real challenge. Sometimes it just can't be done, and one or the other area slips below an acceptable level. This article "School and Gymnastics" presents more details on this area.

4. **Social Issues.** Related to this same issue is the entire question of social life and peer pressure. Gymnasts can become isolated from their non-gymnastic friends through process of their training. There simply isn't enough time to go to the movies, parties, dances, and other normal activities associated with growing and changing. Nothing can be said to ease this real dilemma because the fact of the matter is that gymnastic training at a more advanced level requires sacrifices, and that is one of them. The gymnast's image at school is often mixed at best and the lack of social availability is almost always attributed to "she/he's a gymnast." There is an unwritten understanding that

this label usually means the youngster is not in the mainstream of school related social life.

5. **Motivational Factors.** An additional reason that often becomes involved in this decision has to do with the motivational factors behind participation. Many athletes dream of being a champion and this is a fine reason for doing the sport, but when the road to fame gets tough some gymnasts are not capable or willing to pay their full dues. Related to this notion, of course, is competitive payoff. To continually train and tolerate all of the restrictions that are faced without progress is most frustrating. The technical demands of the sport make success even more difficult to obtain. How long a youngster can pursue an activity where rewards are minimal, and they are always looking up from near the bottom, is an individual matter. But when the return on the investment is not enough, despite the dream and drive, the only option may be to give it up entirely.

6. **Parental Issues.** Another factor that sometimes leads to unhappiness and eventually to leaving the sport prematurely has to do with the degree of parental identification that the athlete experiences. If the focus for doing gymnastics subtly shifts over time, and the youngster finds they are doing it to please their parents, the effort needed to continue often quickly vanishes. The decision to leave gymnastics often occurs during the early and middle teenage years. The sense of social isolation and school demands are highest at this time, but it may also be related to the questions "Who am I doing this for?" "Who's in charge?" This is complicated by the fact that in this adolescent period of life young people are struggling to achieve an individual identity and personal autonomy. It is a time when children need and want to feel a strong sense of some ownership in decision-making and begin to direct the course of their lives themselves. Although gymnastic training can involve some give and take, it is essentially an activity where the athlete places him/herself in the hands of another. Following directions, taking orders, having time scheduled by some else etc. are all aspects of the discipline of gymnastic training. When basic motivational questions are compounded by the need for autonomy, it is not surprising that some gymnasts decide to assert their self-direction and take control over a poor situation by leaving the sport. Parents may be interested in our article, "My Daughter, the Competitive Gymnast."

7. **Injury.** Another important factor in premature quitting of the sport, which is closer to the gym itself, has to do with the number of injuries a gymnast has had and how they were managed. Getting some type of injury in this sport is not unusual, and no matter how hard a program tried to prevent them, such mishaps come with the territory. A gymnast who has an inordinate number

of mishaps, some of which may be serious, is going to be very aware of the price that is paid for continuing. Again responses are, in part, a matter of personality differences, but prevention in the first place and considerate caring management when an injury does occur can do a lot to help the gymnast handle the problem in a positive way. Unfortunately at these times some coaches withdraw attention from the gymnast once the crisis point is passed. This sends a message to the youngster that they are only important in the scheme of things if they are able to perform. Once they are hurt and can't "contribute" their value is diminished. This kind of behavior on the part of the coach falls in the same category insofar as doing subtle damage to a gymnast's self-worth is concerned, as the coach who clearly has favorites on the team at the expense of other athletes. See the article "Psychological Recovery from Injury" for more steps to keeping the gymnast in the sport.

Implications

All of the issues discussed so far are factors that lead to discontentment and may lead into the decision to leave gymnastics prematurely. Many athletes face and deal with these kinds of problems successfully every day to one degree or another. Yet the loss of talented children seems to have accelerated. It is your authors' opinions that the primary cause for this trend in certain programs, and ultimate responsibility for this loss, rests with the professional coach. Dedicated kids have a great deal of resiliency in dealing with school, peer, and parental pressures, but when these given factors are combined with an unhappy training environment and a negative coach-gymnast interaction, the press to leave becomes dominant, irrespective of the personal drive of a child or potential ability.

As pointed out earlier, the most critical factor identified with leaving a sport is the gradual erosion of the psychological satisfaction and general good feeling (fun) that the athlete experiences from participation. Again this has nothing to do with a "hard work" focus but is related to an insensitive working relationship where the adult ego takes priority and motor wonders are driven, without any regard or awareness of the fact that they are basically just children. They may be gifted for sure, but essentially the core of these gymnasts are trusting youngsters, who are hungry for praise and have had little time on the planet to have developed the armament needed to deal with sarcasm, negativism, and assaults on their self-esteem. Most often these attacks are launched by a fiercely competitive adult bent on winning at all costs. The pressure, both internally and externally that these coaches produce, is very real. However, in the long run, programs' devoid of fun and a positive atmosphere usually not only fail to be productive but eventually self-destruct. Unfortunately the extraction of joy that accompanies such programs diminishes the talent pool but also hurts youngsters in the process. As a parent or coach, you may want to read our article "The Decision to Quit" to further your understanding of this important matter.

The implications of these issues need to be taken very seriously indeed. This includes paying real attention to the needs of children that involve matters outside of the gym such as school and social life. Clearly gyms are not guidance clinics, but they should provide a flexible organizational structure that gives out-of-gym issues some degree of priority, when appropriate. Overall there has to be an ongoing awareness of the need to keep "fun" in the experience of gymnasts without reducing quality. It is not enough that lip service be given to the need for coaches to be more cognizant of the psychological and developmental issues of childhood and adolescence. Strong measures need to be introduced to insure that these principles are, in fact, put into daily practice. Program goals and coaching approach should be monitored on a regular basis of knowledgeable owners, directors, or consulting experts in the area. Any national professional coach development system must take into account these non-physical variables and recognize them as being equally important as the technical growth of our coaches.

Chapter Seven

COGNITIVE AND AFFECTIVE PERFORMANCE VARIABLES

T he papers in this chapter are quite technical but important for understanding various variables involved in performance. One of these is the relationship between our cognitive functioning and how we learn a skill which has clear implications in the training arena. In addition, the balance between our affective functioning such as the athlete's arousal state, overall stress, and ability to attend to the task at hand is one of the major factors that results in successful or unsuccessful performance. Many pioneering psychologists have addressed these issues over the decades and these papers attempt to distill their work down to basics and put it in terms that the coach or mature athlete could find useful and informative.

- Right-Brained Gymnasts in Left-Brained Gyms
- The Performance Connection: Part I: Attention
- The Performance Connection: Part II: Stress and Arousal

RIGHT-BRAINED GYMNASTS IN LEFT-BRAINED GYMS

Man has had a long and intense interest in the functioning of the human brain, and the research is not only totally fascinating, but has very definite implications to our sport of gymnastics in all areas, especially the training/learning aspect. We will take a look at one of the phenomenal concepts about the brain and how it affects our learning.

We have written numerous articles focusing on a wide variety of subjects which emphasized the critical connection between physical performance and the cognitive-affective domain of human functioning. This article is no different, however, it is more technical in nature than most but we hope the examples and strategies presented will aid in the understanding of these concepts.

Right and Left Brain Concept

Perhaps the best way to introduce this particular topic is to draw on the experience of educators working with individual youngsters in school. Here are some illustrations that will lead us into the concept of "right" and "left" brain functioning. The student who has said, "Why should I read the directions? I can see how it goes together!" baffles many a teacher, as the boy or girl is confronted by a bewildering array of pieces from a puzzle or model. And the student could, in fact, see how it went together, while a seemingly more able classmate struggled through a decoding process involving following the written directions: "Attach narrow end of Part A to rounded side of Part B" in his efforts to ferret out the information needed to guide their action. The same "seeing" student would protest, "Don't tell me how to get there, draw me a map," while his or her teacher would probably plead, "Don't show me a map, just tell me how to get there."

In the past, such different ways of thinking, ways of remembering (such as "I don't remember what he said, but I can describe the room we were in." vs. "I don't remember where we were, but I can tell you what he said."), as well as problem solving approaches (like "Let's put it out on paper." vs. "Let's talk about it.") have often been explained by simply putting these variations in the everyone-is-different catchall. Continued research sorts out the contents of this catchall into categories of left and right-brained thinking, with promising suggestions for the teacher or coach that could speed up student learning in and out of the classroom and/or gym.

Hemisphericity

Research in hemisphericity indicates that human beings actually have two operative brain sections (hemispheres), each complete in itself and each controlling specific functions. We know that in human beings, those functions performed by the left side of the body are controlled by the cellular constellations in the right part of the brain and those aspects of motor and other functioning seen on the right side of the body are controlled by the left part of the brain. The "dominance," therefore, of a hemisphere will usually result in an opposite handedness, among other things (e.g., left-brained-right handed and right brained-left-handedness). Unlike lower animals, humans, at a very early age, begin to differentiate the data processed by each side of their brains. Their left hemispheres specialize in data whose importance is based in relationships that are built across time. You are using your left hemisphere, for example, when you relate what you are now reading to what you read in the previous paragraph and what you will read next. The left hemisphere has been called the temporal, or propositional, brain, because it perceives significance across time. In essence, it controls language (expressive, decoding, encoding, etc.) functions. The right hemisphere in the majority of people specializes in data whose importance emerges from relationships that must be perceived across space. You are using your right hemisphere when, from the surrounding visual environment, you are aware of where you are in a building, recognize a face or movement or understand a chart, graph or shape. The right hemisphere has been called the visual-spatial brain.

The right and left hemispheres are connected by an impressive and extremely complex bundle of nerve fibers, the corpus callosum, which transmits electric impulses in the form of messages from one brain to the other to produce integrated brain thinking. While brainedness does not always directly determine handedness, an analogy is that we have assigned certain responsibilities to our hands, for example holding a book with the left hand while we point to the word or turn the page with the right hand. No matter how able we are with the right hand, we do most things more efficiently and effectively if we also use the left. In a similar manner, integrated brain thinking is the result of each hemisphere augmenting information processed by the other. Individuals are usually born with a genetic predisposition to use their right or left brains (hands), however, as with handedness; practice has a great deal to do with skill. One only has to consider the right-handed pianist who plays beautifully with the left hand or the craftsperson who uses both hands with almost equal dexterity.

Practice vs. Capacity

Without practice, most skills and processes become somewhat stagnant, so the comfort of using the dominant hand (or brain) often results in minimal use of the subordinate hand or brain. As a consequence, the lack of ability that may be demonstrated in verbal or visual-spatial tasks may be the result of a lack of practice rather than a lack of inherent capacity. Perhaps some of our readers can recall preferring their left hand but being forced to use the right. Such behavior represented a cultural-historical ignorance that believed being a "lefty" was odd. In Latin, the word "sinister" means to be left-sided. Fortunately, modern enlightenment has pretty much eliminated this biased practice in child-rearing.

The notion of "practice" appears to be true of brainedness. Youngsters who can "see" how a model airplane goes together, for example, use their more facile right brains and may not give their left brain the practice of reading and following directions for the model. Other youngsters who comfortably read and comprehend complex written instructions use their left brain and may not give their right hemisphere the practice (exercise) of seeing how the parts go together. The assumption that practice could be as important as native ability is supported by recent research which indicated that measured intelligence can change with prescribed changes in experience. There simply is no way to make everyone learn equally.

It should be obvious that hemisphericity plays an important role in the selection of hobbies and careers. The design engineer, artist, architect, etc., must be able to deal with visual-spatial data in a comfortable manner. The philosopher, writer, etc., must manage temporal, language-based data well and be able to synthesize this material into an idea or understanding. Some people are facile with both hemispheres, and everyone uses both brains to varying degrees, unless, because of an accident, only one is functioning. For many years, the relationship of the left and right brains to learning was only studied in connection with medical cases involving brain damage. In fact, it was from the study of functional pathology related to damage to one brain or to the corpus callosum that much of what we know about hemisphericity emerged.

Coaching Implications

Hemispheric considerations have implications for educators in general who are looking for more effective ways of promoting learning among, and for remediating the learning of, youngsters who are simply not getting it. Obviously, gymnastic coaches are educators in a special sense and these same implications apply to their efforts as they do to the classroom teacher. The findings from an examination of research in hemisphericity suggest that most schools and gyms beam the majority of their instruction through a left-brained input (reading, listening) system, thereby handicapping all learners. The extraordinarily complex motor output required in gymnastics clearly suggests that a narrowed focus of input is not the way to go. Gymnasts who learn well through left-brained input (language) have often had minimal or haphazard practice in using their right brains. Those athletes who learn more easily with right-brained input (visual-spatial) have been handicapped by having to use their left brains without the opportunity of processing the same information through their more proficient right hemispheres.

Leaders in brain research are beginning to suspect that the girl who did well in geometry, but flunked algebra, or the boy who knew everything about a carburetor, but couldn't pass a written test on combustion systems, were both victims of our lack of understanding of hemisphericity—that they are mirror images of the same phenomenon and may represent the teacher's default in understanding, rather than their own.

It has always fascinated us to observe the behavior of gymnasts when the compulsory book first becomes available. Almost immediately, you will see gymnasts adapt a differential approach to grasping the exercises; some reading the text, others looking at the figures, and still others utilizing both. Unfortunately, most of the interpretation involves left-brained analysis: reading the text. We have often heard coaches indicate to gymnasts that, "The picture isn't accurate," or "It is different than the text." One also hears the question, "Is it written for left or right handed?" followed by "What does it look like if you reverse the exercise in part or in total?" Such inquiries reflect issues that are the topic of this article. The implications are that such books should, in fact, have very accurate illustrations, and, in the ideal model, have drawings of the exercises in both "directions." Although this would obviously require additional effort and expense, it would facilitate learning for all gymnasts and save many hours of time used to "figure it out." Likewise, any films developed of the exercises should take this same issue into account.

Coaching Strategies

It is not necessary for the coach to indulge in an elaborate process of diagnosis in an effort to determine which brain a gymnast prefers (handedness can be a good hint). Rather, they can work toward the above three objectives by trying the following strategies:

1. **Presenting information simultaneously to both hemispheres.** Demonstrating or illustrating a skill on a chalkboard or with some mechanical device while giving a verbal explanation or having another gymnast perform the movement while others are hearing the directions are possibilities of this approach. Successful coaches have been using this technique for years, but only recently have we known why and how important the dual input of "seeing" it as well as "hearing" it is in terms of productivity.

2. **Augmenting a stimulus by following it with information beamed to the opposite hemisphere.** Obviously, hemisphericity is only one of many reasons that may affect a gymnast's ability to learn a new skill. Fear, motivation, physical readiness, etc. can also play a critical role. Changing hemispheric input systems, however, can diminish and often remediate a specific skill learning problem (often fear associated with a particular skill may be the effective response to the inadequacy of the cognitive input being received). To

facilitate this opposite beaming, for example, a coach might first say, "Draw out your idea of what you should be doing," and then say, "Tell me what your drawing shows." Or, the coach might begin by saying, "If we mark on the skill illustration chart a critical point, where would it be?" and then follow by saying, "Okay, if we put that into words we would say..." A coach might also ask a gymnast to transfer past learning to give added meaning to the present skill attempt. For example, in teaching a front handspring on beam, the coach might ask the youngster to "see in her mind" a tumbling pass on the floor using a front handspring (assuming here that the gymnast can do the move on the floor) and use words to describe what she did and how. Imagining from past, related experiences not only augments left-brained activity, but also enables the coach to check the accuracy and validity of the gymnast's perception and understanding of the present learning.

3. **Deliberately beaming to only one hemisphere.** This method is designed to give your gymnasts practice in processing one type of information. For example, (a) look at the diagram of the skill and see if you can figure it out, (b) see if you can find three similar angles of the diagram, (c) listen to the directions and see if you can make the figure I am describing, (d) read these instructions and answer these questions, and (e) look at this sequence of three figures in movement and try to draw what the fourth frame might look like.

Professional gymnastic coaches have long realized the importance of supplementing the written or spoken word with pictures, diagrams, etc.—in fact, this is often a major tool in gyms. As technology advanced, more sophisticated audio (left-brained) and visual (right-brained) materials became available. In fact, the marketplace became cluttered and constraints of budget, conflicting information and time needs mitigated against the conscious pursuit of these techniques in a systematic way. Although the kinds of approaches discussed in this article are very time consuming, evidence is clear that they can have a real payoff for the gymnast who is the major consumer! One modern and extremely useful piece of equipment to achieve the ends hinted at in this material is using video recordings. This is primarily a right-brained input system and, augmented by the temporal, left-brained input of speech can greatly maximize, at minimal cost the opportunity for predominately right-brained, left-handed individuals to learn more efficiently. At the same time, of course, it strengthens even more the capacity of left-brained youngsters who can get additional practice with their other hemisphere at the same time they capitalize on their strong suit—the spoken word. As has been emphasized many times before in previous articles, such as "The Art of Feedback," the more we know, are open to, and able to apply in our training efforts with youngsters, the more successful will our program be and individual gymnasts within it.

An Illustration

A basic illustration might make the subtle complexity of this area even clearer. A master technician was instructing a group of 15 young gymnasts in the technique for starting a sprint which involved the thrusting of arm and leg in an oppositional movement. The teacher was facing the group talking about what was required and demonstrating at the same time (clearly teaching beamed to both hemispheres). Three individuals in the group stood out because they appeared totally lost and confused. When the session was completed, the trio of apparently uncoordinated kids was approached and it was found that all three were dominantly left-handed. In a group of this size, this is not just chance. Although the instructor may have turned his back to the group at times, the majority of the demonstration was on a face to face basis so that he could observe the gymnast's activity. Very often, such children as our infamous trio experience a kind of mirroring reversal on the visual receptive screen of the brain and that these youngsters probably would have been able to grasp the concept more readily if the teacher had his back to them a great deal more or if they worked in front of a mirror. Of course, the amount of time needed to do this in such a large group setting would be prohibitive. Implication: in group instruction, it is a good idea to have a model in front of the class with his or her back to the students in addition to the major instructor who may face the class, a real assist to right-brained, left-handed individuals. This may appear very simplistic but is often overlooked in the teaching of skills at any level. The incredible human brain and what we still have to learn is truly awesome!

Application of Findings

What do some of the findings of hemispheric research mean to coaches in the day to day conduct of their gymnastic instruction?

- First, they clearly mandate the responsibility for presenting information in such a way that gymnasts can practice integrating it from both of their hemispheres.
- Secondly, current research findings indicate that whenever a gymnast appears to be missing the point, or "not getting it," coaches should augment the presented stimulus they are already using with one to the other hemisphere.
- Thirdly, the findings suggest that coaches adopt practices that have the potential to increase the gymnast's facility in the use of hemispheres, simple and in concert with one another

THE PERFORMANCE CONNECTION
PART I: ATTENTION

The bottom line in all our work in the sport of gymnastics is to improve that magic result, the performance. Of course, there really is nothing magic about it. Great artistic gymnastic performance is the result of talent, hard work, some luck, and, as we will discuss in this series of articles, the connection between certain psychological and physiological factors. We have entitled this series "The Performance Connection: Attention, Stress, and Arousal" because it is the balance of these things that seems to make for the better performance given the above basic ingredients of talent and hard work.

This first article will focus on the concept of attention as an aspect of this special connection and the important role it plays in understanding the nature of information processing in learning and its limitations when it comes to human performance. In "The Performance Connection: Part II" we will focus on the concepts of stress and optimal arousal in its relation to performance.

Defining Attention

An acceptable definition of the phenomenon was written almost 100 years ago by the experimental psychologist, William James, who suggested:

> *Everyone knows what attention is. It is the taking possession by the mind, in clear and vivid form, of one out of what seem several simultaneously possible objects or trains of thought. Focalization, concentration, of consciousness, is of its essence. It implies withdrawal from some things in order to deal effectively with others.*

Although James's definition is reasonable, modern researchers have tended to avoid referring to "consciousness," what we are aware of at a given moment, in trying to gain a greater understanding of attention. Despite the intense interest in consciousness, experimental psychologists have felt that this notion is nonscientific with one of the major difficulties being that in order to talk about one's consciousness it is necessary to ask an individual to be introspective and search their own minds. It has been clearly demonstrated that people are not very good at describing what is actually going on in their minds and that distortions often occur. Thus, largely because the definitions of attention in terms of consciousness and related research techniques have proven to be so inadequate, other methods have been developed to investigate attention.

A current, prevalent notion is that attention is a limited resource (or capacity) for handling information taken in from the environment or memory. It is believed that when a certain activity requires attention, then some other activity also requiring attention will suffer in quality because there appears to be a limit as to how many things can be attended to at one time. One activity interferes with the other and competes for our attention as it were. These patterns of interference are the basis for the usually operational definitions of attention: If two tasks can be performed as well at the same time as they can be individually, then at least one of them does not require attention. On the other hand, if one task is both performed less well in combination with some other task, then both are thought to require attention. For example, performing skills on the beam requires a great deal of attention; therefore, trying to remember dictated numbers at the same time would be very difficult. On the other hand, one can do mental arithmetic relatively well while walking down a familiar street since walking is a relatively simple motor response requiring little attention. Thus, attention is defined in terms of whether or not activities interfere with each other. If they do, then we say that they "take attention" to perform, or are "attention demanding." This kind of definition has advantages over the definition of attention as consciousness, because it lends itself to experimental operation (measuring the amount of interference between two tasks) and it does not require self-report through introspection.

Structural and Capacity Interference

Thinking about it, we will realize that there is more to this definition of attention than interference between tasks. There can be a great deal of interference among tasks at times and it would be hard to argue that it was due to some limit of central information processing. Returning to our example of beam—if you were required to respond to a series of light stimuli and to perform consecutive turns both activities would suffer simply because the eyes are needed for both tasks at the same time. This is an example of what has been called **structural interference**. If two tasks are performed together that require a receptor system (using the eyes to see) or an effector system (motor response) in common, then the interference will be due to competition between the two tasks for use of the same input and/or output system.

A second type of interference is that which results from the competition for the limited central information-processing capacity of an individual, between two tasks that are performed at the same time. This is called **capacity interference** and is measured as the amount of decrement in one task that results because it is performed at the same time with another also requiring capacity. In this scheme, capacity is the operational definition of the amount of attention required by the task. In order to provide an estimate of the amount of capacity interference (attention) there must be no structural interference between the two tasks. If a performer is asked to make hand movements to visual stimuli in one task and to make vocal responses to auditory stimuli in a second task it would be difficult to hypothesize that these two tasks interfere structurally. The receptors are different and so are the response-production systems. If interference occurred between these two tasks, it would most likely be due to competition for capacity.

Teachers, coaches, parents, and many others have often been heard to say to people of all ages, "Please pay attention!" "Pay" is an appropriate way of putting the request because attending to something has a price—mental energy is spent. The more strident the demand to focus and concentrate on a task, the greater the drain is on our available energy. This is another way to operationalize the notion of attention.

Tasks requiring a great deal of capacity to process, such as gymnastics, often result in fatigue. Based on this idea, it is also possible to define attention in terms of various physiological measures that represent the amount of effort being expended. The most common effort-measure of attention involves eye-pupil diameter. This is accomplished through use of very sophisticated techniques that do not interfere with eye movement. Results of such research clearly show that the pupil diameter in subjects increases substantially when they are under pressure and when tasks are more difficult or complex. The diameter is significantly smaller when the subject is relaxed or the attention demand is low (coaches—next time one of your athletes is about to perform, take a look at their eyes and follow-up with a second look a few moments after they are finished with the event).

In gymnastics, although the motor requirements are extremely complex requiring the fine tuning of sensory modalities, deterioration in attention is usually due to capacity interference (overload) rather than to structural interference (simultaneous demands on same receptor or effector). Careful scrutiny of routine composition to minimize any potential structural interference will increase capacity.

Concepts of Attention

There are a number of additional concepts we need to consider as we look at attention as part of our basic "performance connection." These ideas involve what has been called "selective attention" and "automatic processing." They are both extremely important aspects of attention when it comes to gymnastics and other high risk, high RT (reaction time) motor output activities.

Selective Attention

The mechanism called selective attention has been often referred to in the "party problems" model. At large, noisy parties, attending to one person's spoken conversation with you can be a real problem when there are many other discussions taking place around you. It is quite difficult to ignore those other conversations and often you might find yourself nodding to the person in front of you as if you heard everything they said while in reality you were listening to another topic being discussed within earshot. With effort, however, various conversations can be separated. The findings from research in dichotic listening paradigms and from common observations such as our party model have led to the idea that all of the auditory stimuli received are processed in parallel without attention, and that some mechanism operates that prevents our attention from being drawn to unwanted sources of sound or other distraction. This special mechanism is called selective attention. Simply put, when the sound is relevant to us it is allowed to "pass through" for more intense processing and attention while other, irrelevant stimuli are blocked out. In gymnastics, selective attention is critical since the distractions present at a large competition are numerous and the gymnast must be able to focus in at the specific task at hand with no or very little attention given to extraneous happenings. Our own research in this area can be seen in the article "Psychological Characteristics of Jr. Elite Gymnasts."

Automatic Processing

The second important notion, that of automatic processing, also plays a big part in successful gymnastic performance. In complex movement behaviors such as those found in gymnastics, two simultaneous actions are often executed but do not require the same input and/or output systems (that is, there is no structural interference). Executing a side aerial on the beam and maintaining alignment during the flight as well as balance prior to and after completion of the sequence requires a large capacity to maintain attention. Research has clearly demonstrated, however, that the more a complex motor movement is practiced and becomes part of a well learned sequence–i.e. a routine on beam, the less active attention is needed. This holds true even in such a high intensity sport such as gymnastics. In essence, the movement becomes automatic to a degree and this is referred to as automatic processing. In other words, gymnasts, practice can surely help make things perfect, not only because it gives one confidence and improves the external appearance of our exercise but also because it reduces the drain on our attentional capacity giving us a larger reserve.

Since gymnastic exercises involve an enormous number of high-capacity movements strung together in rapid succession, the attention demands can be excessive and only successfully managed when a considerable number of the movements have become relatively automatized through a great deal of practice. Coaches may want to refer to "A Psycho/ Physical Guide to Training Full Routines" to help their gymnasts reach this level.

Neurologists studying the brain's workings have contributed a great deal in recent years to our further understanding of this automatic processing phenomenon as it applies to complex movements. They are now convinced that the physiological basis for much needed mental economy lies with the system that regulates wakefulness. The reticular activating system (RAS) ascends from the core of the brain and bombards the cerebral cortex with a stream of impulses that maintain cortical activity. When these impulses diminish we become sleepy. A portion of the RAS appears to regulate the degree to which we are "awake" in a highly selective manner. This could be conceptualized as the tuning of our attention. When something becomes more or less habitual through practice, the motor system can move ahead with minimum mental energy output. Should something unexpected occur during this motor sequence (a near fall on beam, a distracting noise, as examples), an immediate re-orienting is required to get back on track. At such times there is a dramatic corresponding sign of activation and increase in attention in the individual's EFG (brain wave). The fact that any change in any aspect of the activity (the routine on beam) will evoke reorienting shows that we are, in fact, constantly perceiving the stimulus involved, monitoring it, and anticipating, with varying degrees of attention being given to separate aspects depending on the amount of automatization that has occurred through practice and the capacity demands of the particular movement. This is the epitome of mental economy in attention.

Demands on Attention

Two other facts neurologists and motor specialists have helped us realize is that the amount of attention demanded increases as the processing comes closer to the response (setting up for a particularly difficult beam sequence usually involves a pause to really focus attention) and that the effect of distractions decreases as the complexity of the main task increases. When about to execute a most difficult sequence it is harder to break our concentration than when the sequence is relatively simple.

An interesting aside here is the fact that the reorienting process described above requires about 150 to 200 milliseconds (ms) or about 2/10 th of a second to accomplish— obviously, this is extremely fast. Upon observation it may seem that humans respond continuously and smoothly with a constant flow of movement occurring as the result of stimulus input. Research has shown, however, that the human motor system appears to be structured by approximately 200 ms and it appears that no two movements can follow each other by less than this amount. This kind of generalization might seem surprising but motor behavior analysis into psychological refractoriness (the delay in response between two closely received stimuli) indicated that this, in fact, is the way humans probably function.

If we visualize the gymnastic exercise, again let us say on beam, as a continuous flow of well-practiced movements culminating in a dismount then we might also hypothesize, based on our prior discussion, that attention demands become greater as the gymnast nears the completion of the particular exercise, that is, the final "response pattern" of the total configuration. Falls from the beam can occur at any time. It is interesting that they often come about when many of the higher demand skills have been executed and the performer is getting close to the dismount. This lapse of attention may indicate that the gymnast has failed to "spread out" the total fixed capacity of attention or that a prior reorientation caused by a fall or bobble earlier in the total motor sequence has drained too much energy from the attentional reserves. You may gain more practical information on this topic by going to "On the Beam: A Gymnasts Guide for Staying There."

Relationship to Performance

It should be fairly obvious how the concepts discussed above are very important aspects of concentration-attention and its relationship to performance. Staying with the beam for illustration, one can observe how the more competent performers tune-in. Watching the eye focus and scan is easy to do and you will note that in such performers there is not "flashlighting" in focus, that is, they do not switch attention from a narrow visual field, but seem to constrict all attention when it comes to any peripheral distractions.

A natural question to ask is: Can one increase the capacity to attend? There are differences of opinion in this regard with some theorists feeling that the capacity to attend is fixed individually by the limitations in the human processing system, while others believe, providing there is no structural interference, that a person's attentional ability can be improved. Although methods for increasing the ability to be attentive are not the subject of this article, a couple of ideas may be helpful. We have indicated that practice can help automatize motor patterns and thereby increase the gymnast's capacity to respond when the attention demands call for it. Moral: practice, practice, and more practice! Beginners on beam sometimes complain that if they run long in their exercise and the timer shouts "warning;" this can "blow their minds." This external probe into their attention, so to speak, has broken it and raised their anxiety. Most gymnasts learn to go right along while working an event despite noises in the background such as floor-exercises music, talking, others warming up, etc. As has been stated by others, the best way to prepare in all areas for gymnastic competition, including the consolidation of attentional capacity, is to simulate competitive conditions during training. Timed warm-ups and exercises, others watching and/or judging, crowd noise, etc.; conducted periodically during training are examples of this kind of important simulation.

Finally, a rather dramatic method, which can only be described as "a brute" is the Massimo Method (for lack of a better name). It can help increase the ability to attend if not the capacity. Using beam again—have the gymnast run through her exercise and at several times during the routine provide verbal distraction, not in the form of random talking or coaching information, but by calling out the gymnast's own name with varying degrees of pitch and emphasis—low/relaxed to loud/authoritative. The personal reference in this kind of distraction requires the use of enormous energy to ignore and maintain attention to the main task. After all, since childhood we have all been taught to respond when our name is called. Eventually, the gymnast will be able to manage this probe, with some exceptions, but it is extremely tough. This drill, all other things being equal, will increase the gymnast's overall attention on the event. Of course, the gymnast should be told beforehand that they are to concentrate on the task at hand no matter what is said. Obviously coaches should also utilize sound judgment in this method and not give such stimulus initially in the middle of a flight series for example. Be prepared for quite a challenge.

Summary

By way of summary to this point:

- Attention has been defined as a capacity for processing information that is related to consciousness, that is limited, and that is measured by the extent to which different tasks interfere with each other.
- Structural interference occurs when the same receptors, effectors, or storage mechanisms are used for two tasks.
- Capacity interference results from limitation in attention. Most theorists agree that the early stages of information processing may not require much attention and that attention requirements are markedly increased in late stages of processing (more complex).
- The ability to block out distractions and selectively attend to a task is seen in more accomplished gymnasts.
- The more a skill is practiced, the more the skill is automated resulting in less required attention.
- Keeping attention requires the ability to shift focus.

In the next article, "The Performance Connection: Part II," we will take a look at the other two critical components of gymnastic performance; namely stress and arousal.

THE PERFORMANCE CONNECTION PART II: STRESS & AROUSAL

We began our discussion of the performance connection in Part I with a rather detailed look at attention as part of this connection. We defined attention (concentration) as the capacity to consciously handle information. It was suggested that we can measure attention by the extent that two tasks interfere or get in the way of each other. Problems in keeping our attention on something result when we need to use the same sense (eyes, ears, etc.) for taking in information or when we need to use the same motor effectors (arms, legs etc.) for putting out a movement. This problem we called structural interference. Another reason for problems in keeping our attention has to do with the individual's personal limitations. This we called "capacity interference." We are all different and this includes our ability to attend to a task. It was also pointed out in "The Performance Connection: Part I" that good gymnasts are able to selectively pay attention to a task and block out distractions. Finally, we said the more automatic a move becomes through practice the less attention is needed to successfully execute it. This makes a gymnast more mentally efficient. By being efficient in this way, a gymnast is better able to control how much he or she lets into the mind for processing. This also allows the gymnast to direct focus from reading outside signs (spotting on beam, looking at knees, etc.) to reading of inside signals (stretch feeling, tension, etc.) in a flexible manner. The ability to shift from broad internal and external focus to narrow internal and external focus is a key for keeping our attention.

Stress and Arousal

In this article we will look at the other two ingredients in our connection. That is how stress and arousal affect attention and influence the level of our performance. Although we can spell out fine definitions of such ideas as stress, motivation, arousal, activation and anxiety in everyday language it is not so easy to separate them in the physical world. For example, when we talk about someone who is highly aroused we can describe such things as a state of alertness, dilation of the pupils of the eyes, an increased beating of the heart, increased sweating, etc. But these are also the signs we see when someone is under stress or highly motivated. We can see that there are difficulties looking at these states in terms of physical measures. However, we can observe differences in actual behavior. For example, both the gymnast who is highly aroused and the one that is really frightened will both have higher heart rates and both be sweating but the one who is afraid will be showing signs of fear (withdrawal, maybe even tears) while the gymnast who is aroused and raring to go will not show threatened behavior. Even their facial expressions will be observably different.

Let's now take a better look at arousal and stress as part of the critical connection. We will define arousal as the degree to which a gymnast is energized. It can therefore range from sleepiness where there is little or no energization to a highly charged state we usually find just prior to competition. In this kind of definition, arousal is neutral, that is, it is simply the amount of energy or effort that the gymnast will apply to the job at hand.

On the other hand, stress and motivation can be thought of as having direction and not being neutral. Stress is usually considered to be a negative emotional state which leads an individual to try and get out of an unpleasant situation. Motivation, usually considered positive, implies a drive toward a satisfying objective such as a good routine and score. Motivation and stress define the direction of the action (gymnastic skills) and arousal level defines the intensity with which the action needed will be approached or avoided. The article, "Locus of Control and Coach Effectiveness" provides more information on this drive.

Optimal Levels of Arousal

Arousal can affect performance in what has been called the inverted-U hypothesis (Yerkes and Dodson). Basically, this idea states that every individual has an optimum level of arousal that leads for that person to a high level of performance. If the gymnast is aroused below or above the optimal level, his or her performance will not be at its very best. Often we have heard coaches say that a gymnast was really "up" for a meet and this is why they were successful.

The implication is that the "higher" we are the better we perform. Actually, there is strong evidence that there is a particular level of arousal for best performance and that too much or too little arousal can cause a marked decline in personal performance. Finding the right "peak" for an individual gymnast is an important challenge.

A significant idea in thinking about level of arousal, ability to attend, and performance is called cue-utilization. The gymnast takes cues from the environment that aid in performance. As arousal increases there is a narrowing in the range of cues that are used. At the same time less important aspects of the surroundings are blocked out and ignored. In addition to the reduction in the range of cues that are attended to when arousal increases, there is an increase in shifts of attention within this narrowed range to different sources of input. This shifting of attention facilitates rapid response when likely things happen but slow and somewhat unpredictable responses when any unlikely event occurs.

Research has shown that high levels of arousal can cause an athlete to direct attention to too many difference sources, mentally jumping around from thought to thought or cue to cue. This usually results in unacceptable distraction. In this situation, some of the sources attended to provide unimportant information causing important cues to be missed. It appears that a gymnast's ability to choose between important and unimportant signals is weakened during overly high arousal. Extreme arousal and stress result in a reduction in the amount of information an athlete can attend to and process. Gymnasts, who by nature have narrow attentional capacity, tend at these times to become rigid resulting in glaring mistakes. What often happens next is that attention becomes focused on the individual's internal state. The gymnast becomes more aware of his or her heartbeat, worried feeling, etc., and gets lost in their own thoughts. Under such conditions of overloaded arousal we often see real panic and "checking" in the actual performance.

Arousal and Competition

The ability to maintain an appropriate level of arousal and accompanying cue utilization throughout a long competition is very difficult. Let's say that a gymnast develops a headache or stubs a toe early in the meet. What can often happen is that the gymnast will shift attention from the needed external focus to internal, becoming acutely aware of the pain and discomfort. This situation usually results in increased arousal wherein outside cues are missed, concentration broken, and routines inappropriately busted. With experience, gymnasts can cope with such distractions because they have learned to "read" the pain in an objective manner (when it is not totally disabling of course) and at the same time emotionally dissociate it allowing for continued performance. They can do this because they have confidence in themselves and can draw on a reserve of past successes to help them during such stress. Beginners, on the other hand, can rarely use associative strategies successfully. Like everything else in the sport, "It takes practice!" and "A Gymnast's Guide to Demonstrating Confidence" can help.

Using the ideas talked about so far, our sport requires a narrow focus of attention during the performance phase. This focus is directed primarily to the external environment for important cues. Different events probably require different levels of arousal. For example, brief high-energy events such as vaulting requires a higher level than the longer, extremely narrowed focus demands made by a pommel horse or balance beam routine. On these events, over arousal would almost certainly lead to deterioration in performance.

Individual Differences

We already hinted that there are differences among gymnasts in terms of "arousability." There are those gymnasts who never seem to get excited, who are apparently low-keyed and cool. In contrast, there are those who become very nervous and even hyper when facing the stress of competition. These precompetitive states do not always predict performance. We have all seen the overtly cool character that blows it totally, while the apparent nervous gymnast may perform superbly when the moment of truth arrives. Both coaches and gymnasts may be interested in the article "Butterflies and Pre-Meet Anxiety."

These differences in arousal-anxiety can be measured by paper and pencil tests. The information so gathered identifies the source of an individual's anxiety. State anxiety is evaluated by asking questions such as, "Are you worried about your performance now?" Positive answers indicate a level of worry about a particular event, and this state of anxiety can vary from time to time depending on the task (i.e. back walkovers are fine but back handsprings on beam are stressful). A second kind of anxiety has been referred to as trait anxiety. It is determined by answers to questions such as, "Are you usually worried about your performance?" "Yes" answers suggest a tendency to worry or be anxious in general. This tendency would not change from moment to moment depending on the skill or event but would be a relatively stable characteristic of the personality. However, evidence is clear that those individuals who are high trait anxious tend under specific conditions, to also be the most state anxious on a given motor task. Thought of this way, trait anxiety is variable that tells us the ease with which an individual can become stressed by the environment.

If arousability in motor tasks is determined by trait anxiety, it would play an important role in deciding how to motivate different gymnasts. The gymnast whose high trait-anxious will reach the level of optimal arousal for a given skill with less motivation from outside because by nature they are already aroused to a given degree. It is easy to see that a coach can over-motivate a high trait-anxious gymnast and that increased arousal may take them over their top and lead to poor performance. The reverse is true for the low trait-anxious gymnast; they may be under-motivated in terms of pressure from the outside. This may all appear obvious but the number of coaches who ignore it is striking.

Skill Attainment

Another important matter we have already touched on in "The Performance Connection: Part I," is that the level of arousal and performance is affected by practice on the skill(s). New tasks can be highly stressful to trait-anxious gymnasts during practice. With increased practice, when a lower level of arousal is established, more success is usually seen. For example, when a young gymnast is attempting a double back for the first time on floor, they are usually more successful on the fourth or fifth attempt. This is not so much the result of some pearl of technical information that was given but is often due to a slight decrease in arousal. Knowing that a gymnast is very anxious means that different methods should be used for presenting technical material in the early stages of learning.

As the level of skill improves with practice, there is a need to increase the level of arousal in order to produce maximum execution. Getting more comfortable with a skill can have its drawbacks since more arousal is required to perform to the utmost. Also, attention shifts from internal thoughts of missing the move to critical external cues. When skills are more highly practiced and the attention demands are lowered through automatization, gymnasts can more easily tolerate high arousal and stress.

Conclusion

The performance connection is extremely important in the learning and executing of gymnastic skills. It is from that point of view that it is the balance between attention, arousal, and stress that results in top flight gymnastics efforts. Some implications for coaching have been suggested as we discussed the interaction of these factors and the connection between the gymnast's physical output and the states of attention, stress, and arousal.

Chapter Eight

—— ΨΨ ——

MASTERING MENTAL GYMNASTICS

Developing and mastering mental skills are crucial to enhancing gymnastics performances. Understanding basic mental imagery and visualization, focus and attention, relaxation and controlling anxiety are all skills which can be learned and mastered. In addition, how to use and apply basic mental skills in training sessions are discussed for both the younger gymnasts as well as the advanced competitor.

Combining your mental skills with the art of goal setting goes a long way in enhancing performance and increasing self-confidence and presentation skills. To establish goals, we explain the fundamental guidelines that are involved in goal setting behavior. Then we provide steps for the gymnast to following in setting personal goals as well as for the coach to use as an effective training tool.

- "The Late Movies" A Young Gymnast's Guide to Mental Imagery Training
- Mental Gymnastics Training for Competition
- Goal Setting Guidelines
- "My Goal is to…" A Gymnast's Plan
- Using Goal Setting as a Coaching Tool
- Top 10 Tips to Goal Setting

"THE LATE MOVIES"
A YOUNG GYMNAST'S GUIDE TO
MENTAL IMAGERY TRAINING

If you think by the title of this article, "The Late Movies," that we are going to talk about the "oldies," you have been misled and might want to stop reading now. We are going to talk about a kind of movie but the screen for this flick is in your head and mind and you operate the video yourself.

Most people imagine things in their heads; we see ourselves as heroes and sometimes picture great adventures, etc. This usually happens when we are daydreaming and surely occurs when we are sleeping and night-dreaming. It turns out that with practice, we can turn our own movies on and off in our heads and picture any number of things while we are wide awake. Rather than simply being a random daydream, we can actually go to a kind of movie file, select a short subject, and run it in our head on our own screen. We can do this in black and white or color. Sometimes you can see this happening at competitions with some gymnasts who appear to be running through their routines in their heads before competing. Some gymnasts actually accompany their mental rehearsal with hand movements and body shifts that go along with the film they are picturing or imaging. Many athletes find this a good way to prepare themselves for an upcoming exercise, just before the starting bell!

We would like to talk with you about using your built-in capacity to show movies or image scenes as a way of helping you visualize and maybe improve the physical performance of learning a skill, or series, or your routines, not by activating or relaxing yourself but by simply "seeing it through." Other things can be tried once you have the knack of it. Research and feedback from gymnasts who have tried imaging suggests that it really helps about eight out of ten athletes. Are you one of these gymnasts? As with everything else, one improves ability with practice. Just as we train and condition our bodies we should give our minds the same opportunity. They work closely together and gymnasts are surely aware of this fact.

Before you can use Mental Gymnastics Training to help with your gymnastics, you need to learn how to open up your theater and get the show going. You need to begin with basic **Mental Imagery Training** or **MIT**. Although MIT can be done very effectively with a coach or trainer guiding or helping to run the film with words, we will focus on the gymnasts taking care of the entire production themselves. Depending on your age, you may need to begin with your parent or coach first, become familiar with the mental exercises, then continue this journey on your own. We'll begin by briefly showing you the progression from beginner to advanced Mental Imagery Training (MIT).

MIT: Beginner Lesson

First of all, let's get comfortable. MIT can be accomplished standing, sitting, walking (when you're good at it) but for openers, we suggest you lie on a comfortable surface on your back with your arms at your side. The point is to settle down as you would for viewing a movie that is going to be somewhere above you, on the ceiling rather than on a screen standing up in front of you. Although many athletes can practice MIT with their eyes open, we strongly suggest you try at first to do the activity with your eyes closed. Wow, is it dark!

Once you are ready for the show, the next thing to do is to take several long, deep breaths and relax. Try to get your mind clear as you may already have some pictures or view spinning around in your head. Some of the scenes can be funny, but no laughing please. Relaxed? Fine. Let's begin.

OK gymnasts, now try to lighten the darkness if it isn't already and try to picture in your "mind's eye" an open, blank space very much like a big, white movie screen. This may take some doing, as young gymnasts we have worked with say that their screens are so large that they can't get any borders around it. That is okay and you should not strain to confine the size of your screen, just try to get it empty of images of any kind. Concentrate and stare into blank space. Now, in the center of the space let a small red dot appear and slowly make it grow until it has filled your screen with color. Any red will do, soft, dark, pinkish, whatever. Try to change the shade of the color while it is filling the screen. After you have done so, let the color shrink back to the small circle and dot then disappear. Breathe and relax. If things begin to pop onto the screen just observe them but don't let yourself get involved. Try and get your screen blank once again. Try the same exercise with different colors. If this is working well, try to see (picture) beams of color going across your screen one at a time or several, whichever is easier for you to handle. Again, clear your screen and breathe deeply.

Remember, gymnasts, this is not a cinch and takes work so don't get discouraged if your screen is a mess and the movie may have to be cancelled for the day because of mental misbehavior. Tomorrow is another day. With your first attempt you might want to stop practice on MIT after simply running the colors as described above. It takes time to build a theater to which only you have the entrance key. It also takes lots of concentration.

If you do stop at this point and begin the next day you should start with this same kind of exercise. Eventually this kind of movie preparation can be cut way down or even eliminated and you can get into the main feature quickly. This is not often the case at the very beginning.

Moving on, now on your blank screen, try to see a clear glass about the size of a basic water glass. It is empty, but clearly there. Now, starting at the bottom, begin to fill your glass very slowly with red juice and stop at the halfway mark. Look at it closely on the screen. Now empty your glass of the liquid and keep the empty glass on your screen. Repeat this and fill the glass with different colored liquids—ugh, gross! Go only halfway up. Always empty your glass and return to the screen with the glass the middle. Should other things pop into the screen, take a look at them, but try to concentrate and return the film to the original blank screen with glass. Now go back to the red juice and slowly fill the glass right to the top edge but don't let it overflow—hold it and empty it once more. Repeat this exercise with different colors. You might want to try to add ice and even a straw to your picture, and that is all right, but focus on the liquid and controlling it in the glass. Finish this exercise in MIT by returning to the red juice, but this time, fill it to the brim and slowly let it run over, down the glass and out onto the screen. Oh brother, what trouble! Clear the screen once again and breathe deeply for a minute or two. STAY AWAKE, GYMNAST! Let's go on with our MIT.

We are now ready to get a bit daring. Clear your screen and now picture a special character from T.V. or the movies, but not a human. Picture them in your mind. Ah yes, there he or she is—try to develop a very clear image of your character. Try not to have them do anything, just stand there and stare back at you from the screen. Isn't this a blast? The next step is to have your character, move around a little. Picture a scene from the movie or invent your own. A real challenge at this point is to add some words at the bottom of your screen briefly describing what is in the picture. This is like foreign films that have a translation at the bottom. Don't get too complicated, but be sure you actually can see the words and read them. Between each step in your mind, breathe deeply and always return to a blank screen prior to starting your projector again.

Going on, try to see some familiar picture like your room. Look around and see if you can picture what it looks like right now. Spend a minute here and then try to picture your gym. Experiment with this part a little—for example, try to see the building, go inside and look around. Take your time. Take a walk through the gym and look at the apparatus, is there a name on it? What colors do you see? Keep looking. We know there's a lot to take in.

Now take a giant step in your mind and picture a family member you know. Get as much detail into the picture as you can. Next picture a familiar gymnast. It could be someone you know or it could be an Olympian. Check out the leotard –cut, color, striping, etc. Observe any spontaneous pictures that appear but again try not to get carried away. Avoid working out on the apparatus in your head this first time. Clear the screen, breathe deeply two or three times and open your eyes. Lesson number one in creating very personal home movies is over.

MIT: Intermediate Lesson

Your next MIT session should begin as the first but you may be able to get the gymnast in the gym much sooner. Again, take your time and begin a new exercise by attempting to see yourself. If you can't get a clear image of yourself at least make the person a gymnast. Try to see as much detail as possible. Next, try to see yourself in the gym, notice what you are wearing, and what's going on in the gym around you.

Great! Assuming that this is the case let's go on from that point and use your movie run for some specific purpose. Pick an event and prepare to begin an exercise in your head. On your screen see yourself or another gymnast(s) preparing to perform a routine. Try to visualize as much of the detail that you can. See the apparatus; picture the mats and the entire scene. Now enlarge the picture of the gymnast and block out other factors except him/her and the actual piece of equipment. If this is all going well then get ready to mount. Breathe deeply. Now mount and go on with the exercise in great detail seeing it in your run through done flawlessly, with perfect form and finished with a nailed dismount. Turn, face the head judge and walk off, to great applause of course! Try very hard while you go through this first set not to repeat any moves. Try to see it without any error all the way.

Now let's go through the exercise on the same event a second time. This time, however, don't hold onto the image too hard. If you make a mistake and end up repeating it, let this happen automatically. Often our minds will make adjustments in the creative picture to correct the flaw in your consciously imagined form because you know what is required. These unconscious shifts allow a "deeper you" to help direct the picture. With practice, we can get to know when to listen to this inner voice. It's like having an extra director to run the show. During this second replay of the basic film, allow any corrections to occur. Try to "feel" the perfect execution to go with the picture. When corrections take place, try to see written at the bottom of the screen the words of correction that go along with the adjustment. Also try to hear them as well in your own voice or that of your coach. (e.g. "line up your hips and go," "block with your shoulders," etc.) When the exercise is complete, praise yourself for a job well done ("Good job, I knew I could do it," etc.). Make sure your corrections and those of your coach are in a positive and constructive manner to help you learn the skills and routines properly. Between each exercise remember to breathe deeply two or three times, clear your screen, and relax before going on with MIT. Run the set several more times with perfection being the goal.

MIT: Advanced Lesson

Other things that can be worked on in your MIT are the flow or pace of the exercise (speed or slow them up in your picture), working on the mount or dismount alone with thoughts being on a solid start and a stuck finish full of energy and class. Proper breathing can also be practiced with MIT, with the gymnast actually working out the breathing pattern while picturing the exercise. One can also have as part of the script a focus on nerves and on being steady. A good example in this area is on the balance beam, where many girls appear to need to fall off because once this dreaded mishap has occurred, they settle down with reduced tension and go on fairly well. MIT can be used to help work this out by seeing the picture with the fall and trying to feel the drop in tension after it occurs. This is followed by a replay up to the point of the fall, making corrections, performing the skill again and going on successfully with the effort being to keep the appropriate tension or activation for this set even all the way from start to finish. Again, this takes lots of practice as there are few miracles in our sport.

Getting back to different uses; you might focus on different parts of your routine where minor or major breaks often happen in reality. In this case, the particular trouble spot is run through several times (not the entire exercise) with mistakes being seen and then worked out in your head and on the screen. Believe it or not, this kind of effort can actually improve your concentration and confidence as well as reduce the habitual mistake. It can also reduce the wear-and-tear on your physical body by mentally working out these issues in your head and having your body really "feel" the correct movements.

Once you get the swing of this activity, there are a number of different ways MIT can be used to help improve your gymnastics. When a technique is coming easier to our home viewers, different things can be looked at or examined during the filming sessions. By the way, doing this after viewing an actual video tape of your effort can really help with the training. One additional variation can eventually be tried if your coach is willing to help with your MIT effort. Together you can make a tape of MIT work with the coach kind of providing the soundtrack for the movie. This obviously has to be planned together with a special objective and event in mind as suggested earlier. The coach provides a kind of verbal accompaniment to the visual picture you see in your head. Part of your MIT would involve the playing of this tape by your bed as you finish the day with one more visit to that much loved, sometimes frustrating gym and a final "look" at your work before you drift off to ZZZZzzzz!

Summary
The title of this article for young gymnasts refers to the "late movies." This is not an accident. It is suggested that you try to begin your MIT by setting aside a period of time (say 15 minutes) each night just before sleep. Lying in bed is familiar, and although you may quickly drift off to sleep, the beginning step in this process will often come easier in such surroundings and privacy. Also, research has shown us that

this last conscious experience may be reinforced while we sleep. A more in-depth look at mental training for more advanced competitors can found in "Mental Gymnastics Training for Competition."

MENTAL GYMNASTICS TRAINING FOR COMPETITION

In the area of psychology and sports, many writings appear that, taken at face value, would suggest a quick route to success. Magic formulas should be carefully evaluated for; in general, nothing can take the place of hard work and dedication. From time to time, however, a particular method has been proven both in the laboratory and in the field to be of help to the striving athlete. There are a number of self-disciplinary types of mental activities which have survived the test of time. It should always be remembered that a basic premise of applied psychology is that all individuals are unique, although there are specific developmental and environmental aspects of the human experience that appear to be universal. It all depends on attitude, motivation, background, readiness and other personal conditions as well as the ability of the professionals to capitalize on the positive benefits of any procedure.

Overview of Mental Training

Exciting work in mental training has been going on for some time and includes experiments designed to make us totally relaxed to those that attempt to get us worked up in a very dramatic fashion. When mental training is used to relax someone, it has been shown that the heart beat can really be slowed down, and that the tension in the muscles can be dropped far below normal. In some approaches, while the body and mind is in a state of relaxation, visualization of skills can be accomplished.

When mental training is used to activate a person it has been shown that the level of muscle tension goes way up as does the heart rate, and that the amount of activation the body gives off increase and last at higher levels than normal for a number of days. This means that the person is able and ready to behave in a very active way (compete) for a longer period of time. It is also very helpful when recovering from an injury. Both learning to relax and getting yourself up are important parts of being a successful competitor in athletics. The above are special uses of mental training and they are usually called upon in close proximity to a competition.

Simply stated, all these methods are a form of self-conditioning which has had some remarkable effects in improving performance. One can utilize the method alone (auto), or it can be accomplished on an individual basis or in a small group using a trainer (coach) who verbally facilitates the mental exercise. The small group or individual sessions which use a special trainer/coach seem to be most effective if morale is high and the team has functioned well together in the past while at the same time respecting the individuality of its single members. It is critical that the trainer be familiar with the sport at more than a passing level since such experience will help maximize his or her effectiveness.

These mental training procedures can be useful in several ways:

- **To improve specific performance on any event**
- **To overcome mental blocks on specific skills**
- **To reduce the number of breaks in routines**
- **To totally reorient the gymnast to an event**
- **To reduce the physical impact on the body**
- **To increase self-confidence in the gymnast**

Perhaps, one of the first skills to learn is imagery or visualization and the most efficient way to explain how it works is through illustration. The process can be accomplished by using various degrees of verbal exchange, depending on the individual(s) involved and the preference of the trainer. It is usually a good idea to try both out to see which appears to work best. In the non-verbal method the trainer (if one is being used) gives limited input during the process, while in the more verbally oriented procedure the trainer is quite active with spoken guidance and suggestion.

In our own work with gymnasts and others, we have taken many liberties with the classic form of the method to fit particular circumstances and encourage others to experiment on their own. If you're just starting out, you may want to read our article on "The Late Movies: A Young Gymnast's Guide to Mental Imagery Training" and go through the beginning, intermediate, and advanced lessons of Mental Imagery Training (MIT). Here is an illustration of a MIT-C session for the more advanced competitive gymnast:

Mental Imagery Training for Competition (MIT–C) Session

Let's take for an example a session between one or two gymnasts or the team and a trainer/coach with emphasis on balance beam or pommel horse; events where concentration and positive thinking are very important and often a problem. For the female gymnasts, you may want to read the article "On the Beam: A Gymnast's Guide for Staying There" to help with that event. The MIT–C procedure goes as follows for visualizing a full routine in competition:

1. **Step I.** The gymnast(s) lie on the mat or some other comfortable area on their backs. Having eyes closed appears best, although some people can visualize with their eyes open. This is an individual matter. There should be no talking. Gymnasts can do this at home alone if not using a trainer.

Often, while lying in bed before going to sleep, many gymnasts go over her routines in their heads anyway and this is just a more formal way to kind of do the same thing and get more out of it. However, they could be making things worse by not knowing how to get the most out of their visualization.

2. **Step II.** The gymnast(s) are encouraged to take deep breaths in an attempt to get physically deactivated and mentally relaxed but not to encourage sleep. (In some forms of activation-relaxation training, sleep is the end result) The trainer assists in this process by helping monitor the rhythm of the breathing through verbal suggestion.

3. **Step III.** The trainer instructs the gymnast(s) to maintain this relaxed condition throughout the exercise, unless they are instructed otherwise. There are times when muscular tension will be required and this will be suggested by the trainer depending on the specific situation.

4. **Step IV.** The gymnast(s) are told (or tell themselves) to begin to mentally prepare for the event continuing the relaxed breathing and reducing tension in their muscles. "Let's begin with balance beam or pommel horse routines. You have finished your warm-up and are now ready to perform on the event. Picture yourself preparing to mount." Every gymnast has their own ritual when they are waiting to perform. The gymnast should go through this procedure in their mind when doing their training. In the group process the trainer will allow time for this to mentally occur. Continue "You are now standing by the apparatus. You are about to mount; so address the head judge. Perform your mount and try to feel the equipment either on your hands or feet depending on your mount. You have now begun."

5. **Step V.** At this point, depending on the specific purpose of the session, the trainer tells the gymnast(s) to picture the mount and continue into the routine. Each element should be seen in full during this initial run through. The pace is important. The gymnast should not repeat a movement in their head and without tensing the muscle groups. Even if they are unhappy with the image seen, proceed until the dismount. When training for a single skill, mastery repeats would be appropriate.

6. **Step VI.** An additional run-through is "performed," but this time the gymnast(s) are encouraged to breathe as if actively working the event and to tense related muscle groups involved in each skill as they picture their routine in their "mind's eye." They should attempt to visualize the element executed to its maximum. The focus is on perfection in this particular drill with coordinated muscular emphasis.

There are numerous variations that are possible utilizing this approach by oneself or with a trainer. Obviously, the gymnast(s) have to take it seriously. Like everything else, it takes time, practice, and a certain degree of faith. The mental training procedure described above is one which deviates from training in ways that we have personally found more effective with gymnasts.

Focusing Your MIT–C Sessions

The following are some other mental imagery training focal points using the same format that you might wish to experiment with on your own or with your coach. Remember that all these session and focal points can be used at various stages in learning, training, and competing routines.

A. **Focus on difficult moments in your routine.** Providing the gymnast has done a particular trick correctly in the past and knows what it feels like to do it right. The effort in this drill is to reproduce the "feeling" through a psychological replay of the movement at the same time you "see" the correct execution in your mind.

B. **Focus on consistent areas where minor or major breaks occur.** This is most successful when you do it yourself or the trainer/ coach works with you individually and knows your exercise well. In this case the gymnast continues the mental run activity but pictures the break in the routine as it usually happens. This should be followed immediately by another mental run through of the routine but this time with the break corrected. The trainer's role in this situation is more active. It is often helpful that the gymnast verbally expresses the error when it happens in their head. ("Oops, got my hips out of line, which felt wrong," etc.) In the "corrected" run through the gymnast makes the verbal corrections to themselves, such as "line up with the end of the beam, breathe and push" and passes the troublesome section with correct technical movements followed by positive verbal reinforcement ("good job", "that's it", etc.) when they pass the place where the break had occurred. Believe it or not, this kind of activity can actually improve your physical performance as well as confidence. Concentration can be heightened in this same manner, especially when the trainer is familiar with the exercise and the problem. The trainer can actually guide the gymnast through the routine, e.g. "Now set for turn, stretch, smooth, ready for handspring, set-concentrate, push, etc." This is even more effective if the gymnast records their voice going through their routine. Make sure to time the routine so what you are thinking is actually in real time. Many gymnasts may find that they are under time and will need to make adjustments.

C. **Focus on flow of entire exercise.** This variation has proven quite successful in all events. The technique is essentially the same as described above except emphasis is placed on the "wholeness" or gestalt of the routine with particular focus on fluidity of movement throughout the routine. (Many gymnasts actually begin to rhythmically move their bodies during this drill although they are lying flat on their backs.)

D. **Focus on mount and dismount.** Again the same basic method previously described is used but the concentration is on establishing stability. Time is spent (mentally) on quick preparation for the landing and "sticking it." Attention is also given to the controlled discharge of energy employed at the mount. (Some gymnasts get so psyched up that they actually overdo for a mount and blow it.) Talking through the mount-dismount phase is also helpful as an accompaniment to the mental move activity.

E. **Focus on proper breathing**. The mental run through drill is carried out as before but with major focus being placed on specific breathing patterns as they relate to the execution of your routine, skill by skill, and in its entirety. Actual overemphasized breathing is encouraged as the routine is seen in the mind.

F. **Focus on being steady.** One of the major problems for some performers is "the shakes." Sometimes these begin before the performer has even mounted and continue throughout the entire routine. For others, they begin while doing the exercise and build up until the gymnast has literally shaken off the apparatus. It should be noted that very often the first fall eliminates or greatly reduces the shakes suggesting that the gymnast has built up enormous tension in anticipation of falling off and once it occurs the biological and psychological system as a whole returns to a more steady state. It becomes pretty evident that the cause of shakes is psychological or just plain nerves gone wild. Even rather successful gymnasts may have a minor difficulty in this area. They have learned to compensate and can perform despite this handicap. If the athlete knows they are a shaker, admit that, and then go on to try and minimize the effect. Rather than eliminate all such nervousness that takes on a physical symptom, the first objective should be to reduce it, if only even slightly. Most importantly, try to get your attention off it and don't overreact to the quivers although they are understandably upsetting. Applying the proper breathing techniques and getting into a relaxed but focused state is best. One thing is for sure: attention must be drawn away from the physical act of shaking. That is to say, neither gymnast nor the coach nor parent should make a major production of this problem. Instead, every effort should be made to calmly redirect the mental energy into the actual, technical performance of the routine. As always, mentally practice consistently steady routines.

Summary

It would be easy for someone to dismiss these activities as not worth the time and effort for the ordinary high school, college, or even club gymnast. This would be most unfortunate indeed since there is growing evidence that such mental and psychological effort can and have improved athletic performance. It is important that coaches and gymnasts alike begin to believe that the marriage of mind and matter can, along with other factors, promote the development of excellence. Just as we train and condition our bodies we should give our minds the same advantage.

GOAL SETTING GUIDELINES

When establishing goals, it is first necessary to clearly understand some of the fundamental guidelines that are involved in goal setting behavior. When setting goals, as an aspect of learning a new skill or preparing for a workout or specific competition, certain principles need to be followed in order to get the most from this kind of activity. Keep a record of these in a Personal Goals Notebook for easy access and referral. Here are a few of our favorites from "Gymnastics Psychology: The Ultimate Guide for Coaches, Gymnasts, and Parents" for effectively setting goals:

1. **Ink them, don't merely think them!** It is a basic requirement of the goal setting exercise that specific goals be written down, not just carried around in the gymnast's or coach's head. There are a number of reasons for this, but the most important is that it makes a commitment to an objective that is formal and noted. You can't alter a goal or suggest you accomplished it, when in fact you did not, particularly if it is on paper, your computer, or phone.

2. **Goals should be stated in terms of physical and mental performance objectives, and not ever in terms of outcome!** This is probably the single most important rule to follow, and it may be the most difficult at times to do. Basically, what the gymnast should be writing down and focusing on during goal setting are the things that need to be done from a performance point of view that will lead to the desired outcome. It is the steps that need to be taken to achieve mastery that is set down as goals, not mastery itself, which is the end result of taking those steps.

    a. **Physical performance goals.** Physical "performance" goals, for example, would include such things as straight legs, straight arms, pointed toes, and literally hundreds of other body segments and form components demanded by any given gymnastic exercise. Additional performance goals would include all of the technical requirements for the mastery of a skill or series of skills. Such things as blocking angles, arm/head/upper torso positions, visual cues "see hands on the horse," speed, landing technique, spotting in turns, and again a multitude of instructions needed to successfully perform a gymnastics effort, are further examples of performance goals.

    b. **Mental performance goals.** Performance goals can also involve behavioral and attitudinal objectives such as "I feel energized" before vault or "take deep breaths and relax before beam," "keep my focus and tune out the audience," "treat each event as a separate meet" and so forth. In all cases, mental performance goals deal with how the gymnast is going to do the skills or approach the routines, not on what an outcome is predicted to be. Your attitude, effort, coping skills, positive self-talk and motivation are examples of objectives to set along with your physical performance goals.

   c. **Outcome goals.** These are the "results" of your mental and physical performance objectives. These are very often not in your direct control and are to be avoided. Examples are individual event, or All–Around scores, placement in a meet, qualifying attempts, and statements such as "stick," "make my flight series," "no falls," etc. If a gymnast is having trouble distinguishing between a performance goal and an outcome goal, it might help to remember that performance goals are those things you need to do with your body and mind, such as "stretch through my shoulders," that will lead to the desired specific outcome, such as "sticking the routine." Performance goals deal with what an athlete can control while outcome is frequently controlled by others such as judges and other gymnasts.

3. **Goals should be positive and never negative in nature, both in form and content.** Positive goals state what is to be done, not what is to be avoided. Negative goals direct attention to the very errors we want to avoid, rather than placing focus and emphasis on correct action or behavior. Positive goals require that the gymnast decide how to reach a specific objective. Positive goals should avoid the word "don't" at all times. An example for comparison would be to say "keep my elbows locked" rather than "don't bend my arms."

4. **Goals should be measurable and specific.** They should not be vague, such as "do the best that I can do," for this is difficult to measure unless you have a clear idea of where you are starting from. Goals should establish a baseline from which improvement can be gradually measured. Again, physical performance goals are superior for they are both specific and can be measured easily. Attitudinal or mental objectives are a little trickier but what's great is that you are the evaluator of your own goals.

5. **Goals should involve realistic objectives.** Goals should be difficult, but seen as challenging rather than threatening and unobtainable. If goals are set that are clearly not in reach, from either an effort or ability point of view, they will not be motivating. Realistic goals suggest that personal judgment is involved. Goals that are based upon a performance baseline that was established one week prior to a competition are quite likely to be realistic. With practice, performance goals can become very "high tech" and "polished," but very realistic at higher levels of competence. For

example, "keep my head in and look down my arm (the lever) at the peak of my blind change."

6. **Goals should be primarily short-term in nature and re-stated as needed.** The majority of the goals should be short-term, such as daily and weekly goals with some extending into a few months. As you keep re-evaluating and adding to your goals, you may find that many so called "medium or long-term goals" were accomplished just based on reaching a majority of your short-term goals. This is the ultimate achievement in your goal setting plans. As a more advanced gymnast, you and your coach can add long-term "dream" goals to your Personal Goals Notebook.

7. **Goals should be evaluated daily, weekly, and/or monthly.** Mutual goal checking off of goals by a coach and athlete after a workout or competition is a useful way of confirming what has been actually accomplished. It is best to evaluate your goals based on your objectives such as at the end of the workout or as soon as possible after a meet while they are fresh in your mind. Evaluate your physical goals according to the goals you set such as "blocking on the horse" or landing 4 out of 5 dismounts. In terms of mental or attitudinal goals you may consider giving yourself a score such as "My focus on beam was an 8 but I felt really relaxed before floor, so I gave myself a 9.5."

"MY GOAL IS TO…" A GYMNAST'S PLAN

The importance of goal setting cannot be overemphasized in sports and a closer look at this idea is very worthwhile. How many of you have heard a young gymnast say "My Goal is to be in the Olympics" where others may say "My goal is to win states this year." These gymnasts might actually achieve their goals and your authors would be the first people to encourage dreams and lofty ambition within the spirit of each young athlete. On the other hand, many long years of experience have shown that some of these visions or fantasies must be kept in their place and reality carefully considered. For example, it is a striking fact that out of the hundreds of thousands of gymnasts competing in the U.S. since 1956, there have been less than 100 men and 100 women who have made Olympic Gymnastic Teams! Unless you are currently pretty well known and a seasoned performer, the chances of you making the next team are indeed slim. It is therefore easy to see if the only goal that counts for you is to make an Olympic or International Team, you have probably set yourself up to be very disappointed, and this goes for competitors of any age.

When it comes to goal setting, those grand dreams should be put on the back burner. This does not mean you abandon your hopes, heaven forbid, but it does mean they are not allowed to become the focus of all your energy so that anything short of them is seen as worthless. Achieving excellence is a long process, and often the process itself and the joy gained from successful small steps, is very rewarding. This kind of approach will help you avoid painful discouragement which might result in your leaving this wonderful sport before you should. The setting of realistic goals has prolonged many gymnasts' career and enjoyment of the sport.

If, in the process of improving and working hard, you should become a state, regional, or national champion, or maybe even the ultimate success of becoming an Elite, that would surely be a most awesome, reward and you'll take it! However, it should be viewed as a great achievement based on your hard work rather than having been the be-all, end-all of your gymnastic participation. In the long run, you will enjoy your gymnastics more if you take it a day at a time. It is interesting to note that many of the eastern philosophies involve the notion that the outcome is unimportant and that it is only the pursuit and moment of action that are of real value. You can use this notion to your advantage in goal setting.

Personal Goal Setting

An important step in goal setting is to make sure that whatever your goals are, that they are, in fact, your own. You need to ask yourself, "What do I really want?" You cannot totally ignore your parents or coaches wishes for you since they are an important part of the picture. Time will be the best judge of their evaluation and opinion. Many young gymnasts are often far more realistic and honest than mom, dad, or even the coach, when it comes to knowing their own talent level. Sometimes it is hard to face this problem because it hurts, and you may be worrying about letting someone else down. But deep inside you know and every day in the gym makes it clearer. You have a responsibility to yourself and you need to sort out what are your own personal goals from the ambitions of those around you, and continually be checking them against the obvious reality. This is a very critical job that needs to be ongoing.

With this as a basic understanding, how do you go about setting goals? The best approach is to set daily goals within a slightly larger picture. In most cases this larger blueprint should be done with the coach and your individual goals part of this picture. A majority of good coaches have this idea automatically built into their practice schedules. If these workout objectives are not individualized, however, they should be, and you need to talk with your coach about it so you can develop your own.

Much of how you set up individual goals will depend on how the training is done in your gym. Many daily schedules include a certain amount of time assigned to a specific event with tasks present. For example, you may be required to do a certain number of skills on a given day on one or more events, or a certain number of elements, passes, mounts, dismounts along with conditioning, etc., assuming that this is how your workouts are arranged. You likely already have some short-range goals established on a daily basis for you and for the team. This training structure gives you a clear idea of where you are going with the group and sets priorities for you individually. Such overall training blueprints provide for the most productive output.

Basic Goal Setting for Skills Acquisition

In addition to the built in goal-setting your coach has set for the training day or week, it is very helpful for each gymnast to develop, on paper, their own personal plan. A good way to do this is to briefly look at a sample involving individual work being done to learn a new skill. The following is a basic example of how a gymnast might go about developing short-term goals in this regard:

Personal Goals Sheet–Basic Skills
- List the skill to be accomplished.
- Note the date the skill should be perfected with assistance.
- Next, put the date which you will be able to perform the skill 5 times unassisted.
- Then, list the date when you can perform the skill at every practice to show consistency.

- Lastly, put the skill into a combination or series and start over with the sequence.
- Evaluate your progress, keep track of your accomplishments, and make notes as to your attitude.
- Keep all your records in a Personal Goals Notebook so you can easily see how much progress you are making.

Obviously, this kind of personal goal setting schedule assumes that these skills are within your reach and that you are doing all the conditioning, both physical and mental, that is required to get these movements on a regular basis. If you are working on developing routines then just change the basic format to include series into passes, passes into a routine and so on.

You will see that the span of time that is covered in this plan is flexible but you want to make sure that the skill is consistent before moving on. Whatever time you set, it should not be viewed as poured in concrete and the schedule may need revision as you progress. When a step is accomplished it should be checked off in your journal and a new goal (skill) added, if appropriate with a new timeline. If the deadline date comes and you have not made it, which is okay, but at that point you need to review what the specific problems are for you with that particular skill. Lack of practice, inadequate preparation, fear, etc., could all be factors influencing success or failure. The answer may be obvious, but you and your coach need to go over the timetable, not only at the time you originally set it up, but also along the way especially at deadline time. This activity will give you something concrete to work towards in a reasonable way. Goal-setting such as the above should be done for each event.

Advanced Goal Setting for Workouts or Competition

Once you are competing on a regular basis, goal setting is still recommended for your workouts as well as your meets. Rather than winning the meet as the major goal, although victory would be just great, perhaps a wiser goal would be to improve on one or two events from your last competition, or to stay on the beam, or to add that new skill. If you have decided you will be number one and that nothing else will really matter or be considered an accomplishment, the odds are that you may be in for a big disappointment. The most important thing is to feel you did the best job you could at that point in time. That way, you will feel good about yourself and the goal of doing your best is always realistic!

In setting personal goals for a daily workout including routines or a specific competition there are additional steps to take which go beyond the type of goals set in training and learning new skills. Many specific goals are set at this time and here is an example to follow. Additional steps and help in setting your personal goals can be found in the articles, "Goal Setting Guidelines" and "Top 10 Tips to Goal Setting." Keep these in your Personal Goals Notebook and refer to them often.

Personal Goals Sheet: Workout/ Competition

- List each event
- List two to three physical performance goals for that event.
- List one or two attitude or mental performance goals for that event.
- Evaluate your goals at the end of the workout or competition.
- Take notes to help with your next personal goal sheet.
- Review your past sheets on a weekly and monthly basis.
- Keep all your records along with your tip sheet in your notebook.
- Share your goals and progress with others. You might be amazed to see how much you have accomplished. Be proud, you've earned it!

Some things come quickly and others take much more time. In gymnastics it is a very individual matter. In this sport, mastery not only requires a great deal of hard work and dedication but also a lot of patience. It is important to realize that the better you get and the higher your skill level, the more difficult it is to get rewards which usually become spaced further apart. In the beginning, provided you are doing proper training, things might appear to move along very rapidly, but as the requirements, both physically and mentally, become more challenging, the overnight kind of positive results are usually reduced, despite the hard work. Progress is often more difficult to achieve. If you have grown to expect relatively quick results or if you have overloaded on goals, you may begin to experience the frustration and disappointment that is often the first sign of a potential burnout. At this point the adage, "When the going gets tough the tough get going," may not be enough. That is why realistic, short-term goals are most important.

Summary

To sum up this brief discussion of individual goal setting:

1. Have grand dreams and ambitions, but keep them on the back burner. Don't allow them to dominate your time in and out of the gym. Use them for inspiration when you are down, but not as your only motivation.
2. Set short-term individual goals, both in the training and competitive phases. These should be part of your gym schedule, worked out with the coach and above and beyond overall team goals.

3. From time to time review things to be sure the goals are yours and not only the wishes of others. Personal ownership is extremely important.

4. Keep a written log in your Personal Goals Notebook of your short-term goals on a limited basis by event, daily or weekly. Medium-term goals will take you up to three-six months as a good guide. Record your progress and even make notes about your attitude. Later in your career, you might set some yearlong or "long-term" objectives, but even then don't place all your eggs in one basket or evaluate yourself on the basis of reaching a single "dream" goal.

5. Above all else, do gymnastics for the actual pleasure of the doing, not solely for the imagined rewards at the end of a rainbow. That way each day in the gym will be fun and satisfying.

USING GOAL SETTING AS A COACHING TOOL

Goal setting is a formalized technique which has been used by athletes and coaches for longer than we may know. It is a psychologically oriented device which has been identified by sports psychologists and other researchers as one of the most effective methods for gaining control of motivation and for centering any training effort. It also has carry-over applications for other aspects of life including school and careers. The basic purpose of this article is to suggest to coaches goal setting can also be used in a very direct way in the actual day to day coaching interaction as well as in preparation for competition as a coaching tool.

Establishing Goals

In order to see the implications and use of this approach in coaching, it is first necessary to clearly understand some of the fundamental guidelines that are involved in goal setting behavior. When setting goals, as an aspect of preparing for a workout or specific competition, certain principles need to be followed in order to get the most from this kind of activity. For a full description of these guidelines, see "Goal Setting Guidelines."

- **Ink them, don't merely think them!**
- **Goals should be stated in terms of physical and mental performance objectives, and not ever in terms of outcome.**
- **Goals should be positive and never negative, both in form and content.**
- **Goals should be measurable and specific.**
- **Effective goal setting should involve realistic objectives.**
- **Goals should be primarily short-term in nature, with medium and long-term goals kept in the background.**
- **Goals should be evaluated daily, weekly, and/or monthly.**

Goal Setting in the Coaching Process

Although there are additional principles associated with formal and successful goal setting, the seven general guidelines stated above represent the essential ingredients for this proven activity. It should be recognized that goal setting can involve the establishment of team and/or individual goals, which can be developed week by week or even day by day. This can take place in the coach-gymnast communication system during real time training. With these ideas in mind, consideration can now be given to the direct use of goal setting in the coaching process. This approach will require some additional time and planning by the coach and athlete, but the payoff in the long run will probably be more than worth the effort.

If we accept the premise that the major task in coaching is to facilitate the gymnast's learning of new skills, and the eventual blending of these into an exercise which meets both the technical as well as aesthetic demands of artistic gymnasts, then we also recognize that the coach-gymnast interaction is essential to the teacher-learner model. Although maximum communication will be encouraged, if there is some mutual give and take in the relationship, it will help increase the pace and content of the learning process. A considerable amount of formal research has gone into studying the dynamics involved in the coach-athlete interaction and we share more of this in "The Art of Feedback: A Model for Coach-Gymnast Interaction." It is generally agreed that this teaching model should provide the gymnast performance information that is designed to bring about technical changes in motor response and, at the same time, positive reinforcement directed at maintaining a high level of motivation. The positive reinforcement part of this equation should be given before the gymnast is provided a critique of the actual performance. If one of the major tasks of the coach is to keep control of both the physical and psychological state and the related behavior of the gymnast during training, it is very important that the athletes' psyche be rewarded as close to the moment of desired effort as possible, as this usually makes the gymnast more open and receptive to "hearing" the physical correction.

Examples of Using Goals in Training

The model being suggested in this article takes all of these learning-teaching factors in mind as well as the basics of goal setting and utilizes them in a relatively simple way, while actually coaching. In this model, the coach should present performance information (correction) in the form of a "goal" for the next effort by the gymnast in a particular skill or set of movements. It is very important that the coach provides only one, or perhaps two, physical or mental performance goal for each attempt!. Our research has shown that our coaches tend to use too much verbiage and psychology tells us that too much technical input at one time results in information-overload for the gymnasts. For example, the appropriate goals-oriented approach to coaching on Vault would involve numerous exchanges of verbal feedback such as the following: "That was an excellent run and arm throw" (+RE-positive reinforcement.) "However, there wasn't much pop off the horse. **Your goal** for the next vault is to see your hands on the horse." (Performance information followed by goal setting input.) Continuing with this particular illustration: following the next attempt the coach might say, "Very good effort and the lift was better" (+RE.) "Now on the next one, **your goal** is to continue the push when you see your hands and block through your shoulders." (Information and goal.) For more explanation of using reinforcement see "Behavior Change: Part I & II."

Using this approach in coaching basically involved the setting of a goal by the coach for each subsequent effort made by the gymnast, after the positive reinforcement has been given on whatever event is being trained. The positive reinforcement should not be provided with each effort, but surely should dominate. Giving +RE seventy-five percent of the time (three out of every four efforts) is a good rule of thumb. Continually used during this kind of training would be the phrases that say "The," "Your," or even "Our" goal. In a very short time the gymnast becomes conditioned to this type of feedback and will eventually ask questions in related terms—"What should my goal be in the next turn?" This method also enables the coach to confirm what learning is taking place and how aware the gymnast is of the progressive learning curve. The coach, for example, can periodically ask the gymnast, "What do you think your goal should be on the next attempt?" This not only opens communication, but it also provides some measure of how much internalization of performance information is taking place. In addition, it gives the gymnast practice in goal setting for what can be valuable self-coaching. Encouraging personal goal setting can also make the coach's goals easier to attain. See the article on "My Goal is to… A Gymnast's Plan" to assist your gymnasts in developing their own goals and being responsible for them.

Goals for Workouts and Meets

A further advantage of coaching through the use of goal setting is that the process can be applied at all levels of training in terms of specific events, compulsory/ optional, actual competitions, conditioning, and all other aspects of training. It can be made as simple or complex as the individual gymnasts can tolerate. It also provides for consistency in coaching input, which is critical for the maximum development of potential.

The "ink it, don't just think it" principle of goal setting should be stressed and utilized in this approach. Assuming a six-day a week workout schedule, a brief meeting with the gymnast(s) on Saturday afternoon at the completion of the workout can be used for this worthwhile purpose. Goals can be mutually discussed and developed for the coming week, involving mental and physical performance objectives (including work volume) and previously set goals can be re-evaluated to determine the success ratio of the prior week's training effort. But don't forget to record them so both you and the gymnasts can see the progress occurring daily and weekly and reward the gymnasts for a job well done..

Conclusion

Using goals and setting goals as a coaching tool is a real challenge as this article indicates. The long range results in terms of both coach/gymnast interaction and the overall productiveness of the workout is worth the extra effort required. The motivation achieved through this method would most likely be very difficult to generate to the same degree by any other technique.

TOP 10 TIPS TO GOAL SETTING

When setting goals as an aspect of preparing for a workout or specific competition, certain principles need to be followed in order to benefit the most from this important activity. The tips can be used by the gymnasts for setting personal goals and the coach can use them to facilitate workouts and competitions, for setting team goals and helping each gymnast reach their own goals. The tips are presented as a handy guide and you can find the principles fully outlined in our article "Goal Setting Guidelines." Here are a few of our favorite tips for the coach and athlete in effectively setting personal and team goals.

Goal Setting Tips

1. **Ink them, don't merely think them!**
2. **Goals should be stated in terms of physical performance objectives.**
3. **Goals should include mental performance objectives.**
4. **Goals should never be stated in terms of outcome!**
5. **Goals should be measurable and specific.**
6. **Goals should involve realistic objectives.**
7. **Goals should primarily be short-term in nature.**
8. **Long-term/dream goals should generally be reserved for the more experienced competitor.**
9. **Goals should be positive and never negative, both in form and content.**
10. **Goals should be evaluated daily, weekly, monthly and seasonally.**

Chapter Nine

Psycho/Physical Training

Many of the papers in this section are written primarily for the athlete with some for the coaches. Everyone should find them interesting as they deal with the mental/ emotional aspect of training with specific recommendations given for certain events. The first article provides the new young competitor the basics on warming-up their bodies as well as their minds, whereas, the article on developing and training routines is geared towards the experienced competitor. Dealing with the frustration of conditioning and how to handle it are also discussed. The article, "On the Beam: A Gymnast's Guide to Staying There" was well received at the time of original publication. Over five hundred gymnasts sent letters describing problems they were having with the event. We hope you can gather some insight to help you with any issues on beam as well and have included a handy tip sheet to help keep you on track.

- Notes for Beginners: Physical and Mental Warm-Up
- "Conditioning…It's so Frustrating!"
- Using Non-Verbal Art Forms to Facilitate Training
- On the Beam: A Gymnast's Guide for Staying There
- Top 19 Tips to "Staying on the Beam"
- A Psycho/Physical Guide to Training Full Routines

NOTES FOR BEGINNERS
PHYSICAL AND MENTAL WARM-UP

One of the most important things you will ever learn in gymnastics is the art of warming up, and it is an art. It takes patience, but it's well worth the time, for the ranks of prematurely retired gymnasts are littered with youngsters who were careless about their warm-up and sustained serious injury. Our bodies are a beautiful and complex network of systems which interrelate and affect each other and it takes some tender loving care to get ourselves ready to do hard work.

Physical Warm-up

Each joint, each muscle group, along with the cardiovascular system (heart, lungs, etc.) must be progressively brought up to peak efficiency before the actual hard training begins. Our muscle system must be warmed up properly. Ligaments and small and large muscles all need to be stretched gradually so they are elastic enough to cope with the strains that will soon follow. They must be ready to respond as needed. I have seen girls come into the gym and immediately drop into a split position without the slightest preliminary warm-up or stretch; such a youngster is looking for trouble. A torn hamstring or groin muscle is very painful and can take many months to repair. In addition, we need to have the flow of our blood in our cardiovascular system maximized so that it can do the job of providing oxygen and rapidly carrying off impurities which are produced during stress. This is how we can build strength endurance. In order for this to occur our heart must be working considerable faster and harder.

So, how do we go about this important warm-up? Every gymnast and coach develops her own set of exercises which should include aerobic activities which gets the heart pumping and the blood flowing throughout the body. This can be in the form of dance, calisthenics, jogging, rope jumping on floor and beam and/or trampoline work. This is usually followed up with total body stretches. Sometimes this work is done alone, sometimes with another gymnast and often in a group setting.

Mental Warm-up

Not only do the parts of our bodies need to be carefully warmed up, but the entire entity must be "awake" as a whole unit. Research has shown that it takes human beings a few hours to completely shake off a heavy sleep. Your body needs time to be both mentally and physically alert. One of the reasons that most gymnastic training takes place in the afternoon or evening, besides school schedules, is that we have been up a long time and are usually fully awake although we may be tired! There is a difference. We have known world class athletes who are due to compete in the early morning who have gotten up at 3 or 4 a.m. to begin the warm-up procedure. In fact, once you begin competing you will find that many competitions begin early in the morning. You don't have to worry about this now, but it is good practice to work out in the morning from time to time, such as weekends, just for the experience. You will feel a real difference from afternoon workouts, particularly if you begin shortly after getting up! (Of course, you also need time for a sound breakfast to replenish your fuel supply and time for this meal to digest). Your coach will make sure you get this practice in due time.

Along with the need to warm-up your body, it is important to warm up yourself from a psychological point of view as well. As your physical warm-up begins to take hold and you "feel" better, your overall attitude improves. The body and mind work together. If you approach your physical warm-up as drudgery, it will not have the same payoff attitudinally as it would if you recognized and believed in the true value of the relatively boring thirty minutes you were about to spend stretching. Lots of girls want to get at the "fun," that is, begin to tumble immediately or start to work on the apparatus. That's one approach, but I can assure you that it is not the correct way to get better at your gymnastics. If you are committed to the warm-up after a short time, you will feel your body energized and that pleasure and your mental gratification over it are interrelated.

If you load the deck in your favor from the very beginning by approaching each aspect of the workout with a positive attitude you will reap the most benefits from your effort. There are some very specific things you can do to train your mind for your workout. For example, going over your moves or exercise in your mind (idiomatic training) is a proven method of helping you concentrate on the task at hand. It is most important to enjoy the feeling of your mind and body working together to achieve perfection, rather than becoming preoccupied with the errors you are making. Learning takes time and patience. Beginners need to know this early in the game.

Everyone has a bad day from time to time. It is the kind of day where nothing you try works and it is most frustrating. Very often the situation deteriorates as you continue and in a short time the tears begin to flow. With experience you will learn how to control this, but you should remember that emotion is natural and healthy, providing it does not block your ability to be rational about your endeavors. A careful analysis of many of these situations almost always reveals some predictors; they are usually evident in the warm-up period. That is why it is so important to approach this time with a clear mind and some enthusiasm. Some gymnasts give into the "bad day" problem, others are motivated to struggle even harder. Some people function best with pressure which comes from within or from without in the presence of the coach or peers and only with time will you discover how you operate best. Allow yourself this luxury of self-discovery. Related to the notion of warm-up is the equally dreaded conditioning. See the article "Conditioning… It's So Frustrating!" for help with understanding and dealing with feelings surrounding all aspects of warming-up and conditioning.

"CONDITIONING... IT'S SO FRUSTRATING!"

How many times has a gymnast said, "But coach...it's so frustrating." It is pretty certain that almost every boy or girl who has taken an interest in gymnastics and trained seriously in the sport has felt frustrated in the gym from time to time and probably said so to the coach, fellow gymnasts, and parents. The dictionary tells us that to be frustrated means to feel defeat, discouragement, and that you are working at something very hard without good results. Very often an insecure feeling goes along with frustration. Thinking about gymnastics, which we all know is a very difficult sport; feelings of frustration are to be expected and are a natural part of the whole training experience.

How many times have you heard about the importance of the fifth event for girls and the seventh event for boys—namely, "conditioning?" Those gymnasts willing to face considerable frustration during this "basic training" part of their gymnastics from the very beginning of their careers can minimize the amount of frustration they will have to deal with as they progress through the sport towards their potential. Hard, long, and faithful conditioning is not as much fun as doing back somersaults on the floor or kips on the bars, but in the long run it is probably more important. It is through conditioning that the body and mind are made ready for specific training in the events. Conditioning provides one of the **"basic foundations"** upon which gymnasts build their collection of new skills and eventually their competitive routines.

Understanding Frustration

There are some things that can be done to help frustrated gymnasts deal with the feeling and even reduce the problem in the future. First of all, you need to remember that frustration is a natural part of all learning in and out of the gym. Surely in school many young people have had the same kind of feelings about certain subjects, teachers, or homework assignments. Some psychologists believe that frustration is the basic reason that learning begins in the first place. When a baby cries, it is a first expression of frustration. The crying is usually happening when the baby has a need that isn't being met and, because it has no language in the early years, the crying is how it makes its feelings known. Child development specialists believe that infants begin to form a mental picture of the person (mother) or thing (bottle) that is usually seen as meeting the need. This "imagining" allows the baby to put off getting what it wants right away. These beginning "thoughts" are really brought on by the frustration that the infant feels.

Some people really get upset when frustrated and can display very bad tempers or bursts of anger. When this happens they usually lose their ability to think clearly and things often get worse. Other people get down in the dumps when frustration comes their way and depression makes it hard for them to continue in the activity they are doing with much success. Still other individuals find that they are doing so with much success. Others find that frustration helps them work even harder and spurs them on with an increased effort. As with most things in life, it is an individual matter and depends, in part, on how such frustrating situations were handled when they were growing up. What is important to keep in mind is that frustration is as natural in life as breathing itself.

Controlling Frustration in the Gym

Athletes can, however, have some control in the matter as well as choice as to when and how much frustration they are going to allow in their training. In our sport, most frustration occurs around learning a new skill and/or building a competitive routine. However, in order to learn the new skills you must have the proper strength, flexibility and endurance to even accomplish the move. Of course, there are different frustrations such as trouble with your coach, scores you receive, and others but the frustration of learning new moves is most common and fundamental in gymnastics. No matter how good you are a certain amount of difficulty or blocked desire is always going to take place during the learning process. However, gymnasts who are willing to face considerable frustration earlier in their careers can reduce the amount they have to face when it comes to dealing with high level tricks and exercises later on.

It is in this area of conditioning that the gymnast has an opportunity to gain some control over frustration.

- One is to decide to skip certain building blocks (or cheat on them if the coach isn't watching) and try to force the body into things it is not prepared to manage. This choice will leave more time for "fun things," but will eventually create high frustration when things don't come easily or at all, because of a lack of good preparation.
- A second option is to spend the large amount of necessary and often grueling time needed to get the mind and body ready. This choice requires a lot of self-discipline and patience. It also can be frustrating because it is often repetitious and rarely exciting.
- Since either choice has built-in, unavoidable frustrations, the gymnasts need to ask themselves if they want to have the frustrating experience at a beginning

point in their training or later when, having neglected to prepare properly, they find themselves progressing very slowly and painfully or coming to a complete standstill. It doesn't take a great deal of wisdom to figure out which is the most sensible choice.

The frustration felt when conditioning can be reduced as the gymnast realizes that the effort has benefits and a payoff in their non-conditioning time on the events. There are also things that can be done to make the "extra" event more enjoyable and challenging. Personal accomplishment journals, schedules with goals, self-vs.-self contests, and encouraging personal slogans are some examples. On the other hand, the frustration felt at a later point in the gymnast's career and training is much more difficult to cope with, since it is unlikely that any amount of effort or repetition will be successful if the basic readiness has been skipped or neglected. There is little that can be done to make those frustrating experiences less painful, because the unprepared gymnast is simply not ready to master what is required. In most cases, it is necessary to go back and fill in the gaps. Few gymnasts enjoy that kind of chore. Keeping a personal log of failed attempts is surely a lot less rewarding in the long run than keeping a record of push-ups done, laps completed, or other drills finished.

It takes real staying power to follow a tough daily conditioning program in gymnastics. Gymnasts are tempted to slack off on the conditioning schedule and need to be helped to keep on target. We have heard young gymnasts complain to their coaches that they are not "up" for their drills or could they skip it "just for today?" The answer must be a firm and definite no! The only exceptions to the rule are determined by coaches and would need to involve the limiting nature of injuries or the highly specialized work that is done prior to competitions by those gymnasts who are getting ready to compete.

This type of training program can't be left to chance but needs to be planned in advance, including all participants right down to tiny tots on very beginning teams. The major responsibility for seeing that this conditioning takes place rests with the coach. Some gymnasts are so inspired and dedicated that they hardly ever need to be reminded about the importance of these exercises, but they are usually in the minority. If you ask a very good gymnast how they managed the self-discipline needed to work on this part of their overall gymnastics you will discover that many feel it is due to the fact that early in their careers, the importance of this activity was stressed by a coach who really felt it was important, rather than just saying so. These coaches motivate their gymnasts by stressing how the physical readiness affects mental readiness, and therefore make the learning of gymnastic skills easier and less frustrating.

Practical Suggestions for Gymnasts

In closing our discussion of frustration, the following suggestions are made to gymnasts:

1. **The number one recommendation is obvious: prepare, prepare, prepare!** When you feel like shortcutting your conditioning, resist the urge with all your strength. This includes all your flexibility, strength, and endurance training as well as any other the coach has developed.

2. **Think of your conditioning as an actual event.** Give it as much attention and hard work as you would the apparatus training. Remind yourself that in the long run, the payoff will outweigh the frustration of the daily conditioning routine.

3. **When you hit a snag in getting a skill, go over the demands of the move.** Talk with your coach to see if there is something special you can do to help get the trick, i.e. in terms of further conditioning. Don't be afraid to back up and maybe leave the skill for the time being while you do some additional work. This is not a negative step, but in fact a very positive action on your part.

4. **Remember that you will experience frustration no matter how hard you work on your preparation.** It is a matter of degree or how much you experience that counts. When this frustration is felt, have patience and stick with it because most things worthwhile involve periods of insecurity and dissatisfaction and take time to master.

5. **Try to stay in control of your reactions to frustration.** This is often easier said than done. Getting your emotions in line is really an individual matter. Everyone has a different threshold for taking frustration just as they do for tension and pain. Blowing your top is usually not helpful, although for some kids, that's exactly what needs to happen in order to go on. Or perhaps a good cry is all it takes. If this is the case for you, try to do it in private and avoid embarrassment. Never let such displays become a habit. See the article "Abuses of Anger in the Gym" to help keep your frustration under control.

6. **Make a real effort to separate out those things that you are really ready for and can do from those things you "want to do."** You simply may not be quite physically ready for a given skill at a given time. This does not make you a "bad gymnast" and eventually you will succeed. When you can do something and are ready for it physically, but won't go for it, you need to work with your coach on psychological preparation and self-confidence. When you want to do something, but are not physically ready (and usually that means not mentally ready either), then you need to focus more on your

physical preparation. They are all related, but each takes a little different tactic or strategy to overcome. This is where proper goal setting can become real important. Refer to the article "My Goal is to...-A Gymnast's Plan" to help you set goals so you will be mentally and physically prepared.

7. **Don't be afraid of challenging yourself.** Taking just one small step at a time beyond your endurance while you are working on your conditioning may reap great benefits. Chances are, you won't faint and this is a good way to see where you are, establish new goals, get a feel for your mental attitude and often reduce your frustrations if any are bothering you at the time.

8. **Talk to your coach and fellow gymnasts.** Talk about your feelings of frustration when appropriate if they're not apparent to everyone! It helps to find out that you are not alone in this regard and you might learn some ways from the experiences of others that you can apply to yourself.

Summary

The kind of frustration that goes along with stretching, strength training, endurance building, and overall conditioning is very real, but also quite different than that felt later when trying to learn a new skill results in little success despite the effort. Gymnasts who don't take this part of their training seriously and try to bug out and avoid the frustration of hard conditioning may seem to be having more "fun" at times, but they are short-changing themselves and setting the stage for real disappointment when they are frustrated in their efforts to progress later on. The smart choice should be clear and it is rarely too late to get on the right track and begin even if you have not up to this point.

USING NON-VERBAL ART FORMS TO FACILITATE TRAINING

Gymnastics is an art form which utilizes non-verbal communication to get its point across to the public. One of Webster's definitions for communication is, "A process by which meanings are exchanged between individuals through a common system of symbols." Communication can be at a wordless, affective level as well as at a verbal, intellectual level.

If we agree that the exercise in gymnastics is to communicate something to an audience (and judges, technically), then perhaps we could borrow from some other artistic endeavors that have the same purpose, such as music. In terms of creating and composing gymnastics exercises on the various apparatus including trampoline and some of the other disciplines, one could conceptualize the objective of routine work through reference to another art form and that the analogy could be extended to the framework of non-verbal communication in general.

Exploring Various Art Forms

The following is an exercise in using various art forms to facilitate creativity in the training of young gymnasts and is especially useful in the development of routines. It consists of discussing art forms such as music, painting, and verbal communication as the gymnasts experiment with movement, dance, and eventually whole routines. The youngster's reactions and responses to these exercises have been most intriguing and we thought we would use this paper to share it with coaches who might wish to engage in a similar venture. Applied psychological research has proven beyond a doubt that intellectual discussions involving the sport one participates in can, and often do, improve actual performance. Esoteric as it may sound, it has some remarkable practical applications.

The initial theme is that the gymnastic performance, besides being indicative of many hours of hard work designed to achieve mastery and competence, is also a vehicle for saying something about the performer and about his/her interpretation of an art modality. In the case of gymnastics, the modality is human body movement in total. As you begin your discussion of creativity and performance, the youngsters themselves will begin to draw comparisons not only from music, but also art and even language structure itself.

Exercises for Exploration

The following exercises to facilitate creativity can be used in a variety of gymnastics disciplines. Here are some ideas which cover composition, tempo, notation, synaesthesia, and structure and language:

- **Composition.** There are some interesting questions to ponder. Ask the gymnasts, "What makes a great musical piece impressive? What shapes and gives the end product the composer's or musicians' personal impact?" With music as a point of reference identify some of those things that contribute to a memorable composition. There are many notations and symbols in music which can easily be related to gymnastic work and, you may want to begin with specific events, such as balance beam performances. Have the gymnasts explore movement and dance on the beam or on the floor while thinking of a particular piece of music.

- **Tempo.** The first concept to discuss is that of tempo. "What is to be the pace of the work?" We recognize that many good compositions involved a change of tempo or key. "How do we achieve this in gymnastics? What should the timing of these changes be? How and when do we move from one to the other, (note, color, or skill)? What do we want the tempo to communicate?" Have the gymnast practice changing the tempo of one of their beam or floor ex passes.

- **Notation.** A second notion to develop has to do with how emphasis and interest is achieved within each tempo that is selected. In music there are notations that tell the artists to play the piece "loud," "with feeling," "softly," "to build up," "sharply," "play large," etc. The same enrichment of composition can be achieved through body tones and movement variation. For example, the subtle body wave followed by a dramatic leap, the graceful poise accented by a sharp movement of the arms, the raising and lowering of the body alignment as we move along the beam, the unexpected focus; all of these build "character" into the exercise.

- **Synaesthesia.** The youngsters can easily bring out ideas about their own work when thinking about it in terms of another form they are familiar with but not necessarily as direct performers. The connections between this and their own physical efforts become clearer for them in reference to another modality—in this case, sound and hearing. They also begin to speak of the images they have when listening to music—an interesting expression of the biological and psychological fusion of sensory modalities that we tend to overlook in gymnastics. We know that some people see a color when hearing a tone—this phenomenon is called "synaesthesia." We could utilize such perceptions in gymnastic training so play around with color as well as assigning a mood or a feeling to the color. Such as if you think and see the color blue does it remind you of cold and ice. Similarly, the color yellow may feel like daisies blowing in the warm sun. Shaping a gymnastic exercise and performing a musical composition can be closely connected in the mind.

- **Structure and Language.** Continue the discussion/ training with the young gymnasts extending it further into the area of music but also painting and other forms of aesthetic human expression. It can be continued to a more concrete experience for everyone—that of spoken language. Talk about the structure of our own speech and the meanings of such grammatical ideas as periods, commas, explanation points, question marks, etc., related to their use to the "gymnastic sentence" or exercise. "Where does the gymnast wish to emphasize a movement with an explanation point, where do we want to pause, (place our commas), how do we pass from one thought to another, as translated to working the beam?"

One thing most gymnasts all agree on is that there should rarely be any "question marks" in an exercise, no doubts, no lack of confident punctuation, and no statement that says, "You tell me." The end result should be a sentence, a paragraph, a sonnet, a poem, a routine, which expresses something important about the content and also about the individual communicating to others through the gymnastic performance. As for the female gymnasts, you may be interested in the article "On the Beam: A Gymnast's Guide for Staying There" to help you perfect such a "sonnet" with your routine.

Coaches, you may be surprised how such an intellectual venture with your gymnasts can have an unexpected payoff in their overall mental training. Consider that experimentation in one art form may end with some applications that can be carried over to other aspects of their training. A footnote: You may be surprised to come into the gym and notice that the gymnasts are making up gymnastic "sentences" and trying to guess what their teammates are "saying!"

ON THE BEAM
A GYMNAST'S GUIDE
FOR STAYING THERE

Let's face it girls, the balance beam is a tough event. It is beautiful to look at, but definitely a tricky challenge. Much of our mail from individual gymnasts involves questions about problems they are having on the beam. Most coaches recognize that competitions are often won or lost depending on the team's performance in this event. It turns out this is often the case for individual all-around honors as well. The basic reason is that beam is the highest risk event for major breaks and 0.5 deduction falls. Just one of these can do the trick when it comes to the magic score. It's tough to fall off the floor and vaulting is over quickly, as is the uneven bars, but the beam makes 1 min 10sec to 1 min 30sec seem like forever. There you are, elevated from the ground about 49 inches and moving around on a four inch log! It stays still, but the gymnast doesn't. Doing what is required and balancing at the same time is a most difficult job indeed.

Coaches, judges, and gymnasts alike seem to agree that the beam is the most psychological of the events. We have spent a lot of time watching gymnasts of all ability work the beam and have asked hundreds of questions of them and of coaches. We have pulled together some ideas that might be worth thinking about and might help you reduce the number of times you mount and dismount during this one event! There has been some formal research done into this very area. Some of our suggestions come from that work, but most come from people who have had a lot of experience under fire. Several may overlap, but we offer them separately for easier reading.

1. **The very best way to improve on the beam is to spend time on it.** We don't mean just standing there feeling it under your feet, but working and working hard every practice. There is simply no substitute for actual time output on the beam in terms of improving your stay-on ratio. Drilling on a line on the floor, etc., is fine and dandy, but it is not the same. Personally, we feel that beam requires the most time and should be treated in a special way when you plan your workout schedule. Actually training on the beam, not just doing difficult routines but drill work as well, cannot be over-emphasized. Besides routine counts, there is another way you can think about your work volume on the beam. Lots of people walk or jog one, two or even three miles a day and think nothing of it. On the beam you have to make approximately 330 passes up and down the length of the beam to walk just one mile. Allowing for about five seconds a pass (and that's darn fast) it would take roughly 27 minutes of continuous movement without a rest or break to make the magic mile. Surely walking one mile a day on beam is a reasonable goal so you can

see, leaving time for rest, bobbles, and the fact that you're not just walking but doing tricks, and you will need about hour on beam at the very least. You can get away with less, but your ability to master this event will be in proportion to the amount of time you put in on it.

2. **Make sure you understand the basic technical demands for staying on.** This is the stuff coaching is made of and we are sure your trainer will make you aware of these but mentally you must be more than aware. These factors must be part of your psychological set and be constantly in your consciousness. Keeping your body in line, eye spotting, shoulders down-necks long, heads up, rear pulled under, tight body, but flexible mind, up on the balls of your feet, etc.—all these should be part of your thinking and be monitored as you work beam. By the way, staying on the balls of your feet serves two purposes; besides impression, it will help you control your body better in an emergency. If you have always trained well up on your toes, then when you do a movement which requires a flat foot or are forced into such a position by a misbalance you will find that your toes are like a small vice grabbing hold of the beam edge. This can really make a difference in your efforts.

3. **Think positive-think straight!** This is easier to say than to do. Before beginning your beam workout, it is a good idea to have a little private conversation with yourself. Stand at the end of the beam and look at the space you will soon occupy. Beam is becoming more like Floor-Ex (theatre in the square) squeezed long and narrow. Get your mind thinking rhythmically. Think about a feeling of lift and dignified carriage. Think that your upper torso is part of the beam, an extension of it, and that you're proud of yourself and what your beautiful body is doing. For the beginner this is not an easy attitude to come by, for you may spend more time getting back on after falling off than you do walking on the beam. You have to start somewhere and be patient. Slowly, but surely, a good attitude about the event will move you toward the accomplishment and sense of control you want on beam but don't believe you can achieve. We have known many girls who talk themselves out of it before they really start. One fall and they are certain that the beam is going to be lousy. Get those notions out of your head immediately!

4. **Use your internal ruler—The "4 inch theory."** There are a couple of interesting ideas around about thinking straight, another important psychological mind set when on beam. We can call this the "4 inch theory"—it would appear that the human body has a couple of built-in measuring sticks that can help on this event. The distance between the bottom part of a person's rib cage (except for very young kids) as well as from the corners of the eyes (across bridge of nose) is approximately 4 inches. There is variation, of course, but essentially it

comes close to the width of the beam. In other words you have a kind of ruler you can use to help keep you in line. If you keep the beam lined up with that rib cage and with the space between the corners of your eyes you can maintain a better alignment. If you try hard enough, you can actually "feel" it work.

5. **Attend to the task and concentrate with all your psychological energy.** No other event takes such sustained attention. You must block out all unimportant sounds and use only the clues you have used to train with. A lot of practice will help with this, as it will make certain aspects of the routine almost automatic. It is not that you want to get into a hypnotic trance, because it is important to be alert and ready for the unexpected. However, you want to be so into the set you're doing that nothing short of an explosion (and maybe not even that) can distract you from the work. Some coaches talk to their gymnasts while they are on the beam. That is fine and you will find that over time you can hear your coach's voice and single-word cues over other louder sounds because of something called selective listening. This should not break your basic concentration. When on the beam, that's where you are, nowhere else. Don't look around to see who is watching, who came into the gym, or for any other reason. Get lost in your work. Some girls talk quietly to themselves while they work and even hum a song or whistle while concentrating. Obviously, you can carry this too far but contrary to some opinion this can help certain people concentrate by providing them an additional internal focus. Try to feel the beat of the movements you are doing and the rhythm of your body in the exercise as we discuss in "Using Non-verbal Art Forms to Facilitate Training." Take things one step at a time. Don't think ahead to the dismount or upcoming move, but put all your attention into the move at hand. How often have you seen a gymnast complete a "big" move only to fall on a very simple element? Reason: usually a break in concentration caused by psychological relief that the previous difficult trick was successful completed. Moral: you can't let down on concentration, ever!

6. **Allow time for difficult drills that your coach assigns in practice.** These should include jump and leap sequences, turns, side spotting and eye focus work while on the beam. Walking the beam with body and arm variation is also time well spent. Cutting down on the number of jumps or leaps needed to cover the length of the beam or increasing the number of full turns you can do from one end to the other is also the kind of worthwhile activity that will help steady you and make for better performance.

7. **Strive for perfection of the movements you have planned for your routine.** Nothing should be random—every finger, arm, head and body position should be planned out. Obviously, conditions will lead to numerous

variations, usually involuntary, but in practice as well as the meet, you want it to be perfect. If it isn't, repeat the move just done until it is right. Sloppiness is not to be tolerated. This requires a great deal of self-discipline for the coach can't watch all your work all the time. It is up to you. If you accept less than correct work in practice you will be shortchanging yourself and the price tag will surely go up in a competition in this event.

8. **Make every reasonable effort to stay on when you're off-balance.** Every gymnast has balance problems, but you should have the idea and the mindset that when the unsteady moment occurs, you will not let yourself simply give up and come off. We have seen many girls, for example, execute a back handspring and land fairly in line, but the upper torso is perhaps slightly off and instead of making an effort the save the skill and counterbalance, they just get off immediately and jump back on again. That's what is called an unforgivable give-away! There are limits to the notion of struggling to stay on—hanging upside down under the beam with arms and legs wrapped around the beam is ridiculous. Not only does it look bad, but also the clock is moving until you hit the ground. If a move really goes, let it go and get on with the routine. At least, however don't quit when a simple adjustment could have saved the day. Again, this needs to be practiced, not just as a part of meet behavior.

9. **Work the beam with the same footwear you plan to wear during a meet.** It is amazing how many good gymnasts use the "feel" of the beam to help them keep oriented and develop greater steadiness. It makes sense to practice in a consistent way when it comes to what is on your feet. Barefoot, or whatever; just keep it the same when you practice as when you compete.

10. **Work the beam up at competition height, whenever possible.** Naturally, there are things that can and should be worked on the lower beam. They are excellent for helping you get confidence in a new skill you are working. When it comes to actual routine training work, you should spend your time working the beam at regulation height. There is research that indicates with strong validity that figure-ground adjustment, even for experienced performers, is not easy. The more you are practiced at competitive "altitude," the better will be your chances of keeping balanced while moving along a stable, narrow surface.

11. **Use your "beam temperature" effectively.** Each gymnast seems to have a personal threshold in terms of the number of warm-up routines needed to be functioning on all cylinders; some get there after two and others may take more to really get clicking. Although the number of routines is important, ultimately it is the quality of those sets that counts. In the end, the one that

matters most is the one you do in the meet —that is what you are working towards. This is another reason for a great deal of practice on beam—to find out what your minimum and maximum "beam temperature" is for your best production.

12. **Learn to breathe properly executing a full routine.** Breath control is very important on all events and beam is no exception. As a matter of fact, poor breath control or holding the breath can cause a little bit of instability and even dizziness, a condition we surely do not want on balance beam. By systematically ventilating your lungs with fresh air, your brain functions best and your control is maximized as is your endurance. This is not a matter of fancy, but of medical fact. Once again, proper breathing does not happen by accident. It has to be planned and practiced.

13. **Don't hold back; express yourself confidently.** Although you want to stay on the beam, you don't want to do so because of modest delivery, but as a result of having perfected your routine. Over cautious exercises stick out like a sore thumb—they lack pace and confidence. When you work beam, go for your movements all the way. Although high leaps or jumps may be scary, they are impressive and dramatic. Believe it or not, they are also easier to manage than a little dinky leap where your body is airborne for a split second, making it difficult to position your feet and body correctly for a solid landing. Constantly remember you are selling your routine. Make it big, put it out, and show it off. Don't get preoccupied about falling off because then, you surely will. Instead, keep the positive attitude we talked about earlier going and move it! As usual this takes practice too. See the article "A Gymnast's Guide to Demonstrating Confidence" for more tips.

14. **Practice mental and physical recovery behavior at all times.** We're not just talking about physical, but also psychological, regrouping. If you have a major/minor break, practice as if in competition, saving the move and going ahead in an unflustered way. Don't get so angry with yourself should you fall off that you can no longer think straight and get lost in your thoughts about the break. If you allow a mistake to blow your mind, it could lead to a collapse of the rest of your effort. It is important to get it out of your head and continue; perhaps even with a slight smile that expresses the attitude —"that can happen to anyone, the difference is, Watch me, now!" Relaunch your attack full blast.

15. **It is psychologically very important to have a sure mount on the beam.** This does not necessarily mean an easy one but one that you do close to 100% of the time successfully. There is nothing more demoralizing than to fall off

on your mount before you have begun your presentation. You end up owing a half point and this can really affect your concentration for the remainder of the routine. For experienced gymnasts, the risk may be worth it and they often will attempt a very tough skill that is not quite mastered. Most gymnasts such as these, however, are able to forget an opening break and go on like gangbusters. This is usually not the case with less experienced athletes. A good start is very important in all the events, but on a beam a positive, confident opening not only gets the judges attention, but gets your mind in a positive groove early.

16. **Put yourself under a certain amount of pressure in practice.** At least several times a week, or whatever your coach has assigned, work your sets with the stop watch. Have the coach or a teammate help with this. This is how it is going to be in a meet and recreating the sound of "warning" and "time" will help you pace yourself and to recover efficiently if you make a mistake. Keep track of your times and set goals to see how you are doing – how consistent you are working. Along the same lines, compete with yourself and keep a record of how you're doing – successful completions, errors, etc. Strive for the top expression and amplitude you are capable of and reward yourself when you're doing a good job. We don't mean have a candy bar, but say to yourself, "pretty good job," "nice routine," "coming along well," etc. It is not crazy to do this. It is a very sound way of keeping your motivation up, and offer critical, but supportive self-evaluation. Your coach will also be doing this (we hope) and so will teammates. The more you rely on self-management the better. See the article "Goal Setting Guidelines" to help set your goals for skills as well as routines.

17. **Set your goals and do whatever it takes to get better on this event.** Establish and set your individual goals for each workout and meet. Know what you need to do to get to the next level in your performance. Have a personal plan and do what you and your coach feels will make you a better performer on beam. See the article "My Goal is to… A Gymnast's Plan" for help in setting these important goals.

18. **Talk with teammates, read about it, and ask questions of your coaches.** Ask questions, read what top gymnasts are saying, and share ideas about beam with teammates and work together. For example, encourage "no fall" in your group when rotating to a specific event. Discipline yourselves with required routine repeats for falls (e.g. two additional routines for each broken set). If you are at a meet and see a really great beam performer, watch her carefully. This is a good way to learn. What has she got that you can actually see? Don't let a good performance get you down but look for ways to improve your

routine. However, don't do this too close to your own performance as you will need time to get into the proper frame of mind before your own performance.

19. **Remember—some days you can't make a thing!** If you're having one of those terrible days on beam when nothing you do works and you simply can't stay on no matter how hard you try—then STOP! Nothing will be gained from practicing poor execution and your mental attitude will probably get worse if you have given it a fair shake. Walk away, take a rest, talk to your coach about it and maybe return at a later time. Also remember that if you have a very bad head cold or sinus infection, your inner ear (site of balance control) may be affected, so it might be wise to work a bit less on such days as well.

TOP 19 TIPS TO "STAYING ON THE BEAM"

The most psychological of all the events for women's artistic gymnastics is balance beam. Let's face it girls, the beam is a tricky challenge. Coaches, judges, and gymnasts alike seem to agree that competitions are often won or lost depending on the individual's or team's performance in this event. For the full description of these tips see "On the Beam: A Gymnast's Guide for Staying There."

Staying on the Beam Tips

1. The very best way to improve on the beam is to spend time on it.
2. Make sure you understand the basic technical demands for staying on the beam.
3. Think positive-think straight!
4. Use your internal ruler—The "4 inch theory."
5. Attend to the task and concentrate with all your psychological energy.
6. Allow time for difficult drills that your coach assigns in practice.
7. Strive for perfection of the movements you have planned for your routine.
8. Make every reasonable effort to stay on when you're off-balance.
9. Work the beam with the same footwear you plan to wear during a meet.
10. Work the beam up at competition height, whenever possible.
11. Use your "beam temperature" effectively.
12. Learn to breathe properly executing a full routine.
13. Don't hold back; express yourself confidently.
14. Practice mental and physical recovery behavior at all times.
15. It is psychologically very important to have a sure mount on the beam.
16. Put yourself under a certain amount of pressure in practice.
17. Set your goals and do whatever it takes to get better on this event.
18. Talk with teammates, read about it, and ask questions of your coaches.
19. Remember—some days you can't make a thing!

A PSYCHO/PHYSICAL GUIDE TO TRAINING FULL ROUTINES

The two-way street connection between physical coaching that goes on with a gymnast and the positive functioning of the athlete's mind has often been stressed as most important. This is certainly the case when talking about the training needed to prepare for a masterful execution of complete gymnastic routines on the various events. From time to time it is necessary to discuss topics in our articles that might be considered to have a direct bearing on actual coaching.

There is a concept in psychology called in Latin, "pars pro toto" which deals with the relationship and importance of parts (pars) to the total gestalt or whole (toto). Numerous authors have talked about the importance of progressive learning in an environment where positive reinforcement and encouragement is provided for both effort and accomplishment. Individual steps toward eventual mastery, taken one at a time in a supportive setting, are probably the basic key for all sound learning. This idea carries with it the built-in notion of patience and psychological endurance, or staying power, as well as planned, motor-skill training and strength development on the physical level.

Assuming that the factors stated above, progressive learning and a positive climate, are present in a training situation for better or worse, it is worthwhile to take a look at the actual preparation of routines for competition. This is a special task that gymnasts and coaches must eventually face, although many would prefer to stick with the doing of "fun" parts and avoid putting it all together as long as possible. Unfortunately, this labor is often put off too long and the result is a very shaky and exhausting performance at best with little real chance of success in competition.

It really doesn't take much to show off an easy skill which you have mastered, but it is a very different matter to go from beginning to end with a full routine with obvious confidence, flair, and physical endurance. Training to do complete routines requires a special **"mental attitude"** as compared to simply doing isolated tricks. If you are still in the stage of developing sequences and series, then see the article "My Goal is to…" A Gymnast's Plan" for steps to get you closer to performing routines.

There are a number of approaches that can be taken to routine training and the one focused upon in this article is surely not the only way to go. It is, however, sound from both a physical, as well as a psychological, point of view and coaches who have used it find that it works pretty well in most cases.

Movement Mastery

First, it has to be assumed that the individual parts (skills) contained in the exercise have been pretty well mastered. Just what "mastered" means is an individual matter for gymnasts and coaches. At the very least it implies that a skill is being executed technically correct more often than not. Ideally, mastery would mean a 100 percent accuracy and completion model. Since we all live and work in a world of imperfection, and surely the gymnastic experience has more uncertainty and risks than many other sport activities, for the sake of this discussion, mastery will mean a nine out of ten success ratio with individual skills. Of course, there will be elements with a greater risk for a miss and other skills that are executed perfectly every time they are attempted. The long range objective is to have the mastered movements dominate a routine leaving the only unpredictable factor being the natural chance associated with any high level gymnastics exercise. Obviously this can be done and those that do are the champions who demonstrate that illusive and much sought after consistency. It is clear that a two-week crash program to get routines ready for a meet just is not the way to go, although far too many try this approach.

Given the fact that the parts are ready and that the gymnast has a clear understanding of the movements as well as a low fear level associated with the exercise, how do we best go about putting it all together? By putting it together we are not talking about what skill beneficial for meeting the overall demands for the internal construction of the exercise, but we are looking at the process for arriving at the actual performance of the desired whole.

During the learning phase, selected individual skills are usually worked on and certain combinations are developed and drilled. Often longer sequences are attempted and in many cases the basic routine is in a blueprint stage both in the coach's and the gymnast's minds. When full routine training is ready to be undertaken the athlete and the coach have hopefully already put down a considerable amount of the needed foundation to build upon making the next step a little easier. See "On the Beam: A Gymnast's Guide for Staying There" for tips.

The next step, full routine training, is a special task requiring an all-out effort of a different type. This process should not be a matter of simply grinding it out but should involve a systematic approach. At this point the gymnast must obtain the maximum level of muscular strength and endurance over a sustained period with a corresponding mental discipline unique to doing full sets.

Specificity and Overload

In full routine training a couple of basic psycho/physical principles need to be briefly discussed. The first of these concepts is referred to as "specificity." This is a scientifically proven notion that suggests that the best way to develop muscular strength for a given activity is to simulate, as close as possible, the actual movement involved in the activity. The greatest development takes place on the specific parts of the body involved in doing an exercise when actually doing the desired movement(s). For example, punching power for tumbling is not developed by jogging but by doing punching type drills. Relating this to the current discussion, the best way to train for full routines is to do routines! Developing the required "mental attitude" for executing routines is also enhanced in this way. This may appear like a simple notion, but it is amazing how often it is ignored.

To carry out this task and remedy deficits in muscular strength and endurance which can show up dramatically when full routine training is undertaken, another principle should be understood and applied along with specificity. This is the concept of "overload." This is a well-known idea in gymnastics. Simply stated, in order to increase endurance, the muscles (and mind) need to be taxed to their sub maximal/ maximal capacity. The way to do this is to continually increase the demands made on the muscle groups involved in doing an entire set. The overall intensity, number of repetitions, etc., must go up in a scheduled and monitored way. Monitoring heart rate and breathing quality and increasing the demands slowly will result in increased endurance. Cardiovascular (aerobic) fitness is involved in this principle since it is the heart that supplies blood (fuel/energy) to the muscle groups and moves weakening impurities out through the bloodstream.

A word about breath control—it is astounding how many gymnasts and coaches take breathing for granted. Actually, it is a very important part of one's training and needs to be practiced just as everything else. Holding the breath can have disastrous effects on your body's replenishing efforts during rigorous activity. It should not be left to chance as a natural part of staying alive when doing gymnastics, but should be consciously worked on when training is taking place. It should be mentioned here that it is important to continually analyze the particular muscles which may require additional concentrated work above and beyond doing a full set. This would represent a kind of extra homework through flexibility and conditioning needed to improve efficiency in the finished product.

Psycho/ Physical Steps in Training Full Routines

Your most impressive gymnasts are those who can execute rigorous routines with apparent ease and with energy left over. In most cases, such gymnasts have trained utilizing both the notions of specificity and overload. With the previous discussion in mind, here's a look at an actual procedure for routine training that is being recommended. As always, the coach has the responsibility to make sure each gymnast is physically and emotionally ready for full routine training.

1. **Step I.** Before you begin, always remember to do your relaxation and visual rehearsals of your routines daily and especially just before each performance. For openers, try to do the entire routine you have planned for competition from start to finish. Some gymnasts and coaches get a nice surprise at this point,

especially if they have followed the above principles in skill development, but in the majority of cases many gymnasts will run out of gas. This is no reason to panic, as it is to be expected until you really get into full set training on a daily basis.

2. **Step II.** The first attempt referred to in number 1 should give you some idea of just how much work is going to be needed in order to achieve set-mastery with dynamics and eloquence. Step number 2 is to divide the routine into thirds. Obviously, this does not apply to vault. On the next attempt, start with the mount and do the first third of the routine.

3. **Step III.** Repeat this same first third with a shorter rest period between each repetition.

4. **Step IV.** Do the same thing with the second, third, and then the last section, including the dismount. At this point you are still working on the partial units only, that is the routine divided into three parts (check your heartbeat throughout this effort increasing your work load at this time by shortening rest periods until your heart rate is sub maximal for each group and breathing is controlled).

5. **Step V.** Now, you can move ahead in one of two ways. You can divide the exercise in half or you can add a given number of elements to the first third extending your effort further into the whole. Whichever you decide, approach the task in a similar manner as given above. Continually cut down on your recuperation time between repetitions. Keep pressing yourself to your maximal muscular output (some gymnasts like to start in the middle and add to each end—a move toward the beginning and one toward the end). We do not recommend this approach, for it should be remembered that you are not only conditioning your body but also your mind for full routine execution. Psychologically, it makes better sense to have your internal mental rhythm moving ahead in a positional beginning to end flow. Doing routines involves a special mental attitude and a real desire.

6. **Step VI.** The above method, over time, should definitely begin to pay off. Your energy output will become more economical with each effort and your fatigue level lowered, as each body part is more properly utilized. At this point your mental imagery rehearsals and training before you go to bed at night and at other times, should involve entire routines rather than single moves or sequences.

7. **Step VII.** Step number 7 is to go for the entire set. This should be done over and over again gradually reducing your recuperation periods between exercises to the absolute minimum.

8. **Step VIII.** Just as you build your productivity on each event, your approach to the all-around effort should be the same. Remember specificity and overload. Do the all-around program when each individual effort is ready in a similar way as you prepared for the single exercise. You will note that in the highest level of competition the gymnasts often go through an exercise in or near to its entirety during the warm-up. This is usually evidence of proper routine training and of a gymnast who is ready both physically and mentally prepared for the competition.

Finally, from a psychological point of view, nothing will build a gymnast's confidence more than entering a competition with a sense that his or her routines are solid, under control and ready to be shown. There are no shortcuts to this kind of readiness and serious gymnasts must be prepared to put forth the enormous number of hours of hard work and discipline that are required if they hope to realistically reap the full harvest of their individual potentials.

Chapter Ten

MEET PREPARATION AND COMPETITION

I f you, the coach, and the team have not properly prepared for an upcoming meet, the results may be disastrous, to say the least. In many other chapters we have identified the mental, physical, and emotional prerequisites for enhancing gymnastic performances. Here, we will focus on issues directly related to the competition arena.

The first article addresses the psychology behind judging and its implications for coaches and the athletes. Several were written for the athletes themselves such as the discussion on the development and display of confidence. It is detailed and points out a most interesting connection between the concepts of confidence and vigor. If anyone has ever experienced "butterflies" the night before or the day of competition we offer some valuable advice. Lastly, how you present yourself at an actual competition as well as the steps needed to be taken by both the gymnast and coach are discussed. Understanding these concepts and following the guidelines will help you ensure a productive, competitive season.

- The Impact of Psychological Factors in Gymnastics Judging
- A Gymnast's Guide for Demonstrating Confidence
- "Butterflies" and Pre-Meet Anxiety
- Personal Presentation: "Putting Your Best Foot Forward"
- Meet Presentation Guidelines

THE IMPACT OF PSYCHOLOGICAL FACTORS IN GYMNASTICS JUDGING

Regardless of how well a judge has mastered the technical rules and regulations concerning the gymnastic competition and the evaluation of exercises, there are many other factors which may affect the score. These are primarily conscious, preconscious and unconscious and are simply not found "in the book." Before going on, a definition of terms seems appropriate. By conscious factors we mean those biases, decisions, or actions that we are aware of while engaging in any behavior—i.e., judging. Preconscious factors are those influences which are just below our level of awareness but which can easily be brought to the conscious state through second party identification (we are told about them). We would recognize them quickly. Unconscious factors, the most influential and difficult to clarify, are those which we are totally unaware of and which cannot be brought to the conscious level without varying degrees of psychological intervention. All of these factors can be operating at once and usually do although a single level may be more predominate at a given time than another.

This article is primarily directed at the unsung heroes and heroines of the gymnastic competition: the judge. Coaches and gymnasts should find it of considerable interest as well. The following observations are based on our experience as judges and coaches and through informal discussions with judges. Although we all "play the game," we would not want to make a value judgment as to the ethical considerations involved! Consider the following example:

An Illustration

You are judge number three. You have taken your seat on the floor and are waiting for the first competitor to make his or her appearance for the Floor Exercise event. This is a very important dual meet. You have not seen these teams before in competition. Had you seen them in action at another time, psychological factors, primarily conscious and preconscious would have already begun to have an influence. Evidence suggests that some officials often evaluate what they expect to see rather than what they actually see because of prior knowledge of the gymnast's exercise (we might like to pretend that this doesn't happen but it does and it affects the score). On with the example: You have heard and know from experience that one of the coaches is particularly critical of judges and this is a home meet for him. You are a bit anxious and, of course, want to do a good and accurate job. Such anxiety can serve a useful purpose as it helps an individual focus his attention in a more controlled manner. The first athlete performs—you develop your score and it is presented (open system). Although you are in range your score is the lowest—the crowd reacts, the coach folds his arms and glares across the floor at you, several gymnasts on his bench turn to one another and talk. One points in your direction. You may feel a flash of increased anxiety (pre-cognitively or unconsciously determined)—a natural response indeed in a Roman arena! Alas, even with great control and considerable experience, psychologically relevant factors are about to enter the evaluation process. Response at this point will obviously vary. It is conceivable for example, that a judge at this juncture might consciously raise the score of the next competitor from that team a few tenths or even more. Recourse to this behavior is often determined by unconscious factors relative to the officials need for acceptance and approval and his/her tolerance for anxiety. It is apparent that if one has a need to be a "good guy," gymnastic officiating should be avoided as an avocation!

Such a situation described, unfortunately, still occurs in gymnastic competitions especially at the lower levels. Audience, coach and gymnast pressure of this type is unavoidable. The level of each official's psychological response to this natural and basically healthy phenomenon is solely an individual matter. A little more understanding of the psychological factors involved as well a few definite guidelines can be provided.

Recommendations

Perhaps the most crucial recommendation is that the judge make a real conscious attempt to keep him or herself aware of these factors and their impact in order to help minimize their overall effect on the evaluation process (gross bias towards one team, a situation sometimes encountered, can usually be diagnosed with ease and remediated quickly). It should be noted that many coaches use a working knowledge of the effect of these factors to keep the "pressure" on.

There are additional psychological factors which influence the process of evaluation at a more subtle and superficial level. Personal appearance and presentation of the individual gymnast can have a definite psychological effect on an official. Again, here it is often a highly individual matter with each judge and primarily determined by preconscious variables present in his or her personality structure. Such matters are far too complex to go into in a limited paper. However, it should be emphasized that judges continually must struggle to identify these subjective judgments and recognize their effect in the process. Some other examples of these factors are: personal appearance, reputation, national or racial origin, manner of speaking, stature, judges favorite event or skill, etc.

There are other factors, outside of the technical rules, which effect the evaluation from a psychological point of view. Besides such matters as personal appearance (cleanliness and neatness of the uniform) already mentioned such variables as method of addressing the superior judge and panel, facial expression, crispness of final address, being ready to perform before the officials (not keeping them waiting), exit-dismount (some judges get very irritated when a male gymnast undoes his suspenders immediately upon dismounting) response to a break, recovery ability, and others all contribute to that illusive concept of general impression which is so important in the evaluation constellation.

Finally, here is a brief philosophical observation. Rollo May in his book, "Psychology and the Human Dilemma" makes the point that man's basic problem or dilemma is that he is both object and subject at one and the same time. When he studies himself and his behavior (psychology, sociology, anthropology, etc.) as an object for investigation he is also the observer. Therefore the bind of knowing what really the "true" facts are and what is the result of distortion by his own being in the observation process is critical and irresolvable.

For all our efforts to objectify the evaluation of a gymnastic performance (and we do an ever improving job in this regard—F.I.G., etc.) there simply is no infallible way to eliminate ourselves as subjective filters through which the more objective technical criteria must be applied and interpreted. It seems that this may well be a positive thing after all and that perhaps we should not become preoccupied with attempting to eliminate all such personally psychological variables from out of evaluation endeavors. If one accepts the above position, it is apparent that we could not be ultimately successful despite all our efforts. Of course, we must and will continue to refine our procedures of evaluation and become increasingly cognizant of the effect of such factors as discussed in this paper in order to produce the most objective score possible. However, it would seem appropriate to joyfully recognize the fact that we are trapped by ourselves as vulnerable beings participating in something which is essentially quite human.

A GYMNAST'S GUIDE FOR DEMONSTRATING CONFIDENCE

What is that special quality that past Olympians demonstrated and today our new top elite and Olympic gymnast's exhibit that catches our attention almost immediately? Surely the high level of their exercises is one thing, but there is another quality that also makes us take notice and it is sometimes called an "air of confidence." We have all heard such statements as, "He showed great confidence in that set," or "She appeared very confident and self-assured on beam," and other positive comments about someone's work. What is really being talked about when these statements are made? What is this quality called confidence and what things are seen that give the impression of an "air of confidence?" More importantly, how can you get it if you don't have it now?

Defining Confidence

To find the most basic meaning, we can turn to the standard dictionary for a formal definition. Webster's Dictionary defines confidence in a number of ways:

- It is faith, trust
- A feeling or awareness of personal powers
- A reliance on yourself
- The quality of being certain

Most dictionaries give other definitions as well and they all come down to describing a person whose state of mind and behavior is marked by easy coolness and a freedom from uncertainty or embarrassment. Most definitions stress the fact that a confident person is one who has faith in him or herself without any suggestion of being conceited or arrogant. A truly confident person is one who has self-control and discipline when under stress, rather than a person who talks a good game when there is no real challenge present. The confident athlete often has a quiet modesty that is backed with a strong and dignified personal power. The falsely confident individual may brag a lot but will not be able to come through when the pressure is on. We have all met both types of people in our daily living both in and out of the gym.

Personal Confidence

Confidence is obviously not something one goes out and purchases in a supermarket or pizza parlor. It is clearly a state of mind, a mental attitude that develops over time from the very experiences of our lives. If a person has never had a real success at anything or has constantly been told that they are not good or doing well it is nearly impossible to build the kind of inside feeling associated with personal confidence. People who have always been put down are often shy and negative about themselves, even when it is clear they have ability. These individuals are often their own worst enemies, expecting to fail and fulfilling their own predictions. They exhibit little self-esteem or respect.

At the other end of the extreme is the youngster who has always been told everything they do is just great, that they are tops, and no matter what happens they should think of themselves as number one. Such individuals often expect success without putting out the effort needed to reach their goals. The confidence shown by such a gymnast is often very false because it has been based on false information and dishonest feedback about their efforts. This may develop a snobby attitude, but also these people may withdraw like those who experience constant criticism. This happens when, contrary to what they have been told, their false self-image and sense of confidence is bombarded by their actual gymnastic experiences. Often they become very distrustful and tend to avoid or ignore all forms of feedback or efforts to help from the coach and others. As in most things in life, neither extreme is desirable. The confident person is probably one who has received honest, helpful criticism but also positive input that says "you're okay" and has worked hard for what they have accomplished.

Rarely do we meet someone who has no confidence at all, particularly in the sport of gymnastics. The very nature of gymnastics would tend to discourage a youngster with little or no self-confidence from taking part in it as they would be afraid to do anything. It should be said that if a youngster can get started and under good conditions, gymnastics is a wonderful tool for building confidence. We do, however, meet young gymnasts who need to develop and show a greater "air of confidence" in their work. The question is, how do we go about developing it?

Mastery and Confidence

In other articles such as "A Psycho/Physical Guide to Training Full Routines," we talked about the importance of mastering movements and routines as a crucial part of really being ready for competition. Often we have said that the gymnast who goes into a meet physically prepared has a real psychological edge over the gymnasts who feel that their preparation has not been what it should. Physically unprepared gymnasts are obviously nervous, uncertain of themselves, and not able to concentrate because they worried about making it through their routines. The more physically ready you are to perform, the greater will be your mental readiness. One system feeds the other in a positive, supportive circle. Therefore gymnasts, one way to gain a more total feeling of confidence is to be as highly physically ready as possible. This means hours and hours of very hard work and output. It means repetition after repetition and a level of motivation that lets you push yourself to the limit of your endurance. The physical and sometimes emotional pain that goes with this type of effort has a payoff in competition. Just remember that your physical preparation underlies a confident attitude.

Competition and Confidence

We can all see a confident gymnast the moment he or she steps on the floor and usually before that if we have been watching during the pre-meet warm-up. These individuals have a selling quality about them and create a special impression right away. One thing that can be seen immediately is personal appearance. The moving nature of gymnastics makes keeping a neat appearance difficult. However, it is important and needs to be given attention as part of a confident and controlled image. For example, girls should select a hairstyle that is flattering but that also stays together and out of the face. Rearranging your hair during the competition suggest a lack of complete preparation. There should be nothing going on during the meet that distracts from a personal look of sureness. Generally speaking, a sharp and organized appearance is of value.

Competition Warm-up

Your warm-up for competition can help establish a sense of confidence that fellow gymnasts, judges, and the audience will be able to see. The warm-up should be well planned and full of energy. When your turn on an event comes during warm-up it is damaging to your image to stumble around trying to figure out what you're going to do. This should all be worked out with your coach ahead of time not only because it will help you mentally and is more considerate of fellow gymnasts, but also because it helps promote a picture of certainty. You should go quickly and go hard. Sometimes officials watch the warm-up prior to the actual competition on a given event. Unconsciously at least, they are often impressed by an efficient gymnast who does not waste motion and appears self-assured. If you totally blow a skill during your warm-up it may affect your confidence and increase your nervousness. In such cases the judges, although not intentionally doing so, will be waiting for that part of your exercise to see if you make it or not. Clearly you can see how your physical readiness will always contribute to an "air of confidence" and the total evaluation process.

Remember, that in part, **"you are your exercise."** If you have not prepared well you won't be able to show your routines confidently with the form, pace, energy, and daring that is needed. Don't overload your exercises. Select connections which show your strengths and takes away from any weakness. In other words, plan your routines in a way that allows you to show them, not just do them, from beginning to end.

Presentation

Another important ingredient to showing an **"air of confidence"** is your presentation during the actual competition. When you know you are soon to be up, get ready well in advance and never keep the officials waiting. Walk firmly with good posture and class. Remember it is a performance and part of performing, besides the actual tricks, is you the gymnast. Look smart, proud, and alert. Go to a spot you have selected beforehand and be ready to present yourself to the superior judge. There should be no confusion or fumbling around at this point. Be with it and ready before the judges are and when you get the nod return it with a slight bow or smile. Don't overdo it as that will also ruin the impression you are trying to get across as much as will a failure to acknowledge the panel.

If during your exercise you have an unfortunate break, a real possibility that happens to the best in a sport as demanding as gymnastics, recover quickly and with confidence. Know what you are supposed to do, don't stand around pouting or looking in a daze. Although certain damage has been done in so far as your score is concerned, a confident recovery which shows good physical and mental preparation can often reduce the severity of any penalty. Such recovery behavior can impress people in terms of your self-control and coolness under stress, both aspects of confident behavior. See the article "Personal Presentation: Putting Your Best Foot Forward" for more tips.

When you have completed your exercise, for better or for worse, don't forget to once again acknowledge the superior judge. It is good manners as well as psychologically a wise place to leave off. Always be pleasant but never hysterical. Letting your temper or disappointment show if that is the case will not get you anywhere. Try to be professional even if you're not quite there yet! Try to put some energy into your exit, even jog or move off faster than your approach. At the very least try to show you have something left. The right mix for you in this regard will come from experience. The kind of "closing statement" you make says something about you and your work and can leave a "mental echo" that the judges may hear in their heads as they figure your score. Remember the evaluation process is not as clean cut and objective as we would sometimes like to believe. That critical extra tenth on your score can, in fact, come from something that is not directly connected to your actual physical performance. Any honest judge will admit that this is true—and thank goodness it is!

Vigor and Confidence

Another interesting concept perhaps related to confidence demonstrated by these top athletes, can be found in a psychological inventory assessment called the "Profile of

Mood States" (POMS). This assessment has been used to identify and even select elite athletes in a number of sports. The research using this test identifies a pattern called the "iceberg profile" which was found among the most successful elite athletes. This name was picked for the profile because of the peak found at the top of the pattern among the best performers. These athletes score way below average on the POMS in such things as tension, fatigue, and confusion. At the peak of the profile for these athletes is a characteristic which is called vigor. Vigor is defined in Webster's Dictionary as; "active bodily or mental strength or force, well-balanced growth, and intensity of action." Based on our own research with talented young gymnasts as we demonstrate in the "Psychological Characteristics of Jr. Elite Gymnasts," it is probably safe to predict that for a successful elite gymnast "vigor" would also be found at the top of their profiles. That is not just an energetic delivery of an exercise but also a kind of attitude and mastery that an individual shows.

Perhaps in thinking about confidence we should think of vigor. This definition sounds very much like the personal quality of confidence we have been discussing. Maybe vigor is the basic component in achieving an "air of confidence." If we think about one of the USA's top gymnasts, we think of a very confident performer. Surely their energy level and vigor is extraordinary and he or she is a super example of the connection between these two important ideas. So gymnasts, approach your gymnastics with as much "vigor" as you can and it is very likely you will find that your level of confidence will increase and show in your work.

Summary

As we have seen, confidence is much more complicated than many think. It is more of a mental attitude developed over time based on life's experiences than a skill we learn. We cannot wish it to happen although many gymnasts sure wish they could. However, there are things you can do and practice to gain that "winning attitude" and "air of confidence." Remember, the more physically ready you are to perform, the greater will be your mental readiness.

"BUTTERFLIES" AND PRE-MEET ANXIETY

A day or two before an actual competition, most gymnasts begin to experience some odd sensations usually associated with being nervous or anxious. The closer the competition becomes, the more these feelings are felt. They can involve the feeling of "butterflies in the stomach," trouble with sleeping, dry mouth, an increase in heart beat rate, a higher level of perspiration, a dramatic increase in the number of times the gymnast yawns or goes to the bathroom, and usually a lot of thoughts moving around inside the athlete's head having to do with the upcoming competition.

The nature and degree of these pre-competition jitters is an individual matter. It usually is a function of how much competitive experience a gymnast has had, the degree of physical preparation they have done, the overall readiness the athlete feels they have attained, and a matter of how they are psychologically wired together. Some gymnasts are much more prone than others to get anxious about the meet situation. There are gymnasts who get nervous about everything, and their anxiety is general and very strong indeed. Others just get uptight around the actual competitive situation and some of the training accompanying it. The degree of anxiety is no ironclad measure of how the athlete will actually perform. Too little tension can lead to as many mistakes as can an over amount of competitive anxiety. The ideal level of arousal is again an individual matter, and has been discussed in articles dealing with peaking and optimal attention and arousal levels prior to competition such as "The Performance Connection: Part I & II"

Pre-Competition Anxiety

In addition to an individual's basic tolerance for stress and innate level of anxiety, the general factors underlying pre-meet anxiousness are such things as fear of failure, concerns about letting someone down, a worry about losing control during the actual competition and feelings of inadequacy. In many cases, a critical source of pre-competition anxiety is the perceived difference between what the gymnast feels confident to perform and what the actual competition will demand for success. When the gymnast feels they are up for the challenge and that their exercises are well prepared, the amount of pre-meet tension experienced will be less. If the athlete feels they are not ready to compete in a specific situation at a certain level, then the degree of worry can be crippling to performance, and most of the gymnast's thinking will become negative and self-defeating.

In a short-term endurance/power sport such as gymnastics, exaggerated nervousness can be emotionally draining and can have a direct effect of how much energy is actually available for use in executing the routines. In addition, it is difficult for a very anxious gymnast to focus concentration on the controlled channeling of power. When athletes are overly tense, they generally turn their thoughts inward to focus on the uncomfortable feeling of being anxious, which is an inappropriate and costly use of attention. Movements practiced to near perfection to a point where they can be executed automatically can suddenly now require constant thought, which will further interfere with the gymnast's ability to recover from errors and adjust to performance difficulties.

Sport psychologists who work with athletes are often asked about "nerves" and what can be done about pre-competitive anxiety. Of course, the majority of athletes don't ask about this problem, either of gymnasts or coaches, let alone a professional consultant. Many simply develop their own approach to controlling uncomfortable tension, and if the self-developed methods work, that is wonderful. There are some things, however, that can be learned from psychology that will help reduce the amount of time needed to work out your own solution, and, at the very least, might make your suffering less acute.

Reducing Pre-Competition Anxiety

The best way to reduce pre-meet anxiety and try to prevent the "butterflies" from every invading your body is to learn and practice a few proven mental strategies before you ever enter the competition arena. Some of the strategies are the building blocks for many of the other techniques such as your basic physical and mental readiness along with relaxation and visualization training. Look over them all and try them one at a time and keep building from there. Many of these strategies are helpful to most, some only for a few, and others may have their own way of dealing with the "butterflies." In the long run, do whatever it takes to be prepared, confident, and feel good about your performance.

Physical and Mental Preparation

One thing is certain from the beginning: It is a total waste of time and energy to worry about things over which you have no control. The judging, what gymnasts are entered in the meet, the type of equipment, the temperature in the gym, the size of the crowd, etc., are all things that are not in your power to influence. The one thing, however, that you can take responsibility for is your personal mental management. This arena belongs to you and, although your coach can be of assistance, ultimately the way you play the psychological games rests with you.

As noted earlier, a very important source of anxiety is a sense of inadequacy. Therefore, it is a given fact that the most crucial mental preparation that will help reduce pre-competition stress is directly related to the degree of physical readiness the gymnast feels. There simply is no substitute, psychologically or otherwise, for the feeling of confidence that comes from entering a given meet knowing you are physically ready to perform at your best. Going into a competition with uncertainty about what moves, or set of moves, you are going to be able to successfully execute, or maybe even survive, is a sure way to raise anyone's anxiety to a high level and guarantee failure.

With this observation about the importance of physical and mental preparation offered as a fundamental principle and rule of thumb, the following strategies may also be useful to gymnasts in dealing with pre-meet "butterflies."

Mental Gymnastics Skills

Mastering your mental gymnastics skills is one of the first places to start in avoiding pre-meet anxiety. Learning how to relax and managing your breathing will help you become focused on the task at hand. Visualizing your routines performed correctly as well as learning to cope with mishaps in your mind, goes a long way to ensuring a great performance in the meet. See the article, "The Late Movies: A Young Gymnast's Guide to Mental Imagery Training," for more information on relaxation and visualization. You also want to make sure you are setting goals for each competition. These should include mental goals which have to do with your attitude as well as performance goals which have to do with your physical performance. You should focus on a few goals where you can see some improvement in your performance and not focus on the outcome of the meet. You will want to read the article "My Goal is to… A Gymnast's Plan" with help in setting these goals.

Optimal Level of Motivation

One thing that can often help with this anxiety is to become aware of the things that psyche you up and get you to an optimal level of motivation for performing. Leaving out the contribution that your coach or a sports psychologist could make in this regard, the best source is from your own past experience. The idea here is to try and identify those things that help you become aware that you are mentally ready for a great competition. This kind of mental sorting out can be referred to as a "flash back-flick up" method. The gymnast should think back to a meet situation where they not only did very well score wise, but they also felt mentally ready to be in. You're trying to "flash back" in your memory to a meet situation that you emotionally wanted to aggressively move forward rather than retreat from; one where you sensed victory and were hungry for success. Once this recall is established, then the task is to "flick up" the associated feelings to the current competition and once again recapture those feelings of being mentally prepared. It may help some gymnasts to write down what mental thoughts were associated with the feeling of being ready—how were they different from not-ready types of feelings, and what behaviors were connected with the positive feelings? The entire point is to begin to understand and identify the factors and feelings that are connected in your mind that motivate you for competition and, also, what factors get in the way and make you overly anxious. When you begin to focus intently on the current competition, and are in fact excited about it, you are probably entering your peak zone for performing well.

Performance Cues

Related to this notion of flashback and flick up is the idea of developing a non-technical performance cue. This technique involves identifying a word, series of words or vivid image that is associated by you, personally, with success and competence. Reviewing a past performance where you felt at the top of the game is, again, usually the way to come up with this kind of personal motto or power starter. For example, if one of your best performances is associated with your intensity and strength, you might come to the word and image of your performance at that meet which reflects an aggressive approach, such as "go like a tiger," "attack with a capital A," etc. One gymnast said that his greatest career performance to date is connected in his mind with the smell of popcorn, which was being sold at the meet. Part of his immediate mental preparation is to recapture that powerful sensory experience prior to competing. He claims he actually smells popcorn even when there is none around, and that is his cue. Incorporating this performance cue into your preparation as a way of getting on task and reducing performance jitters takes practice, but can eventually become second nature to use.

Focusing Attention

Another technique that is used to reduce anxiety and get in focus can be referred to as the "green light/red light" method. Simply put, when you are in green light mode, you are relaxed, practicing deep breathing, chilling out and letting yourself survey the competitive situation in an unbounded way. As your actual turn to compete gets closer, you have conditioned yourself to send a message from the brain to the central nervous system that says, or maybe yells, "red light time." That "internal alarm" is your cue to turn inward and away from all distractions and outside stimulation. This is the time that you focus complete attention to the challenge of performing your routines to the maximum. You no longer relate to any other athletes, nor pay any heed to what they are doing; for now, you become a closed, self-contained person with total concentration given to the approaching task. When to turn on the "red light" insofar as timing in the meet is concerned is solely an individual matter. It is probably not a good idea to do so too soon, as such intense mental control requires considerable energy to enter into and to maintain. Pre-meet nervousness is simply not part of you at this time, and although you do not want to become physically "tight," you do want to be mentally narrow in focus. Some athletes help themselves enter this state by actually seeing the colors green or red fill their mind screen, as a way of starting the attention process.

Using the "green light/ red light" method can be practiced in your normal workouts as well so it will feel more natural in a meet situation. For example, on a day when you're doing full routines, practice going from green light into red light mode. Make sure you let your teammates and your coach know what you are doing. In addition, your coach can have the team practice their focusing skills. For example, the coach can say "Today, we've got a meet this weekend so there will be no talking around the chalk bucket. As soon as you chalk-up, go into "red light time." You'll be amazed at how focused your gymnasts are and how productive your workouts can become. In fact, in our experience, most of the gymnasts who have worked under this situation, love it.

Thought Management

Sport psychologists have often talked about the notion that thinking negative thoughts is a prime contributor to pre-meet anxiety, and that "thought stopping" is a most important technique for reducing this nervousness and gaining self-control, which is so important for a good performance. Your authors do not exactly agree with the traditional idea of "thought stopping." Thoughts, in fact, cannot be stopped cold in their tracks once they come in consciousness. They have happened, and that's it. What can occur, however, and what is a more accurate label is that "thought management" can take over. This involves recognizing the negative thought, examining its origins, and then doing something about it. The gymnast's task when a negative, non-productive idea pops into his/her head is to arrest it from expanding and creating increasing anxiety; basically bringing it under control not by denial, but by using it against itself.

This technique involves a number of steps that take many more words to describe than it takes to carry out:

> For example, let's imagine that the gymnast is preparing to compete on the floor and gets the thought that they might over or under rotate the opening pass of a double back salto. This negative thought immediately raises the level of anxiety being experienced by the gymnast. Once that concern has surfaced into

consciousness, it makes no sense to try to stop it, since it has already occurred and the damage is done. Rather than trying to get rid of it, the gymnast should first recognize it for what it is, with a mental correction that uses imagery and a heavy dose of technical self-talk input. The gymnast should take a deep breath and mentally visualize the opening pass on their personal theater screen we all have in our heads, and imagine that double back completed perfectly with no rotation issue. This picture should be followed right away by the "inner coach" reviewing the specific performance goals that must be accomplished to successfully execute the particular skill. In this case, the voice would emphasize, for example: "fast hands off floor, good set and arm lift, strong back, full extension through legs, etc." Once this internal conversation has taken place, the skill should be pictured, once again, with perfect results. With this combination of mental strategies, visualization, imagery rehearsal and self-talk, the gymnast will most likely find they have managed the negative thought content that led to an elevation of pre-meet tension and that they will be back in positive control. At this point, it is also a good idea to give yourself some praise for taking charge and dealing with the negative thought. It is very appropriate to say to yourself, "Well done!"

Triggers

Eventually, some of the intervention methods used to reduce pre-competition anxiety discussed in this article will become more or less automatic. Until experience and practice have taken hold of your mental preparation, it is sometimes necessary to rely on some kind of personal "gimmick." This serves to trigger the needed strategy when you begin to feel an overabundance of "butterflies," or when negative ideas begin to spin around in your head. One of our favorite triggering devices for reminding a gymnast to bring into use some of these mental game techniques is the introduction of minor pain as a personal signal. Nothing gets our attention quicker than discomfort on the physical level. It is very difficult indeed to maintain a specific thought when it is suddenly interrupted by a sharp and distinct pain. As an example, try the "rubber-band trigger." Wear an elastic hair band slightly loose around your wrist. At the first sign that you are losing focus and getting anxious, you privately (don't make a display of it) pull the band as far as needed until it will snap back against your wrist.

Believe us when we say that the instant pain created by this simple movement is very definite, and if you do it several times, the sting will remain in your thoughts for some time after the first snap. This is a gimmick and the idea behind it is that you have made an agreement with yourself beforehand that when you use the rubber band, it is your signal to immediately get off the negative stuff and begin to practice other techniques for the management of your pre-competition anxiety. Obviously this is a beginner's method for dealing with your anxiety and should not be used for a long time, but many seasoned competitors have used it. A week or two of workouts should be enough. Gymnasts have reported to us, after successfully using this triggering starter motor, that in subsequent competitive situations they find themselves rubbing their wrists where the rubber band once was, and that the act of rubbing serves to remind them to get into their mental game right away.

Summary

The various methods described in this article for dealing with pre-meet anxiety and stress that often occurs with competition are not sacred, nor are they the only ones available. For some gymnasts, one or two techniques may work, for others all may be of help, while for still others, none will be effective. As a matter of fact, sometimes psychological tools can create more difficulties than they solve, especially in the case of young athletes. In the end, it will probably be more a matter of the personal constitution of the individual gymnast that will determine how much of the "butterflies" and other anxiety-provoking things, such as random negative thoughts can be brought under control, than it will be a matter of skills from the discipline of psychology. As with all things worth doing, however, developing a possible bag of tricks to manage your mental gymnastics game requires patience, practice and persistence over extended time.

PERSONAL PRESENTATION
"PUTTING YOUR BEST FOOT FORWARD"

Many of our young readers have been in competitions, some at the beginning level and others at the advanced or above level. We have often spoken about the importance of preparing for such meets: the necessary timing for arriving at top efficiency, the conservation of energy, the mental-attitudinal factors associated with peaking, the content of the pre-meet workout schedule, etc. Along with their physical exercises gymnasts bring to the actual competition a personal psychological state which will either enhance or deter from their performance. Confidence versus concern, rested vs. overworked, defeatism vs. positivism, normal performance tension vs. diffuse anxiety, physical readiness vs. routine unsureness, and many others are just part of a gymnast's physical/psychological constitution on the day of a meet.

There are many factors that go into a successful competition on an individual level. Obviously the actual physical delivery of the routines is primary and without a confident and clean performance, obtaining the desired score just is not going to happen. Given the fact that your physical and mental preparation are most important, what other aspects of your gymnastic effort can have at least an indirect and often a direct effect on the outcome? The answer is your "personal presentation with a capital P." This article will consider some of the things that have to do with presenting, and although they are not as significant as your actual execution, can still have a positive payoff when it comes to the bottom line, your score.

Coaches often tell their gymnasts not to worry about factors over which the athlete has no control when in a meet. Such things as the temperature, the athletes who are in the competition, the apparatus, the lighting, and dozens of other variables are things in which you cannot control. This is sound advice, for to do otherwise, is to waste valuable psychological energy that needs to be utilized on concentrating on the task at hand. One of the competitive factors, however, that you can have a very substantial influence on, is how you "present" at these meets. That is an aspect of the competition that you have total control over. So, let's learn the best way to "put your best foot forward."

Physical Appearance

This somewhat elusive concept of "presentation" begins before you even get to the competitive arena itself. It is extremely important that your physical appearance be carefully attended to prior to competition. You should arrive on the site, with your personal appearance impressive and under control. Hair management is extremely important. If you have a short cut, many of the problems are automatically eliminated. If you have longer hair that you like to wear up, make sure it is very secure. Pins, barrettes, clips, and hair bands, falling out during the meet is not acceptable. Ponytails are fine, again if they are neat and securely tied. The goal is to be a class act from start to finish. How you look, including your hair and attire, is a crucial part of setting up this classy appearance. Last minute touch up is acceptable, but more than that can be a distraction, as you try to ready yourself for the physical act of competing. It goes without saying, of course, that your leotard should be clean and well fitted. Pick colors that flatter you, your eyes, and your hair if you're an advanced gymnast. The right combinations can really have a startling effect on people. Most gymnasts change, following warm-ups, to a second competition garment which makes a great deal of sense, not only because it is hygienic, but also because it represents a crisp, fresh start.

Entering the Gym

When you actually enter the gym, "presentation" expands, and now we are talking about how you appear to the gathered audience and fellow competitors. Judges don't enter into the picture yet, as they usually are not around until the meet is ready to begin. The picture you want to paint to the crowd and other athletes is of someone in control of herself, who is confident and looks it from the very beginning. Gazing around as if in shock is counterproductive to your "psyche out" efforts with other gymnasts. There is absolutely no question that your entrance and how you warm up etc. has a real impact on other athletes. Anyone who thinks otherwise is naïve indeed. It has been proven that your level of focus, intensity, and certainness, can affect other competitors and work to your advantage. We have seen gymnasts taken out of a competition before it began, due to the powerful presence of another youngster who distracted them, and took them off their own game plan. Even the slightest effect is worth achieving, when it comes to being a real competitor.

Apparatus Warm-up

Your actual warm-up on the apparatus should be planned well ahead. You (and your coach) should know exactly what you are going to do during timed warm-ups and during the touch. This kind of quiet but obvious organization, augmented by non-verbal communication between yourself and your coach, is all part of your overall presentation as a gymnast. This kind of focused behavior can be most disconcerting to a less prepared gymnast who is waiting her turn. There should never be a display of confusion or, most importantly, any panic or loss of emotional control. At a broader level if you are going to an event saying a prayer, you are simply not ready to give your best effort. Apprehension and a lack of confidence are very apparent at these times and it gives the competition a definite edge which can be capitalized on, depending on how aggressive they are in the meet situation. Judges are also aware of this kind of over-determined anxiety. They are only human, and they may end up waiting for the mistake you seem to communicate is going to happen to take place, rather than concentrating totally on what they are seeing you do.

Once the warm-ups are over, and the lineup has occurred, your presentation now goes to another level which can again have influence in a less subtle and direct way. March-in is important and if you will review meets you have been in, it is a sure bet that someone stood out because of the way they looked at this pre-competition point. This includes dress, head held high, confident steps, appropriate flair, and excellent posture. A kind of pleasant detachment is recommended over a "playtime" approach at this important moment!

Presenting to the Judge

Presenting to the judges before competing, signals the beginning of genuine "presentation" at the highest level. Always be ready. It is not a good thing to keep a panel of officials waiting while you're chalking up or indulging in some other out of touch action. Your coach is part of this process, but basic independence and self-control, in this regard, is behavior of choice. Salute smartly prior to "showing" your exercise with authority. Extremes should be carefully avoided; no scowls, or looks that say "heaven help me." Hysterical smiling or overdoing in any form should be avoided. The best look is one that says, "Now let me show you how it's done. Enjoy it as I will." When you dismount, don't forget to address the judges once again, and this last impression is very important. Remember failure to address the judge has an official deduction in the Code of Points (.1). Every tenth counts as you surely know from past experience. If you have made a mistake, don't pout or present a face or body language that suggests you feel suicidal or that the world has come to an end. Making an error is part of the game, and it should not be shown that is has demolished your composure. Outstanding recovery is impressive, and judges sense it on a preconscious level, at least.

When you have finished a routine, leave the competitive area with energy, not dragging off as if all your resources have been drained away. If you have had a great performance and garnish a fine score, it is appropriate to celebrate in a somewhat dignified way, but do so out of the judges' view and with some degree of control. If you distract from their duties, they will remember it next time you are evaluated. In addition, you don't want to create the impression that a good performance comes as a real surprise to you and is such a rare occasion that it requires screams, and that a general party atmosphere be established in your honor. Again primary responsibility for this rests with your coach, but you have a role to play as well.

Awards

The art of presentation does not end when the competition is over. If you should be fortunate enough to have placed in an event or the All-Around and there are official awards to be given, it is important that you continue to project the image you have developed. It should be a rule of thumb that you do not take the victory stand looking disheveled or sloppy. A team warm-up or leotard is the way to go, not in a T-shirt or street clothing. A tailored and confident attitude needs to be maintained at this time as well as during the competition.

Summary

Like anything else worth doing, having a sense of presentation, as discussed in this article, takes practice. In most successful gyms, presentation is practiced on a regular basis. In addition to having simulated meet conditions where gymnasts march in, perform routines which are judged, "presenting" is also practiced in this setting. Coaches, judges, and the general audience will often comment on how sharp this or that team looks. Such an image does not come about by accident and that in part is because of this level of attention to detail. The article "Meet Presentation Guidelines" provides a detailed list for both the gymnast and coach to follow for achieving and mastering presentation skills.

Remember, gymnastics is a performance in the fullest sense of the word. It not only involves the execution of routines, it is also a "show" in its own right. It has a specific set of rules concerning the manner of performing and has a definite entertainment value. Part of the showmanship of the sport has to do with the impression left, not only by the exercise performed, but also by the person performing it. Just like a solid stick upon dismounting remains in the judges' mind, so too does a disciplined class act. It is surely worth the time and practice necessary to perfect this aspect of gymnastics.

MEET PRESENTATION GUIDELINES

Do you know how important presentation skills are in competition? Actually, they are pretty significant and they begin before you enter the arena and continue until you exit. We all know how important physical preparation is and hopefully you're preparing mentally for competitions as well. But did you know that presentation skills can also contribute to the overall impression of the team or individual gymnast and may affect the outcome of a meet? In fact, one of the ideas for this article is based on numerous comments by judges of all levels.

You may ask what presentation skills really are and what do they have to do with meet preparation? Well, we've all heard of one's attitude. According to the dictionary, "attitude" can be defined as your "bodily posture" or "manner." This attitude and bodily posture are easily seen in the personal presentation you convey throughout the entire competition and are noticed by coaches, teammates, judges and the general audience. As a matter of fact, the idea for this article is partially based on comments made by judges concerning the importance of the gymnast's presentation and etiquette in the competitive arena.

Before we begin, let's see how well you pay attention to presentation. How often have you seen a gymnast land a dismount and practically go into hysterics? Or how about the gymnast, who has had a fall on beam, finishes the routine, then gives a half salute and sulks as they walk away from the event?

What impression do these athletes give you, or did you even notice? You can be sure the judges, coaches and the audience noticed and formed an opinion of that athlete. So what impression are you giving to everyone at a meet based on your attitude and presentation? Let's take a look at some skills you can work on.

Guidelines for Meet Presentation

There are five important areas to focus on in "meet presentation." They begin with home preparation, how to enter the arena, what to do during general and timed warm-ups, proper etiquette in front of the judge, and end with the awards. Let's look at each area:

1. **At Home Preparation:** The concept of presentation begins long before you reach the arena. It is extremely important that your physical appearance be impressive, under control, and portrays a "class act" from start to finish. You should always arrive on time and well prepared, with only last minute touch-ups acceptable.

2. **Entering the Arena:** Once you actually enter the gym, the notion of presentation expands and now includes fellow competitors, coaches, and

parents. You want to portray a picture of yourself, to others, that shows you are focused, in control and secure in your skills and preparation for the meet. Besides your own confidence, it has been proven that this attitude can affect your competitors and work to your advantage. In fact, some gymnasts can be taken right off their own game plan due to the distractions caused by the powerful presence of another athlete or team.

3. **General Team vs. Timed Apparatus Warm-ups:** Well-planned warm-ups are a must for a successful competition. You, your team, and coach should know exactly what you are going to do during the general and timed warm-ups as well as the touch.

   a. **General team warm-up** should be planned by the coach and go accordingly. A set routine done in group unison, whether there are 2 or 20 gymnasts, should warm-up your body and your mind for the meet.

   b. **Timed apparatus warm-ups** also need to be planned but on a very individual basis. You must be so confident of your skills, that the warm-up is just that, a "warm-up" before the execution of a well-practiced and perfected routine.

   c. **Touches** may be even more critical due to the limited time element. What you execute in the touch is often based on the timed warm-ups, so it is crucial that you and your coach know exactly what to do.

   d. **Mistakes in warm-ups** can happen for a variety of reasons. In the event that something doesn't go as planned, take a deep breath, relax, and refocus on the task at hand. You and your coach should also have a plan of action if this occurs.

   Apprehension, nervousness, or lack of confidence will definitely be noticed by the other competitors, coaches, and even judges. Staying strong and composed should set the stage for your own physical readiness as well as your mental preparation for the competition.

4. **Judges and Judging:** The idea for this article, as stated before, is partially based on numerous comments by judges of all levels. Personal presentation and proper gym etiquette are extremely important and can affect your score. Yes, of course, the execution of the skill is paramount, but the delivery of the routine as well as your attitude and bodily composure, are also important.

   There are a few things to keep in mind when it comes to actually **addressing the judge**:

   a. When you step up on the apparatus to salute the judge, this begins the actual "presentation" to the highest level. You and your coach should always be ready when the judges are. It is not a good idea to keep a panel of judges waiting.

b. When you salute the judge, it should be done with confidence, authority, and a genuine smile. Let them know you are ready to show them what you've got.

c. Upon dismounting, your presentation is crucial and should always reflect self-control.

Here's where some athletes make **presentation mistakes:**

d. Hysterical smiling, jumping for joy, or overdoing it in any form should be avoided. Are you conveying that you have never hit your routine before or have never made a certain skill?

e. Perhaps you did an okay routine but gave only a token salute to the judge at the end. Are you saying you could have done better?

f. When you do salute, do you wait for the judge to acknowledge you back? The judge may have been writing notes and was looking down at their paper when you saluted. Proper etiquette dictates that you stay and salute the judge until they signal you, often with a look and a smile back to you as well.

g. What do you do if you made a mistake? Are you pouting or presenting a facial or body language which suggests defeat?

Remember, outstanding recovery is very impressive and it shows your solid confidence in yourself and your skills. So while saluting and exiting the event do it with the energy and confidence in which you entered, no matter what the outcome of the performance. This is not to say that you are expected to act like a robot, on the contrary, you should show genuine enjoyment, satisfaction, and pride at all times.

5. **Awards:** The art of presentation does not end when you perform your last event.

a. You should stay on the floor until all your teammates and other competitors have finished their performances as a show of support and respect, not to mention the possibility of disturbing another gymnast's focus and concentration.

b. If you were fortunate enough to place in an event, you should report to the awards stand with a neat appearance, wearing your team's warm-up suit or leotard, and a tailored and confident attitude. Offer a respectful smile and a sense of gratitude for getting that award.

c. Upon exiting the arena, you should continue to project the **image** you have carefully crafted during the competition.

Special Tips for Coaches

Here's an important note for Coaches: none of this matters without **practice, practice, practice**. You may be asking yourself what does meet presentation have to do with training and practice? Well, the answer again is everything. These skills in the five important areas of presentation ought to be practiced before a competition just as you practice routines. But don't wait until the day before a meet to work on these skills. Begin at least a month before the season starts and practice occasionally during the season as necessary. Give your gymnasts every opportunity to feel confident, prepared, and in control so they will shine at every meet.

Here are a few practice tips to incorporate in your workouts:

- Practice basic presentation and etiquette skills
- Practice individual and team march-ins
- Practice warm-ups and touches
- Hold "mock" meets with pretend judges
- Hold pretend award ceremonies
- Give scores on presentation

Summary

Remember, gymnastics is a performance to the fullest extent, involving both the execution of routines but also a manner of performing providing an entertainment factor as well. Part of the sport has to do with the impression left by the performance as well as the impression left by the gymnast performing it. In fact, many of the successful gyms around the country do practice their presentation skills. Next time you are at a meet, pay special attention to the aspect of presentation and who seems to be in control. Or reflect back on your last meet to see if anyone stood out that you believe deserved a "10" in presentation. I'm sure they made an impression on you and others as well. So set yourself up so you get the next "10" in presentation.

It is surely worth the time and energy to practice these seemingly easy, but potentially important tasks. A polished performance combined with impeccable presentation skills can only lead to a **disciplined class act** in the minds of your teammates, coaches, parents, judges and the audience.

Chapter Eleven

Balancing Family, School, and Peer Relationships

The following papers touch on some very sensitive issues when it comes to the young athlete involved in a level of training which takes a great deal of personal commitment. The articles concerning mothers and their daughters and the appropriate level of their involvement in gymnastics have remained most controversial, at least from the perspective of some parents. However, many of these are also required reading in a number of gymnastic training centers across the country. The discussion dealing with school and issues that come about for youngsters in gymnastic training has prompted considerable mail.

Parents and coaches should pay close attention to our articles about changing gym programs or moving as they concern everyone involved in the process. Another paper in the collection got its impetus from our work with a national champion and her parents when she faced a critical decision. Lastly, if you or your gymnasts are focused on the Elite level, some important information and facts need to be considered.

- "My Daughter, the Competitive Gymnast"
- Parental Involvement in Competitive Gymnastics
- Parenting Commandments
- School, Peers, and Gymnastics
- Changing Gyms: Pitfalls and Strategies
- The Decision to Quit

- Leaving Home to Train: A Critical Decision
- Elite Level Gymnastics and Reality

"MY DAUGHTER, THE COMPETITIVE GYMNAST"

This article is a little different from others that we have written because it is primarily directed to the mothers of competitive female gymnasts. We hope gymnasts and coaches along with other key family members will also look at the ideas presented as it may help them understand and cope with some issues which might often be experienced or felt but left unsolved. The focus on the female gymnast and their mothers may appear biased. This direction was taken because, for the most part, it is the mothers who are generally more directly involved in this aspect of their daughters' lives at a young age. In addition, due to the maturation age of male gymnasts at high levels, the issues to be discussed as well as the mother's involvement are not usually seen to this extent in the mother-son-gymnastics relationship. However, it is important to recognize that the influence of both parents is very significant for children of either sex and their respective roles in the rearing process will determine the nature of their specific input. Therefore, in this article, we will briefly examine only the "mother-daughter-gym" interaction.

Emotional Investment

Probably the most critical thing to realize at the onset, although some parents may want to deny this fact, is that mothers usually have a substantial emotional investment in the activities of their daughters. We don't mean to imply in any way that this is unnatural or harmful in and of itself; it is all a matter of degree and underlying parental motivation. There are those mothers who share the joy of their children's accomplishments, support them at times of disappointment, encourage them to persist, and provide an ongoing model for commitment and good spirit. On the other hand, there are those mothers who have become over-involved in the athletic lives of their youngsters, who see the child as the ultimate extension of themselves and who take the gymnast's successes and failures as very personal reflections of their own performance record. This kind of living through child interaction places a great deal of pressure on the gymnast at several levels and is usually destructive in the long run, often resulting in an uptight and unhappy youngster. Of course, from another point of view, there are girls who thrive on this type of psychological connection, use it all too effectively to manipulate the parent, rely on it to keep going, and generally reverse the process to the point where their preconscious and sometimes even conscious motivation is to please their mothers. We have known gymnasts who have remained in the sport because they didn't want to let their moms down (and dads for that matter). Such justification is ordinarily not in the best interest of the child. Wanting to please others is a healthy aspect of the motivational system of many athletes, but when such desire is over-determined and no other clear and rewarding reasons appear to exist, trouble may very well be on the horizon for everyone involved.

There is not a great deal that can be done about these situations once they have become entranced. Every individual case is different and the historical background varies in each mother-daughter relationship. Perhaps the most important thing is to recognize that it can and does happen. There are some signs of potential over-involvement which can be identified: constant inquiry, in a third-degree fashion into how the gymnasts skills are progressing, continual pressure to move up through the system, the presence of gymnastic talk in and out of the gym whether the child is there or not, an overreaction to scores received in a meet – high or low – and dramatically sharing your elation or anger with your daughter, omnipresence at competitions, derogatory remarks about the performances of other gymnasts, overt statements questioning the coach's ability, and many other such symptoms.

Over-Confidence

One big problem in this area is the mother who is convinced she has produced America's answer to the next Olympic Champion! This is a theme which has become more and more prevalent in recent years partially due to the great deal of national and international media coverage given to gymnastics. It can occur at any age but seems most common in the younger years, when a naturally fearless youngster is constantly doing better and better and seemingly learning skills at an alarming rate and are therefore endowed, in the ambitious parent's mind, with limitless potential and extraordinary talent. Alas, this is not always or even often, the case. Enthusiasm is important and we would be the last ones to stifle spontaneous motion or ignore latent ability, but it is crucial that these evaluations be accomplished by professional coaches and that parents keep things in perspective. If you imagine you have a potential Olympian living in your house at age 7, you will be very disappointed when reality comes home to roost; especially if you have built unrealistic dreams around this outcome. A parent once openly shared her fantasy about this—"I imagined that my daughter was interviewed on national TV and in front of millions of people thanked me for helping her achieve this success." We all have such personal ambitions and fantasies to one degree or another. At least this mother was honest about it and could recognize her related behavior and its effect on everything she did regarding her daughter's gymnastics. When it doesn't work out the way one has hoped it is conceivable that not only will the parent be very disappointed but also quite angry at the daughter who hasn't measured up. Beware! It might help to remember that since, and including, the 1952 Olympics, there have only been about 100 female U.S. Olympians in gymnastics. If you count those who repeated on teams, the number is even less. The article on "Elite Gymnastics and Reality" paints a good picture for both mother and daughter on these issues. Obviously, the odds against this eventual result are enormous and growing every day!

Physical Presence in the Gym

Most gym schools have rules about parents being present during lessons or training. Some mothers find these very hard to tolerate and conform to, but these controls are established for a reason; avoiding showing-off behavior and preserving concentration being just two. Experience has clearly shown that parents in the gym can often mean problems for the youngster, directly or indirectly. Watching through a one-way mirror may be better but in some cases even that degree of distance is too artificial. We have talked to gymnasts in such settings who know full well that their mothers are watching them and discussing their work with other mothers, and for many daughters this is a very uncomfortable feeling. Under the same condition, we have seen other gymnasts completely relaxed about the whole thing knowing their mothers have brought something to do while they are waiting, who may take a look from time to time without commenting about it later, or who couldn't care less if their parent's nose was glued to the window. Coming into the gym from time to time at the child's request and with the coach's permission, to see a specific movement, etc., is a different kettle of fish altogether, and very appropriate. Often mothers will take on a job in the gym such as helping with the bookkeeping, organizing some fund raising activity and the like, as an aspect of a parent booster association or related group support system. This too, is quite a different matter and a legitimate avenue for a kind of vicarious participation, provided it is kept rational in character. Again, it is all a matter of the basic fiber of the daughter-mother relationship and how it has developed in regards to independent functioning primarily outside of the gym.

Although attendance at competitions is a fun thing for many parents and their children, we strongly recommend that from time to time, no parent be present during a competition. Let the gymnast be on her own completely, insofar as parents are concerned. The presence or absence of the parent at a meet may or may not influence performance. For most gymnasts, whose reasons for being there are personally solid and who are intent on the competition, parents in the audience are totally insignificant. Once more, it is an individual matter, but still worthy of consideration. The parent who proudly announces, "I've never missed one of my daughter's meets," may not be providing the ideal model that the statement overtly suggests.

Summary

In an article such as this, it is not possible to address all the implications of the mother-daughter-gym interaction. We have tried to at least highlight some basic issues and provide some food for further thought. We cover additional information in the article "Parental Involvement in Competitive Gymnastics." In addition, we have provided some suggestions for both parents of young competitive gymnasts dealing with these issues in the guidelines entitled "Parenting Commandments."

PARENTAL INVOLVEMENT IN COMPETITIVE GYMNASTICS

What is the most appropriate level of involvement in your child's sport and how is it established? Ask anyone and you will get a multitude of answers. There are parents who rejoice in their children's accomplishments no matter the outcome, encourage them at times of disappointment and give them the stamina to persist while providing an ongoing model for commitment and good spirit. On the other hand, there are those parents who think their child can never do well enough or have become over-involved and see the child as the ultimate extension of themselves and take their children's successes and failures as very personal reflections of their own performance record.

Here are nine basic guidelines to help you determine the most appropriate level of involvement in your child's sport whether they are just beginning competition, a teen with a few seasons behind them, or even a collegiate competitor. It is important to recognize that the influence of both parents is very significant for children of either sex and their respective roles in the rearing process will determine the nature of their specific input as well as the outcomes. These are by no manner exhaustive; however they highlight some of the issues surrounding the parent-child-gymnastics interaction.

Parenting Guidelines and Commandments:

1. **The number one thing to remember is that this is your child's thing.** If you feel because you pay the bills you can get into their gymnastics anyway you wish, then we suggest you are 100% wrong and it would probably be better to try something else.

2. **Your involvement should be on your child's terms as much as possible.** This is most difficult to determine when we are speaking of 7 or 8 year olds. However, even at this young age there are clues that will come from the child (how easily she separates from you, etc.). At this level, it will have to be a judgment call by you and only you can determine, perhaps in consultation with the coach, where you are coming from. For latency age and up into adolescence, let the youngster call the majority of the shots about her gymnastics and your participation in it.

3. **Encourage, transport, show interest, but not intrusion.** Your child may very well resent interference, although tolerating it on the surface. Please try to avoid any prolonged whisper sessions with the coach!

4. **Don't be afraid to ask your child if they want or don't want you at meets.** If they say they'd like you to come, fine. If they don't wish you to be there all the time or perhaps not at all, try not to make them feel guilty

about that decision. In the long run, you will be doing your child a special service they may not overtly thank you for but will appreciate inside on a psychological level.

5. **If you think a practice or meet didn't go well, be as supportive as possible, low keyed, and cool.** We're not recommending that you restrain all the emotion—that would be unnatural, but try to keep it in perspective. Share the pride of success, but try to avoid slipping into a depression when things don't go right. It is the coach's job to analyze what happened or didn't, in terms of the youngster's gymnastics, not yours. Avoid obsessing about the outcome and try to remember you have a very crucial impact on your child's attitude at these times. Reading the article "My Goal is to…" can help you understand your child's motives and goals.

6. **At competitions, if your child has had a "bad" meet let the coach handle it.** In fact, who's to say it was "bad?" Stay off the floor, away from the judges and other gymnasts. (We once actually heard a parent say to another gymnast other than her own daughter, "My kid really got shafted, don't you think so?") It might appear an insult to the intelligence of our readers but such things do in fact occur.

7. **Monitor your involvement.** From time to time review your involvement and your feelings about yourself in relation to your child's athletics. This is easier said than done since most of us are blind to our own true motivations. It is surely worth the effort however, for you might just recognize a problem as it is emerging and before it becomes serious and irreversible.

8. **If you should have more than one child in the sport, stringently try to avoid making any comparisons.** Their individuality in terms of self-worth and competence will be self-evident. Treat them as separate entities but equally in terms of your investment in their work.

9. **Be natural and follow your common sense.** Let your own common sense and intuition about your individual youngster determine the track you run on when it comes to their gymnastics. It is a better idea to play by ear, not by a predetermined script.

These basic guidelines are primarily directed at the parents of young athletes, even teens and college-aged gymnasts; however, this information is pertinent for the family members involved as well as the coaches. Hopefully, some of the ideas presented may help everyone with a child in sports, acknowledge and understand some of the issues which might often be experienced or felt but left unsolved. **Talk** with your child, **share** your feelings, and mutually **work together** so that your child can experience the best gymnastics has to offer.

PARENTING COMMANDMENTS

Here are nine basic guidelines to help you determine the most appropriate level of involvement in your child's sport. These are by no manner exhaustive; however they highlight some of the more important issues surrounding the parent-child-gymnastics interaction. For full descriptions see the article "Parental Involvement in Competitive Gymnastics."

Parenting Commandments

- **The number one thing to remember is that this is your child's thing.**
- **Your involvement should be on your child's terms as much as possible.**
- **Encourage, transport, show interest, but not intrusion.**
- **Don't be afraid to ask your child if they want or don't want you at meets.**
- **If you think a practice or meet didn't go well, be as supportive as possible.**
- **At competitions, if your child has had a "bad" meet let the coach handle it.**
- **If you have more than one child in the sport, avoid making comparisons.**
- **Monitor your involvement in your child's sport.**
- **Be natural and follow your own common sense.**

SCHOOL, PEERS, AND GYMNASTICS

First of all, it should be obvious that serious training in gymnastics requires a very big commitment of time. If you're going to the gym three or more hours a day, four, five or even six days a week you are making a real decision about how you organize your life. Most public schools are in session five hours a day and if you add on your gymnastic training program, including transportation to and from the gym, the day is pretty well filled up. There isn't much time left for anything else to go on, to any great degree.

Having worked in public school and university settings as well as private gymnastics clubs, we personally spent a great deal of time talking to and working with school age youngsters and college athletes. The students talked to us about problems they were having in school, with work, teachers, peers and parents and any other matters that they are concerned about all the time. Over the years that we have been in our sport, we have talked to hundreds of young athletes about issues surrounding school and we thought it would be useful to share some of our observations with you.

Mental Organization

One of the things that we have observed, contrary to what someone might expect, is that most gymnasts are pretty successful in school. As a matter of fact, many better gymnasts are often better students. One of the reasons for this is that serious gymnastics training forces you to be very well organized. In the gym this organization means you have to follow a program that gets the job done. This is usually managed by the coach who works out a schedule that allows for rotation among events, compulsories, optionals, conditioning, dance, etc., so that your time is used efficiently. If it isn't, you'll be in the gym until the wee hours of the morning and will soon fall down with exhaustion!

This kind of gymnastic organization carries over to your out of the gym life as well. Order is important to most gymnasts who like to have a predictable schedule to follow. Included in this planning is when to do your homework, your chores, special studying for tests, religious school, etc., and how to divide what remains of the day into periods that allow you to manage your out of the gym time with equal efficiency. It appears that this type of sound and careful planning is an almost automatic thing that comes from participating in gymnastic training. You will find out that without it, either your gymnastics or your schoolwork will suffer. At times, the pressure in this regard can become great and youngsters lose tempers with parents, parents with children and tears often flow. Everyone usually recovers with patience and mutual understanding about the frustrations.

Not only do gymnasts tend to have tightly organized days they also appear to have tightly organized minds as well. Mental organization is not just a matter of chance. It is a good idea to actually write out a daily schedule which includes how you will approach your various responsibilities each day. Included in this should be some period that is just your own, that doesn't belong to the school or gym. This is a rest and relaxation time to be used as you want in a private way and shared only if you wish it to be. This is a very difficult piece to come up with because by the time everything else is in place there may be precious little left. We feel it is very important, however, to try and fit this in as often as possible, even if it is just 15 or 30 minutes. Your parents need to help and cooperate in this effort.

We are often asked my opinion about the bottom line, that is, if push comes to shove, what should have priority, gymnastics or school? Being gymnastic fanatics, deep in our hearts we hear a whisper which says, "Gymnastics, gymnastics!" but in our rational minds, we know that the answer must be school. If one has to choose because of the pressure of doing too much, we would have to vote in favor of school work, since the young person's education in today's world is very important. If you are such a talented gymnast that your world-class performance would suffer from a reduction in gymnastics while you are getting caught up in school, then you should probably be in a special educational arrangement. We don't mean this sarcastically, as many top notch national and international gymnasts have drastically reduced their school attendance in order to concentrate on their training. Whether they finish high school in three, four, or five years is irrelevant, and that is a decision that they make in consultation with parents, school officials, and coaches. In addition, the availability of alternative learning programs, such as homeschooling, tutoring, and online high school have made an impact on this issue. One word of warning; besides the emotional upset that can take place when there is too much tension keeping up with a very tight and demanding schedule as we described earlier, there is also the possibility that one can become physically sick as well.

Peers and Friendships

Another matter that gymnast-students often talk to us about has to do with friends. In our past interactions with highly motivated and involved gymnasts, suggest that what relationships they have that might be called friendships are usually with other gymnasts. Sometimes they will have one or two non-gymnastic friends but this is not the general rule. Why should this be the case? Well, one thing we have already made clear—you're not available very much to do other things like going to parties, the movies, the arcade, etc. If you are not in the gym, you are home studying. It is pretty tough to build or maintain a relationship when that is the case. Other gymnasts know what it is like and are in the same ball game, hence it is easier to develop and keep a friendship with someone like that with whom you have a lot in common. Other kids get tired of hearing you say, "I can't go on Saturday because I have to be in the gym." They don't understand and after a few times they will give up trying. You can try to get non-gymnastic friends or potential friends involved as spectators, going to meets, and even a workout from time to time but sitting in a balcony watching someone else do gymnastics is hardly the basis for a lasting relationship among preteens and teens. There is little we or anyone can say about this that will make it better. It turns out to be a fact of life when you have decided to dedicate a large chunk of your young years on the planet to competitive gymnastics. Don't fret too much about this, however, for our follow-up with many gymnasts suggest that when their competitive careers end or become less intense (college for example) they have no difficulty making or maintaining friendships, although at first they may be a bit rusty at it!

Image in School

A related problem some gymnasts have shared with us has to do with their image in school. Where is this mysterious person going who disappears immediately after school? Why aren't they here doing sports? What is this gymnastics anyway? How come a couple of days a week they seem to be on a special schedule, leave early or even absent when others are supposed to be in school? We don't like her because we are jealous, but we won't let her know that is the reason; we will pretend it's just her as a person. "Hey Susie, let's see you stand on your hands or do a flip." These are all aspects of social kinds of issues that many gymnasts may face in school.

There are a couple of things you can do to lessen the discomfort that sometimes goes along with being considered "weird" or the "odd person out." For one thing, be proud of your gymnastics ability. Don't keep it a secret and share what you are doing with classmates. This shouldn't be done in a show-off way, but with modesty. If you can "educate" the other students to what you are all about you will gain greater acceptance. Gymnasts in elementary school often excel in all areas of physical ability and in games or athletic tests of one kind or another. This can single you out in a positive way and you should not hold back in order to avoid being considered special. As a matter of fact, you are special and your ability, not your mouth, will demonstrate this to others. Keep your teachers informed about your activities and discuss any problems with them. One gymnast arranged with her coach for her entire class to come to the gym one day for a fun get-together. This not only cleared up some of the mystery about gymnastics but gave the youngster a new basis for relationships.

The kind of issues we have been discussing can be less of a problem at the high school level especially if you belong to the high school team and compete for your team. This can make you very popular indeed with kids of the same and opposite sex. In high school many of the difficulties more or less take care of themselves. The gymnasts who stay with club programs and do not compete with their school teams face similar problems, however, as the younger gymnasts, except they have age and maturity on their side. They all face the potential problem of time available to socialize and participate in the normal activities of teenagers.

Summary

In closing, let's summarize some of the major points made in this article:

- Training in gymnastics takes a great deal of time. Write out a daily schedule for yourself that will make your out-of-gym time, as well organized, as your gym time.
- Allow for about 15 to 30 minutes a day just for yourself. No gymnastics, no school work, no chores.
- Be patient with your parents, etc., when time pressure begins to wear on everyone's nerves.
- Be proud of your gymnastics. Share what you are doing with classmates, teachers, and family, etc., as appropriate.
- Don't be embarrassed by your physical ability. Let it speak for itself, however, remain modest.
- Whenever possible educate people in your life (friends, grandparents etc.) to your sport. Bring them to the gym; invite them to meets or related social activities.
- Being an accomplished gymnast can often mean being somewhat isolated from the social mainstream of school life. Do your best to minimize this but don't worry about it, it goes with the territory. More often than not, it evens out in the long run. Enjoy your gymnastics while you can.

CHANGING GYMS
PITFALLS AND STRATEGIES

Although changing gyms is not an everyday event in most well run programs, it is common enough, within the sport, to warrant some examination. If the change is due to a family move to a new geographical location, it is an entirely different matter than one that involves moving to another program. In the latter case, the move often reflects some degree of dissatisfaction with the current training situation. At times, it is less a matter of total dissatisfaction than it is a notion that the individual growth of the gymnast will be better realized in a new setting.

Sometimes a change of gyms is quite appropriate. Although the youngster and his/her parents may like the coach and the general setting there may, in fact, be justification for a move. For example, if a program can only take a talented gymnast just so far and not beyond, because it does not provide a comprehensive experience, then the change is often warranted and less stressful. In the majority of cases, however, this is not the usual reason for leaving.

The purpose of this article is to look at some of the issues surrounding changing gyms such as the parent's role as well as from the perspective of the coaches involved. Some recommended strategies for reducing their impact on everyone concerned will be presented. Major focus will be on issues for coaches and gymnasts when the decision to move has been made. These changes, when they do occur, often have built in problems for coaches, parents, and gymnasts, both in terms of the program being left **"departing gym"** and the new one being entered **"receiving gym."** This is true no matter how harmonious the decision has been made and carried out.

Parental Role

Parents, most importantly, need to be clear about their role and influence in this decision and be responsible for assuring that rational behavior will prevail. If possible, it would be worthwhile for parents to receive some neutral consultation from a professional in the sport prior to making any final decision.

Often, parents and gymnasts want to keep the idea of changing gyms a "secret" from the current coach until the last minute. We feel this is a serious mistake and highly recommend that if a new local setting is being considered, it be discussed openly and honestly with the current coach as soon as feasible. To do otherwise, besides being highly unethical, places the youngster under a great deal of unnecessary pressure. Open dialogue may be more painful and will not eliminate all problems, but it can surely serve to reduce future difficulties.

Departing Gym

Unless the coach is a saint, and that is most unlikely, there are almost always some residual feelings of resentment about the gymnast who has left the program regardless of how smoothly the move was managed. Obviously, this is particularly true if the athlete was a top notch competitor in the gym being left behind. In reality, this kind of move can definitely do real damage and disrupt the winning edge of some competitive teams. In these cases the resentment sometimes manifests anger, and animosity can be severe. It is perfectly natural for a coach, who has developed a youngster over a number of years, to be hurt and emotionally bothered about the fact that he or she has lost a good gymnast after so many hours of commitment. Coach reaction is basically a matter of the personality of the individual and their level of maturity, as well as a factor of time, in the specific program.

Recommended Actions by the Coach of the Departing Gym

Experience has shown that time does heal most such wounds, but there are some actions that the coach, losing such an athlete, might want to think about taking more immediately (other than crying or having a temper tantrum!):

1. **Open discussion.** Obviously, the first thing to do is to be very clear as to why the move took place, and that is one reason that the open discussion referred to earlier is so important. If that has not occurred, we strongly recommend that the coach seek out the answer in a rational manner. This is not a way of altering or changing the decision but is a method for understanding what went wrong, if anything, in a particular individual case. Unfortunately "gym jumping" can be contagious, and it is not unheard of for several youngsters to leave when one does, especially if friendship bonds had developed between the different gymnasts and their respective parents. Being reasonably sure as to why the move happened will allow the coach to possibly modify behavior or program elements that need to be addressed in order to establish more "holding" power for the future. In most cases, however, such a move involves an individual athlete, but an ounce of special exploration is surely worth the effort—not only to get answers to nagging personal questions, but also to stabilize the program.

2. **Team conference.** Another important action the coach, losing a gymnast, might want to think about is to have a frank discussion with the other gymnasts about the move. Such a discussion can help deal with any myths or rumors that have begun to develop among the remaining athletes,

and can help the entire training effort get back on track. Coaches need to carefully avoid bad-mouthing the gymnast who has left. Negative comments can only detract from the issue being considered, and can lower the respect that the children have for the coach. In such a discussion, the coach should maturely present the issues in a calm manner, answer relative questions, and allow the gymnasts to respond as they wish. This does not have to be a big deal, but such a forum can eliminate future issues and help further establish a coach's integrity with his or her team. Choosing to do this is again an individual matter, and highly dependent on the coach's ego and group discussion skills. Refer to the article "The Coach: Gymnast Conference: Listening and Other Art Forms" for suggestions on running this meeting.

3. **Talk to the "receiving coach."** An additional step that a coach, losing a gymnast, should seriously consider is to discuss the change with the new receiving coach. Most local programs know each other and very often compete against one another during the competitive season. It is very important, to professional coaching, that such moves be managed in an adult and responsible manner. In many cases, coaches sign contracts that prohibit them from working in other local programs for a given time period, should they leave their current position. There are no such restrictions on gymnasts and it is important that communication between programs be kept open, since the guiding principle for all professional gymnastic coaches should be a focus on what is best for any individual child. In the fierce competitive business climate of today's gymnastic programs this may appear naive, but we suggest that such behavior is, in fact, not only honorable, but in the long run very good for "business." Such positive and sensitive actions are communicated around, through the club-school network, and can have a very real effect on the image and reputation of any given program as well as the individuals who direct them.

4. **Termination conference.** One of the most difficult things to accomplish, at this time, is to swallow one's pride and wish the departing youngster good luck. This can be handled through a letter, but often a face-to-face meeting to clear the air is most appropriate. The age of the youngster is a factor in the decision, but such a "termination conference" is reasonable with early adolescent and adolescent gymnasts. Once more, it is an individual matter and primarily contingent on the maturity of the coach. In some cases such a meeting is simply too difficult for all parties concerned, and that

is understandable. To be successful and productive, a final meeting should only take place when both the coach and gymnast are comfortable with such a process.

5. **Future behavior.** A danger that needs to be stated out loud, although one would like to believe that it is not necessary, is a warning to coaches about their future behavior towards a gymnast who has left their program. Your authors have witnessed some unforgivably immature, downright cruel and irrational behavior on the part of coaches, including those on the national level, who have lost a good gymnast and encounter them for the first time since the move at a competition. In one Elite meet, while a gymnast was warming up on floor ex, a former coach came onto the floor and told the gymnast she could not use the music nor choreography because it was not her property. It was temporarily resolved but the damage was done. Fortunately, the gymnast was mentally tough and she performed a decent routine. It may seem incredible, but more often than not it does happen. We have even known of cases where a coach deliberately prepared the other team members to be rude and even worse, to put former team members down in every conceivable way during the course of a competition. It should be obvious that such behavior is despicable and intolerable in adults who purport to care about young people. Even benign neglect, in the form of ignoring a former club member, is better than overt hostility although that stance is also borderline at best. Again, this is why some form of planned "leaving off" conference is so critical at the time of departure.

6. **Be aware of the "mood" of the team.** As mentioned earlier in this article, friendship patterns usually develop between gymnasts and their parents among the youngsters and adults in a given program. There is little that the coach, losing a gymnast, can or should have to do about this issue, other than to be aware of it and alert to the level of unhappiness and residual moodiness that might be present among remaining friends of the departing youngster. The adults will have to manage the problems themselves, as it is the price that is paid when the decision to leave is made. In time other patterns of social interaction develop in the new setting, but that is not the coach's immediate concern.

Receiving Gym

In a local gym change, there are special problems that the receiving coach needs to be aware of and prepared to address:

Recommended Actions by the Coach of the Receiving Gym

7. **Team acceptance/rejection.** One obvious difficulty is the level of acceptance or rejection by the new teammates of the latest arrival. If the arriving gymnast is quite talented, this issue is usually significant. Although the new athlete may represent an asset to the team and its overall performance competence, he or she also serves as a threat to the current team members at a variety of levels. This becomes even a greater problem if the receiving coach, in a legitimate effort to make the newcomer feel welcome, gives special attention to the new gymnast. Jealousy, envy, and a sense of abandonment are emotional responses that may be displayed by original team members, particularly when some neglect is involved. Coaches, who want to demonstrate how "powerful" they are to the new person, may also vary their usual behavior towards the existing team members. This can only serve to make matters worse. Rarely are these negative feelings on the part of original team members overtly expressed, although that can occur. More often their frustration is shown by team members ignoring the new gymnast, or even isolating them from the group's informal social interactions in the training setting. Such behavior, along with some snide comments, is not atypical for preadolescent or adolescent youngsters. The best way for the receiving coach to handle this difficulty, again involves anticipation and prevention.

8. **Team conference.** It would be a mistake to make a mountain out of a molehill, since a certain degree of "initiation" by other members of the team is normal and to be expected, prior to genuine acceptance. In addition, experienced and mature teams take the whole thing in stride and there often is no issue. However, the receiving coach may want to seriously consider having a team meeting prior to the new athlete's arrival, to air out any concerns in this regard. If this meeting is not held, the receiving coach needs to carefully monitor the situation and intervene when appropriate so things do not get out of control. It is also important that the coach monitor his or her behavior as well, insofar as over-attending to the needs of the new gymnast is concerned. Uncharacteristic doting behavior may raise the emotional temperatures of original team members unnecessarily. Given time and sensitive management, most of these kinds of problems mitigate themselves as team members grow to appreciate and accept the new arrival. Again, it all takes time and involves the coach's judgment and level of personal maturity.

9. **Monitor coaching comments.** An additional difficulty that the receiving coach may face has to do with manifest differences in coaching style and approach to gymnastics in general. It would be very easy for a receiving coach to "put down" the past coach even on an unconscious level. This is usually a

subtle matter and involves such comments as "we don't do it that way here," "no wonder you're having so much trouble with that move," "that technique went out with the dinosaurs," and many examples too numerous to articulate. The new coach must make a real effort to avoid this kind of thing; not only because it is unprofessional, but also because it may well reduce the level of respect that the new athlete is building with you in the new setting, regardless of your reputation as a good coach. Past loyalties are not easily transferred, even when the prior circumstances might not have been ideal. Making such comments, as illustrated above, may alienate the arriving gymnast, or even create some resistance in the new setting.

10. **Adjustment period.** Another related problem that the receiving coach may have to contend with is the idea that they are going to "fix" everything that they have inherited in terms of the new gymnast's performance abilities. In an effort to have the arriving athlete fit in and conform to training and performance expectations as soon as possible, the receiving coach may both technically and emotionally overload the new gymnast's processing circuits. It is very important that the new coach be patient during this adjustment period, both on a technical as well as an attitudinal level. As the new youngster's comfort level increases, he or she will be better able to take in and utilize performance feedback without comparing the data to that received in the old setting. In most cases, the coach-gymnast communication system will gradually develop and training can move ahead free of baggage from the past gym, which might otherwise interfere with the new teaching-learning model. See "The Art of Feedback: A Model for Coach–Gymnast Communication."

Summary

The discussion in this article concerning changing local gyms, although not exhaustive, touches on a few of the crucial issues that need to be recognized by both the coach losing a gymnast from a program and the coach who is inheriting the athlete. Most gym changes involve a certain unavoidable degree of discomfort and adjustment by all parties involved. With that as a given fact, it can be managed less painfully when:

- Communication between gymnast, coaches, and parents is open, direct, and as complete as possible.
- Preventive strategies are employed on both ends of the equation.
- Adjustment time is freely given for everyone concerned.

THE DECISION TO QUIT

"It just isn't fun anymore." "I'm getting tired of it." "Sometimes, I'm in the gym and realize I don't want to be there." This illustration represents quotes which were taken from a conversation with a sixteen year-old gymnast who had been involved in the sport for close to six years with two years of high level competition. They were spoken during a meeting with the athlete to help the youngster sort out her feelings and decide whether or not she should stay in gymnastics.

When you have spent nearly half your time on the planet doing a certain activity such as gymnastics, which was the case for this gymnast, it is not an easy thing to decide if you should change your lifestyle and retire at an early age. Many young gymnasts, however, who have begun their gymnastics careers very early in life, are facing this issue in increasing numbers. In the case quoted above it is relatively clear that to continue in the sport with such strong feelings consciously coming to the surface on a regular basis is quite foolish. There are coaches who would say that everything should be done to keep the gymnast going and, up to a point, we agree with this position. On the other hand, long experience has shown that when the point of alienation from the activity is very dramatic, it is mentally unsound and emotionally harmful to continue. To do so may also eventually lead to physical injury, as a gymnast's mind is not where it should be, and a break in attention at the wrong time can result in a serious accident.

Considerations for the Gymnast

The reasons youngsters arrive at this point are numerous and it is not possible to cover all of them in one article. However, there are some basic struggles that contribute and lead to such a moment of decision and they are worth considering.

1. **Social frustration.** A growing awareness of the social consequences and sacrifices that often go along with high level training is a major contributing factor in a gymnast's wondering, "Why am I doing this?" "Is it really worth it?" "Should I quit?" The answers to these questions that are arrived at by gymnasts are primarily the result of individual differences among the athletes. The fact that these questions arise, to whatever degree is probably a reflection of a universal experience all athletes face at one time or another.

2. **Degree of satisfaction.** One of the factors that can make a difference in the final outcome when it is triggered by social frustration is the degree of psychological satisfaction and general happiness that the gymnast experiences in the training setting. It takes an enormous degree of

motivation to sustain effort in the gym when there is a lot of negative feedback or where the overall climate for artistic endeavor is far from ideal. This is even more critical in light of ongoing school pressures. If there is an absence of camaraderie or friendship in the gym and a total focus on fierce competition, it is quite likely that certain gymnasts are not going to be able to handle the situation. Obviously, this is more the case in settings where the coaching philosophy is to produce champions and win at all costs. This attitude may work for a time, but eventually programs that are insensitive to the development needs of youngsters are apt to fail and literally stop producing. Too many will leave too soon and, most unfortunately, for the wrong reasons.

3. **Physical injuries.** Another important factor in the decision to quit or not often has to do with the number of physical injuries a gymnast has had and how they were managed. Getting some type of injury in this sport is not unusual. Surely, everyone strives to minimize them but injuries somewhat come with the territory. A gymnast who has an inordinate number of nagging mishaps or a few serious ones is going to become aware of the price paid in this area and begin to evaluate the wisdom of continuing. Again, responses are a matter of personality differences, but prevention in the first place and considerate, caring management when an injury does occur can do a lot to help the gymnast handle this problem in a positive way. See the article "Psychological Recovery from Injury" for more information.

4. **Personal drive and commitment.** An additional factor that often becomes involved in the decision to quit has to do with the "reason" for participating in gymnastics. Kids are motivated to do gymnastics for many reasons but in order to keep going one has to have a very high personal commitment. Dreaming of being on TV or a national champion is a fine reason for beginning but the road to fame is rough and few are capable or willing to pay their dues. To continually train and tolerate all of the restrictions that implies without progress and results is most frustrating indeed. The technical demands of the sport in our day make success even more difficult to obtain. Just how long can a youngster pursue an activity where the rewards are minimal and they feel they're always at the bottom looking up? Not very long. There is simply not enough return on the investment to keep the gymnast going, despite the dream, without extraordinary drive.

5. **Parental involvement.** Another factor that often creeps into the conflict over whether to continue to do gymnastics or stop has to do with the degree of parental involvement that the athletes experiences. If the focus for doing gymnastics gradually changes and the youngster finds they are

doing it to please his/her parents then the great effort needed to keep going will often diminish rather quickly. This is particularly true, as it becomes clearer to the gymnast that their parents are in fact competing or living through them. Sorting out "who is doing what for whom" becomes a real issue especially as the gymnast matures. Spurts of progress will begin to grind to a halt as the lines between the individual athlete and significant others become blurry. Parents and gymnasts may be interested in "My Daughter, the Competitive Gymnast."

6. **Personal identity.** As with our opening illustration, the decision to continue or leave the sport often takes place during the early and middle teenage years. The sense of social isolation and school demands referred to earlier often lead to the dilemma at this age. However, there is an even more critical reason that this choice may rise to the forefront during adolescence. This period of life is normally marked by a struggle to achieve an individual identity and personal autonomy. It is a time when youngsters need and want to feel a strong sense of ownership in decisions, and to begin directing the course of their lives themselves. Although gymnastic training can involve some give and take, it is essentially an activity where the gymnast places him/herself in the hands of another. Following directions, taking orders, having your time scheduled by someone else, etc., are all aspects of the discipline of gymnastic training. There is one area, however, where the youngster can exercise a powerful option and that is the "choice to stop" when others may wish them to continue. Asserting one's self-direction in this manner leaves little doubt as to who is ultimately in charge. Depending on the degree of autonomy felt in other areas of their life, this internalized psychological struggle to get control can often be acted out successfully through this important decision.

7. **Individual potential.** There are of course, things that can be done inside and outside of the gym to reduce the chance that a gymnast will stop participating in the sport before they have reached their potential. But who is to say what that potential is? One coach will say a specific youngster would be a good optional gymnast, another coach might consider that same gymnast a mediocre compulsory gymnast, while a parent might feel they have an Olympian on their hands. In the last analysis, an individual's potential is measured by what they in fact do. If they remain active long enough to realize more of their potential it will probably be the result of developmental soundness, educational security, sensitive parents, and caring coaches rather than from a manipulation of their environment. For those who leave so called "prematurely" by the adult standard, it may in reality mark a most healthy decision despite some burnt fingers and bruised egos. Additional research and

factors leading to leaving the sport prematurely are discussed in the article "Reasons for Dropping-Out."

Checklist for the Gymnast

Here is a basic checklist to go through before making such a major decision in your young life:

- First of all, make sure what you are feeling is not just the result of a bad day or spell. Every athlete has these feelings once in a while and with time and renewed effort they often pass. In other words, don't jump the gun.
- Share your feelings with your coach and parents in any order. It is extremely important to determine if you are being listened to. If you are threatened at this point by either a parent or coach, you need to think very hard about their attitude and your motivation.
- Sometimes a change of setting, a new gym, can help but often the issues are within you and changing locations will do little good in the long run. However, it is worth some thought if the "place" appears to be the problem.
- If at all possible share your concerns and dilemma with someone you trust, preferably an adult who has nothing whatsoever to do with gymnastics or any investment in your participation in it. A neutral opinion can be most enlightening (teacher, youth leader, etc.).
- Make a list of pros and cons for staying or leaving. Be honest with yourself and give your list time to develop. Review it regularly.
- It may be necessary to take a trial "retirement" and see how being away from gymnastics feels. For many gymnasts the answer to quit or not to quit comes quickly when this is tried.
- If, after very careful thought, your negative feelings persist as with the girl in the beginning of this article, then, sad as it may be to realize, your gymnastics is probably no longer worth it and your career should come to an end.
- If you have given it your best shot and considered all the factors involved openly then you can make this difficult decision without guilt and with a sense of accomplishment at another level, you have grown-up a little more.

Illustration

Continuing with our sixteen year old national champion, we had the opportunity to meet with her to discuss her feelings and then with the gymnast and her parents together where the decision was made to leave the sport. Some genuine tears were shed and the youngster's mother admitted that she would miss the excitement involved in having a top notch child to watch and share this kind of experience with over the years. Her mother went on to say that she appreciated, supported, and respected her child's decision. This honesty helped the meeting end on a positive note with parents hugging their youngster. The gymnast's courage and the parent's behavior were moving and all deserved a medal. It would be wonderful if all such difficult moments could be managed in such a mutually supportive fashion.

Summary

In closing, we want to give a word to parents and coaches. If the decision to stop doing gymnastics is difficult for the youngster, it can be equally disheartening for parents and coaches. At this time, the gymnast needs your love, support, understanding, and rational behavior. Coercion, guilt trips, (e.g. "How can you do this after all we spent?"), anger, or an attitude that communicates that you want them to stay with it despite their feelings or to feel that you, as the adult, always know what is "best for them" is to entertain a dangerous myth that could backfire in the future. It is important to remember that the child's best interest should be the only consideration at all levels by everyone involved.

Finally, perhaps this article is misnamed, since quitting has a negative ring to it. It might be better to consider this a "decision to change" and move on to other equally gratifying things in life.

LEAVING HOME TO TRAIN
A CRITICAL DECISION

Over many years we have received a number of letters from parents asking our advice and assistance in making a crucial family decision. This pivotal question has to do with whether or not a daughter or son should move away from home in order to train in gymnastics at a special setting. With the increase in popularity of many disciplines of competitive gymnasts, such as rhythmic and tumbling and trampoline, we are seeing more gymnasts searching for specialized programs. There are a number of clubs across the country that have accommodations for youngsters, or who locate appropriate housing for them to live in, while training at the particular club. These programs often have national reputations, and are designed for very special athletes who are elites or have elite potential. All of these programs engage in a vigorous evaluation of the youngster's gymnastic talent and readiness for such a step, as well as a consideration of other factors that could make such a move a success or failure. Most clubs do not make this decision lightly, and have a heavy responsibility to weigh a host of related issues. The parents have an even greater responsibility in this regard.

Focus in this article will be on factors that the family needs to carefully consider when this kind of move is being entertained, even as a remote possibility. Although this is not a common situation that many families with gymnasts face, it is hoped that the discussion will have broader implications of interest to any parents whose youngsters are involved in high-level competitive gymnastics. Coaches should also find this information helpful and may want to share this with their parents.

Questions to Ask

A first important question to answer is why such a move is even being thought about. In most cases, it reflects dissatisfaction with the current training situation. At times it is less a matter of dissatisfaction, as it is a sense that the youngster's gymnastic growth will be better enhanced in a more concentrated setting. Both of these reasons are legitimate, if we are talking about a highly gifted child whose potential is obvious and proved to some degree or another. In most cases, the potential receiving clubs own evaluation will take care of many such myths, but this is not always the case. Therefore, before even letting this idea take root in your mind, you need to discuss it with a professional gymnastic coach who is not a relative and who has or currently trains the child. Some parents want to keep this notion a secret from the gymnast's current coach. We feel this is a mistake, not only because it puts the child under terrific pressure, but also because it is highly unethical. We strongly recommend that if you feel your child needs a new setting, not just a new gym, but one that involves leaving home for a period of time, that you deal with this issue openly and honestly with the child's current trainer. A change of local gyms should involve the same kind of mature behavior which we discuss in the article "Changing Gyms: Pitfalls and Strategies." In some cases, the recommendation to leave is proposed by the coach, and this is obviously a different matter altogether. If this is not the case, and it usually isn't, involve the current coach in your thinking, well before any decisions are made. Worrying that you will hurt his or her feelings is not an acceptable excuse.

A second question to ask is whose idea is it to make the move. Many youngsters have aspirations that far outstrip their actual capacity, and parents who foster the idea that going away from home will be the ultimate solution is often promoting a dangerous illusion. Along the same lines is the parent who believes their child is the next Olympian so they go in search of a program away from home. Parents may wish to read "My Daughter, the Gymnast" for more insight. We have actually spoken with some parents who have been thinking about this kind of very disruptive move simply on the basis of the youngster's spoken desire to do so. No early adolescent, or even adolescent, and surely no younger child is in a position to make such a decision. Obviously, parents should not make this kind of decision unilaterally without a great deal of research and without a continual dialogue with their youngster. Every case is unique, but in all cases the child's overall well-being should be the determining factor, not solely her gymnastics.

Parental Considerations

If this kind of move is being contemplated, it is absolutely essential that a preplanned visit or series of visits take place before finalizing any decision. In many cases, a clearly defined trial period is indicated, and this will usually help everyone to arrive at a more rational decision with a greater degree of comfort than otherwise would be possible. Along with an on-site exploration and trial, the following is a partial list of major factors which we feel need to be carefully considered in arriving at a conclusion about the wisdom of such a move. These come into play assuming it is absolutely clear that the child's gymnastic potential is such that an intense, away from home training setting is indicated, and that no modifications in the existing situations are feasible.

1. **Age of the child:** It is our personal and professional opinion that no child under the age of twelve should leave home to train in gymnastics, regardless of the circumstances. The reasons for this are complex and too lengthy to be discussed in this article, but they involve multiple developmental issues.

2. **Financial considerations:** Parents need to be absolutely clear as to the actual total cost of this kind of effort, and certain that they and other members of the family will not be making a disproportionate sacrifice beyond reason to

support a live-away gymnast. It will be hard enough on the child without having to carry a burden of guilt, feeling that others are doing without, in order that he/she can have this opportunity.

3. **Emotional stability:** Under no circumstances, irrespective of age, should a child with any history of psychological instability or difficulty, be considered for this kind of effort. This includes diagnosed learning problems.

4. **Level of maturity:** It is very important to discuss this kind of decision with your child's pediatrician or a mental health professional to help determine the child's emotional readiness for this move. Some children can manage being away from home with relative ease, especially when a regular schedule of visiting has been incorporated into the plan. For others, this decision, although appearing sensible at several levels, can have long term effects and cause serious emotional damage to the youngster. Previous separation experience can provide some indication of readiness, but not a definitive measure, especially if the conditions associated with a prior absence were quite different (overnight extended camp, etc.). This is a very unique exposure and professional consultation should be sought.

5. **Siblings:** The child's age in relationship to his/her siblings is an additional important factor. Often, chronological and emotional closeness to a brother(s) or sister(s) can be a deterrent to successful adjustment in this kind of dislocation. Parents with an only child, as well as the youngster themselves, will find this decision extremely difficult to make with any true certainty.

6. **Proximity of training setting to home:** Accessibility is important. The child needs to feel their parents are available, not on a check-in basis, but at least spiritually. A setting closer to home can foster this kind of security, versus a program on the other side of the country. If there is a choice available, and most factors are equal, choose the facility nearer home.

7. **Educational concerns:** These considerations are of enormous importance. Most gymnasts are very good students, at least with academic goals of a very high order. Questions in the area of quality of the new academic structure, as well as the implicit cognitive disruption of a move, need to be addressed.

8. **Social issues:** In addition, leaving home usually brings an end to existing peer relationships during the adolescent period of life. This may be less crucial for gymnasts, since such high level athletes usually have little time for intense peer relationships and most often form bonding interactions with other gymnasts. However, the issue is still significant and needs to be carefully evaluated. The basic educational blueprint has long-range implications, and must be thoroughly thought out prior to making any move.

9. **Medical and related issues:** These areas are relatively self-explanatory and require little comment. It is very hard on a young child to be sick, when away from home. Response patterns, as well as emergency procedures, need to be carefully developed and understood by parents, child and the supervisory staff of the host setting. Such apparently simple things as the child's diet need to be considered (kosher, vegetarian, etc.).

10. **Parents' ages and health:** Moving away is tough in its own right, but if the child is worried about their parents' well-being while they are away, it will be defeating the very reason for going. The child will be distracted and fragile. Parents with any special issues, in this regard, should carefully evaluate their impact by themselves or in consultation with a professional.

11. **Criteria for evaluating success:** Prior to making a final decision, it is important that a plan be developed within a specified time frame for evaluating the degree of success of the move. This plan should not only involve an assessment of gymnastics, but of overall adjustment. "What if…" questions should be anticipated, including criteria and the process to be used to end the live-away situation, if appropriate. This should be clear to everyone involved and not seen as a punitive or "expecting the worst" measure, but as a preventive strategy.

12. **Review of the climate of the setting itself:** Along with the educational and related issues discussed earlier, it is important to get a sense of the feel of the proposed home away from home. Does the child have peers in the program who have moved? Are there any children in the same grade and circumstances? From what part of the country? What about the quality of supervision? What is their religious affiliation, etc.? Is this where you want your child to live if they must, in fact, be away? Of course, all the special gymnastic requirements need to be present as a given condition. It is often helpful to talk with parents who have children in the program who are also live-aways. Parents sharing with other parents and kids sharing with other kids about their experiences can help to answer many questions.

13. **Total family move.** Although not common, there have been several cases on record where the entire family has moved to a new location to facilitate their child's gymnastic training. This total familial disruption presents its own set of very special issues and difficulties that are not the subject of this article. In these cases, the child does not face the same separation problems, but there are other, larger separation and relocation questions that are crucial and must be examined. In the few successful cases that we are familiar with which involved total family moves, the youngsters were clearly identified as

Olympic-level athletes. See our article "Elite Level Gymnastics and Reality" for more insight.

Summary

In summation, for the kind of move discussed in this article to have a real chance of success, the child must leave as free of guilt or worry as possible. They must also be highly motivated with an obvious positive attitude, evidencing a sense of joy and anticipation, with the expressed feeling and belief that her parents and family are 100 percent behind them in this endeavor, with a clear idea of special procedures and a timeline for evaluating the experiences from all points of view. In our opinion, no such move should be considered unless all other possible adjustments, including changing to another, more local setting, have been identified and examined. In the final analysis, and putting it succinctly as possible, when there is any doubt in anyone's mind, do not do it! On the other hand, we have known many gymnasts, some of which we coached ourselves, who went on to train away from home with great success.

ELITE LEVEL GYMNASTICS
AND REALITY

The International Gymnast Editor forwarded a letter that had been written to the magazine by a former gymnast, which suggested the possibility for an article in this column. After reading the letter, it appeared that it did provide a topic that would be of interest. Having received permission from the author to reproduce the letter, it is provided below with some modifications designed to insure anonymity of the writer.

> *Dear Editor,*
>
> *I am a fan of your fantastic magazine [IG]. Although I no longer participate in competitions, I still enjoy your magazine. Keep up the good work. The purpose of my letter is not to get it published in "Letters to the Editor," but to suggest an idea for an article to you and your staff.*
>
> *Being from the part of the country I am, there is little exposure to elite level gymnastics. My coach tried to take several girls, including myself, to the elite level last year. The transition was too hard for us, and we were not mentally ready for it. I think the main cause of our problem was our attitudes. We were used to being some of the top gymnasts in the area, but when we went to an elite level meet, we were nothing. We psyched ourselves out during warm ups just watching the other gymnasts.*
>
> *After that season, I quit gymnastics altogether. I think an article on making the transition to the elite level would be useful for coaches and gymnasts. There is so much involved, mentally and physically.*
>
> *Sincerely,*
>
> *Ex-Gymnast*

It is difficult to know what aspect of this letter to address, since it has several clear implications for gymnasts, parents and coaches. First of all, it should be stated that the experience described in the letter is more common than one might suspect; as a matter of fact, we receive letters and phone calls from gymnasts and parents from all over with similar issues, and not just at the elite level. Trying for any level when unprepared is a mistake, particularly elite. We will address various issues brought up in the letter in our discussion on elite level gymnastics.

Elite-level Gymnastics

Perhaps it would be most appropriate to begin with an overall statement concerning elite athletic effort, in general, and then speak specifically about gymnastics. The elite level is the epitome of excellence in amateur sport. Participation at this level is extraordinarily demanding and requires tremendous amounts of dedication, commitment, sacrifice and personal fortitude. It is the world-class level, and although many aspire to achieve at this level, relatively few are successful in reaching their highest objectives. The elite level is the fine tuning arena of motor effort where the physical, cognitive and emotional realms of personal endeavor must come together in a unique harmony. It is for the mentally tough, the highly disciplined, intrinsically motivated and, in a nutshell, "cream of the crop."

In gymnastics, specifically, the above observations apply, but the nature of this activity at the elite level also demands an effort directed, not toward a single type of motor activity or teamwork, but toward mastery of concrete exercises in separate complex events. In addition, three concurrent demands are continually present: physical endurance training, concentrated flexibility training, and specialized mental preparation. There are few other sports pursued by women (or, for that matter, men) that present so many challenges on the long road to top competence. Added to all these requirements are the high risk factors associated with world-class gymnastics today, which further serves to eliminate and self-select successful participants at the elite level.

Most elite gymnasts we know and have known in the past have totally modified their life style for the sake of their training. Many have tailor made school programs, and a substantial number have even physically relocated to take advantage of specific training opportunities or recognized programs focused on the development of excellence. This is not to say that every gymnast at the elite level must be a world-class performer, but it should suggest that elite athletes have the demonstrated capacity to be successful at the national level and the potential to eventually be world and/or Olympic athletes. Many gymnasts would like to call themselves elite, and may even be competing under that label, as a result of having made it into the group through various geographic zone-qualifying competitions (regions also like to claim they have elites, and sometimes politics is involved). However, a good number are really not of the caliber associated with that level and this is usually true, not only in terms of their individual development, but also their long-range competitive production.

Coaching Obligations

It should be obvious that to attempt to enter the world of elite gymnastics, either prematurely or even at all based on any illusions, can lead to the kind of outcome described in our reader's letter. Sometimes even more destructive results are seen on a psychological level, and, most unfortunately, sometimes on a physical level as well. In reading the letter, it appears that certain obligations on the part of the coach were not met.

There is not enough information provided in our reader's letter to know if she and her teammates were at the appropriate entry level (Level 10) or if they had the kind of exposure and experience mandatory for attempting to qualify for elite. However, their combined experiences of basically being paralyzed and "psyched out" during their initial effort suggests that they were not ready at any level for the attempt. If this is the case, and apparently it was, the responsibility for the negative experiences of these young people rests entirely in the lap of the coach. We have met coaches who are quite anxious to get a gymnast into elite, and, in some cases, it is a matter of personal pride and ego enhancement for the coach. It feels good to say that you or your program produces elites, or at least one. It takes a very mature coach to objectively evaluate a gymnast's overall readiness and to consider the painful consequences, at an emotional level, of the discovery that the gymnast is totally outclassed by the competition. Striving to achieve elite status is a legitimate coaching goal, but not at the sacrifice of the athlete or by ignoring reality.

Our reader's letter also suggests that in her home state, there were not a great many elites or elite gymnastics training settings. The same difficulty she describes, however, takes place with gymnasts from locations that have many elite programs that could be observed. Again the responsibility for not providing aspiring gymnasts with guidance and an opportunity to do some preliminary "reality testing," rests with the coach. It is his or her professional obligation to honestly evaluate the potential of the athletes under their charge and to determine if, in fact, they are ready for elite and have the slightest chance for any success. Success is not defined here as making it to the elite level, but trying for this level without leaving the initial experience with a feeling of utter defeat and incompetence. Taking a risk is part of the game, but it should only be done when determining factors have at least been considered. Calculated avoidance is the best strategy to prevent ego damage, for both the coach and gymnast, whenever there is substantial doubt about the outcome.

The letter also states that the "main cause" of the gymnast's problems was "their attitude." The negative attitude being referred to is directly due to observing gymnasts of far greater ability, and becoming psychologically shattered with a consequent loss of focus, as a result of seeing their superior skill. There is no question that this can happen to gymnasts, at all levels, and it has frequently been seen at work at different competitions. The degree of this shock reaction is a personal matter, but, in this case, it would not have occurred if the coach had done proper homework and prepared the gymnasts. If it again appears that the coach is being faulted, that perception is accurate. No matter how great the level of the coach's ambition, the amount of parental pressure, or gymnast's desire, this situation was clearly inappropriate from all perspectives. If the misguided reason for this venture was to teach the gymnasts a lesson and shock them into realizing that although they were "tops" in their area, this was not the case elsewhere, the strategy clearly backfired.

The counter argument to this conservative attitude concerning this issue of readiness, is one that proposed that the level of challenge should always be just out of reach and that with physical and emotional nurturance, provided by a technically skilled and personally sensitive coach, the gymnasts will be able to make it through a reasonable degree of disappointment and be inspired to train even harder. This is, in fact, a very valid position. The problem is to define a "reasonable degree" and to encourage coaches to act in a skilled and sensitive manner. Along with the notion that nothing less than going for gold is of value for kids, are certain erroneous concepts that are often bantered around some high powered gyms that supposedly motivate athletes. Among these are such themes as "no pain, no gain," "practice makes perfect," "your drills become your skills," and others. In actuality, however, there can be much progress without undo suffering. No degree of practice will compensate for a basic lack of talent and, although important, skill acquisition is more a matter of a gymnast's psychological/physiological ability to make corrections, than it is the rote application of repetitive drills. Without a certain degree of measureable success in reaching challenging goals in all areas, the will to prepare gradually declines and no amount of cheerleading can alter the situation. See "Coaching the Team: Part I & II" for more insight.

It is hoped that our readers do not misunderstand the intent of this article. The purpose is not to dampen drive, and it is very important to have lofty ambitions, high objectives, and even inspiring dreams. On the other hand, it is equally important not to distort reality and unnecessarily set a gymnast up for bitter disappointment and perhaps alienation from the sport. Young children and teenagers are not in the position to have the information needed to make certain decisions concerning their place and level in gymnastics, although they should be involved in these issues as much as possible.

The wisdom to make these determinations rests primarily with the professional coach, just as the duty to protect children from emotional damage rests, to a large degree, with parents. In the long run, gymnasts should be guided one day at a time with systematic progressive learning, to rise to their highest level of ability, which is both recognized and rewarded. The wish and tendency to jump ahead, and perhaps skip certain steps on the way, may seem exciting, but it may also mean that the gymnast has skipped a building block or a fundamental step that will impede progress at a later time. In the sport of gymnastics, patience is an extremely critical virtue.

Elite-level Checklist

Finally, here's a suggestion to those coaches and gymnasts who are thinking about the "elite" level. Perhaps it would be of some assistance to consider the following as a type of fundamental checklist:

- Has the gymnast regularly scored in the top three All-Around at a Level 10 state meet?
- Has the gymnast placed in the top three All-Around at a Regional Level 10 competition?
- Does the gymnast have full difficulty in all optional events?
- Has the gymnast's work been compared with the output of recognized elites on a national level?
- Has the gymnast had a comprehensive appraisal by a coach other than her own?
- Has the gymnast received active encouragement from a beret judge who has evaluated elites on a national level? If not, such an assessment should be arranged.

If the answer to most of these basic inquiries is a resounding "yes," then you need only go for it!

Afterword

Congratulations!

We hope you've enjoyed *Gymnastics Psychology: The Ultimate Guide for Coaches, Gymnasts, and Parents*.

The articles and observations presented in this volume are the end product of 100+ combined years of experience acquired in the academic arena as well as the competitive athletic environment as gymnasts, judges, and coaches. Our primary goal is to share what we have learned with our fellow coaches as well as the athletes and their parents who face multiple challenges every day. It is our hope that you will find ideas in this comprehensive guide that can be translated into action within your own specific situations.

Coaches

If you're a coach, many of the articles addressed to you were based on extensive research within the coaching and gymnastics clinics settings. Even though the research took decades to collect, the information correlates to today's training and it is still imperative that you pay attention to the findings and assimilate what you can to incorporate into your own training regimens. Some of the articles provide guidelines especially when it comes to the interaction with your athletes. In the final analysis, how you interact with the youngsters under your charge will define who you are as a mentor.

Gymnasts

If you're a gymnast, many of the articles were written with you in mind. Some were to provide you with concrete tasks to work on and others to show you how to improve your composure and confidence to be the best athlete you can be. In fact, we used your input, or other gymnasts just like you, during our research studies to develop suggestions and guidelines for the coaches as well as your parents so they can better communicate with you about your gymnastics.

Look over your own situation and pick one thing you want to work on first, and go for it! Put it in your Personal Goals Notebook and work out a plan to achieve it. Sharing this with your coach and perhaps your parents will be a great start.

Parents

If you're a parent or family member, we thank you for bringing these wonderful young children into our lives. We are all blessed and somewhat changed by our interactions with them. You will discover that many of the articles are directly related to decisions that have to be made in relation to your own involvement in your child's sport. These are not easy tasks but taking some of the ideas and suggestions may help make your home a more gymnastics friendly environment.

To Our Gymnastics Enthusiasts

To everyone else involved in the sport of gymnastics, whether you are a gym owner, judge, official, instructor, staff, or other support member, we thank you for your dedication to the sport. Hopefully you will reap some benefits from the insights presented in this volume of work.

Special Gift

As a special gift, we are offering a bonus for each of you to help enhance your gymnastics involvement even more in whatever aspect it may be. We have a few different bonuses just right for the coach/gym owner, gymnast, or parent so don't delay and get yours now. Just go to the following link to get your gift. Don't forget to get on our mailing list and we will let you know when our workbooks, audios, and videos are ready for you to enhance your gymnastics' experience.

From Your Authors,
Doc & Dr. Sue

BONUSES

Are You Ready to Realize Your Peak Potential?

If so, follow these simple steps and we'll keep you posted on the latest tips, techniques, and secrets in Gymnastics Psychology!:

1. **Sign up** on our priority mailing list to receive your **Bonuses** and special messages to help you **Reach Your Goals**:
   - GymnasticsPsychology.com/bonus
2. Please leave us a **Review** if you like what you've read, at:
   - Amazon or Barnes & Noble for "Gymnastics Psychology: The Ultimate Guide for Coaches, Gymnasts, and Parents"
   - Please leave a **Testimonial** on any topic in the book which helped you at: www.GymnasticsPsychology.com
3. Join us on:
   - **Facebook** : Gymnastics Psychology
   - **Twitter :** Gymnastics Psychology
   - **YouTube Channel** : Gymnastics Psychology
   - **Text** us at: **707-5 GYMTIP**
     - You'll receive 5 Gymnastics Tips each month
     - (Some Fun, others require practice, but all to help you Reach your Potential!)
     - You'll also get Previews and Coupons for the "Gymnastics Psychology Guidebooks" and audios & videos when they become available.
4. Check out our **Gymnastics Guidebooks** on:
   - Gymnastics History & Research
   - Coaching Psychology
   - Coach/Gymnast Relationships
   - Motivation

- Fear
- Health & Well-Being
- Stress & Anxiety
- Goal Setting
- Mental Gymnastics
- Psycho/Physical Training
- Performance Psychology
- Meet Preparation and Competition
- Psychological Preparation Programs
- Gymnastics Parents

ABOUT THE AUTHORS

Dr. Joe Massimo

Dr. Joe Massimo, affectionately known as "Doc" throughout the gymnastics community, began his career in gymnastics in 1950 and has remained active in the sport ever since. As a competitor, coach, and judge in the 1950s and 1960s, he was appointed to the United States National Coaching Staff in 1969 as a special assistant. This represented an historic moment in the growth of competitive gymnastics with an emphasis placed on developing a "mental strategy/game plan" coupled with a vigorous physical training regimen. Having graduated from Harvard University with a Master's and Doctorate in Clinical and School Psychology, Dr. Massimo focused on helping grow the sport of gymnastics in this country. He was very involved in the transition of power from the American Amateur Athletic Union (AAU) to the United States Gymnastics Federation (USGF) propelling our teams into an international presence while working with several World and Olympic teams over the years.

In the 1980s and 1990s, Dr. Massimo, while continuing his coaching, was a master clinician and lecturer on the national circuit. Serving on the United States Association of Independent Gymnastics Clubs Sports Medicine Council, "Doc" was inducted into their Hall of Fame in 1993, and was inducted into the USA Gymnastics Region VI Hall of Fame in 1994. Appointed to the USA Gymnastics National Athlete Wellness Network as a Sport Psychologist in 1997, he has been listed in the World Sport Psychology Sourcebook, U.S. Olympic Committee Sports Psychology Registry and International Society of Sports Psychology.

Although, many thought "Doc" worked full time in gymnastics, he was the Chief Psychologist for a school system in the suburbs of Boston for nearly 30 years. Supervising a staff of 23 psychologists, he was charged with providing services to 18,000 youth within the context of school and their families. Dr. Massimo also found time to teach as an Asst. Clinical Professor of Education at Harvard University, Asst. Professor of Psychiatry at Boston University School of Medicine and Adjunct Professor of Sport Psychology in the B.U. Graduate School of Education as well as the University of Massachusetts. His clinical work in psychology has been published in every major journal in the United States. He has written nearly 100 articles in the field of gymnastics psychology and coaching and co-authored 3 books and many e-books.

Based on his school and educational background, Dr. Massimo is a strong proponent of supporting a healthy relationship between young athletes, their parents and the teachers and coaches who work with them. As the author of many articles and books about psychology and gymnastics, he found time to be in the gym every day. In addition, Doc has also worked with competitive age-group and Olympic gymnasts

as well as elite athletes from the following sports: figure skating, kick boxing, swimming and diving, soccer, ballroom dancing, track and field, bobsledding, and golf.

Today, even though he is retired, "Doc" Massimo continues to spend his time in the gym welcoming the young students and parents, coaching, and having "psych sessions" with the gymnasts. He loves all the kids, regardless of the age or talent, and could not think of a better place he would rather be.

Dr. Sue Massimo

By the time she was thirteen, Dr. Sue Massimo, knew what she wanted to do with the rest of her life, which was to work with kids in sports. As a competitor on three YMCA and AAU sport teams, she competed at the Regional or Junior National level in gymnastics, swimming and water polo and garnered a National YMCA Youth Fitness Championship. She was influenced by a coach, Mr. Tom Thrailkill, who encouraged her to attend the national YMCA Leader's School for youth instructor/career development program for nine summers and thus became dedicated to pursuing a life of teaching and coaching.

In college, she discovered a new athletic interest that moved her away from competitive gymnastics. Using her gymnastics skills, she became a member of the Florida State Flying High Circus, performing aerial acts, requiring strength and flexibility in choreographed routines.

Her academic pursuits in college included sport psychology, fitness and exercise science, biomechanics, and motor learning. She became an assistant athletic trainer and was certified as a Master Fitness Specialist. Research became her focus when she supervised the Biofeedback Research Laboratory for Sport Sciences at the Boston University, studying stress management in sports. Her doctorate was awarded to her in Sport Psychology and Human Movement after conducting several research studies on the psychological attributes of young competitive gymnasts.

Dr. Sue has been an Elite Gymnastics coach and age-group coach to both men's and women's teams. She has provided psychological skills training to the National Junior Elite Development Program, as an Assistant Sport Psychology Clinician for the Sports Medicine Council of the United States Association of Independent Gymnastics Clubs as well as the National Open Gymnastics Program. Her writings can be found in professional and mainstream periodicals and books. She has written nearly 50 articles in the field of gymnastics psychology and coaching and co-authored 3 books and many e-books. Besides gymnastics, she has worked with young athletes in horseback riding, water and snow skiing, swimming and sailing. To all, she encourages, "pursue your dreams."

LIST OF ARTICLES
BY THE AUTHORS

The material presented in *Gymnastics Psychology: The Ultimate Guide for Coaches, Gymnasts, and Parents* is based on the following original articles by Dr. Sue Massimo and/ or Dr. Joe Massimo. They were primarily published between 1969 and 2007 in *Modern Gymnast, Mademoiselle Gymnast, Technique,* and *International Gymnast* Magazines. Articles published elsewhere are noted as such.

- *Abuses of Anger in the Gym* (May, 1987)
- *Amateur's Guide to Psyching-Out Behaviors or Being Disliked Made Easy, An* (January, 1980)
- *Anorexia Nervosa: A Psychosomatic Illness* (February, 1982)
- *Art of Feedback: A Model for Coach-Gymnast Communication, The* (October, 1984)
- *Behavior Change and Reinforcement: Part I* (July, 1984)
- *Behavior Change and Reinforcement: Part II* (September, 1981)
- *Butterflies and Other Moving Things* (October, 1991)
- *Changing Gyms* (May, 1988)
- *Coach-Gymnast Conference: Listening and Other Art Forms* (March, 1986)
- *Coaching the Team (The Role of Adult Authority: Part I)* (August, 1989)
- *Coaching the Team (The Role of Adult Authority: Part II)* (November, 1989)
- *Coaching through Goal Setting* (November, 1991)
- *Coach's Guide to Nonverbal Communication* (October, 1984)
- *"Dear Doc"* (December, 1977; August, 1982)
- *Decision to Quit, The* (January, 1984)
- *Defense Mechanisms and Gymnastics* (June, 1974)
- *Different Strokes for Different Folks* (September, 1986)

- *Elite Level Gymnastics and Reality* (March, 1991)
- *Fear in Gymnastics ("I'm Afraid to, etc.")* (May, 1976; January, 1981)
- *Gender Differences-Coaching Implications* (May, 1990)
- *Guide for Coaches and Gymnasts for Understanding and Coping With Fear (Summation), A* (May, 1984)
- *Guide to Routine Training (Full Sets), A* (July, 1980; July, 1986)
- *Gymnast's Guide for Demonstrating Confidence* (February, 1985)
- *Gymnast's Guide to the Late Movies, A* (July, 1983)
- *"Help, I'm in a Slump"* (September, 1988)
- *"I'm Afraid to...continued" (Some Coaching Strategies)* (June, 1976; May, 1981)
- *Impact of Psychological Factors in the Evaluation Process: Getting to the Judge, The* (June, 1977)
- *Issue of Ethics (Code of Conduct), The* (May, 1994)
- *"It's So Frustrating"* (November, 1985)
- *Key to Success: Part I, A* (October, 1976)
- *Key to Success: Part II, A* (March, 1977)
- *Leaving Home to Train* (July, 1987)
- *Locus of Control and Coach Effectiveness* (April 1984)
- *Male Coach–Female Gymnast* (January, 1976)
- *Mental Training Drills* (March, 1978)
- *Mothers, Daughters, Gymnastics* (November, 1989)
- *My Daughter the Gymnast* (November, 1978)
- *"My Goal is to…"* (March, 1986)
- *Notes for Beginners: Physical and Mental Warm-Up* (July, 1975)
- *On the Beam: A Gymnast's Guide for Staying There* (March, 1983)
- *Open Letter to Dan Millman: Psychological Aspects of Gymnastics, An* (December, 1971)
- *Performance Connection: Attention, Stress and Arousal: Part I, The* (July, 1982)
- *Performance Connection: Attention, Stress and Arousal: Part II, The* (December, 1982)
- *Promoting Self-Esteem* (March, 1989)
- *Putting Your Best Foot Forward* (November, 1993)
- *Psychological Preparation Program,* In *National Technical Notes* (July, October, 1994; January, April, July, October, 1995*)*
- *Psychological Recovery from Injury* (April, 1985)
- *Psychologist's View of Coaching: Part I (An Introduction), A* (October, 1987)
- *Psychologist's View of Coaching: Part II (Guidelines), A* (November, 1987; November, 2007)
- *Psychology and Safety in Gymnastics* (June, 1996)

- *Psychology and the Gymnast* (March, 1969)
- *Reasons for Leaving* (October, 1992)
- *Research Report: Gymnast's Perception of the Coach: Performance Competence and Coaching Style, The* (June, 1978)
- *Right-Brained Gymnasts in Left-Brained Gyms* (April, 1982)
- *Role of a Psychologist in a National Training Program, The* (May, 1977)
- *School and Gymnastics* (October, 1983)
- *Some Thoughts on Coaching: Part I* (August, 1975)
- *Some Thoughts on Coaching: Part II* (September, 1975)
- *Understanding and Managing Fear* (March, 1993)
- *USAIGC Report-Psychological Characteristics of Jr. Elite Development Program Gymnasts* (August, 1982)
- *Using Non-Verbal Art Forms to Facilitate Training* (June, 1975)
- *We Have a Problem* (January, 1982)
- *"What I'm Afraid of? What do I do about it? Who do I tell?"* (March, 1990)

CPSIA information can be obtained at www.ICGtesting.com
Printed in the USA
BVOW07s0143180214

345245BV00016B/337/P